HENRY WARD BEECHER

HENRY WARD BEECHER

Spokesman for a Middle-Class America

Clifford E. Clark, Jr.

University of Illinois Press
Urbana   Chicago   London

Publication of this work was supported in part by a grant
from the Andrew W. Mellon Foundation.

Library of Congress Cataloging in Publication Data

Clark, Clifford E   1941–
Henry Ward Beecher : spokesman for a middle-class America.

Includes bibliographical references and index.
1. Beecher, Henry Ward, 1813–1887. 2. Congrega-
tional churches—Clergy—Biography. 3. Clergy—United
States—Biography.
BX7260.B3C6   285'.8'0924 [B]   78-1721
ISBN 0-252-00608-9

for my wife and for my parents

Acknowledgments

Many friends have helped, both directly and indirectly, in the production of this book. Without attempting to name all of those to whom I am indebted, I should mention particularly Sydney Ahlstrom, Donald Fleming, William G. McLoughlin, Theodore Baird, William F. Woehrlin, and John Ludden, who all read drafts of the book and offered their generous comments. Together they have given meaning to the phrase "the community of scholarship." I would also like to thank Anna J. Merritt, who prepared the index.

During the decade I have worked on this book, my thinking and ideas have also been strongly influenced by the writings and teachings of Martin Duberman, John L. Thomas, John William Ward, Hugh Hawkins, and Kirk Jeffrey. Their commitment to analytic toughness, their scrupulous concern for accuracy, and their regard for literary grace has been a continuing source of inspiration.

I am also grateful to Amherst and Carleton colleges for faculty research grants that have helped bring this book to publication.

Finally, my debts to my parents and my wife and family are too numerous to mention. Without their interest and encouragement, this book would never have been completed.

Contents

Illustrations following page 140

Prologue

When Henry Ward Beecher died in 1887, he was universally recognized as having been one of the most popular preachers in America. A public funeral was held and the entire city of Brooklyn turned out for the solemn procession to Greenwood Cemetery. ". . . all in all," wrote E. L. Godkin in *The Nation*, "the American people will hardly ever see in the pulpit or on the platform any one who could so easily put an audience into the heroic mood, and who on the whole used his great power for such noble ends." *Harper's Weekly* agreed, adding simply that "Beecher has been among the chief leaders, a true tribune of the people, loyal always to the most generous hope and thought and effort and he dies as he would have died, with all his force unabated, and upon the field of battle."[1]

The many tributes that were showered upon Beecher after his death are not only testimony to the enormous influence he wielded in his own time, but they are also important clues to the sources of his popularity and success. As the references to heroic leadership and military prowess attest, Beecher stood in the popular imagination as a crusader against the vices of the day. He represented the fervent idealism, militant democracy, and aggressive moralism that characterized much of American culture in the middle decades of the nineteenth century.[2]

Beecher's success as popular prophet had many sources. Clearly his unusual ability as a public speaker was one of the factors that contributed to his appeal. "He was the most remarkable preacher of his time, the most popular, the most influential," wrote Godkin. Others agreed, pointing to his skill at painting verbal pictures that aroused the imagination and excited the enthusiasm of audiences from coast to coast. Still others singled out Beecher's personality as the key to his effectiveness.[3] "The same temperament that made him powerful in the pulpit gave him equal power upon the platform," wrote a reporter for *Harper's Weekly*. "The manly heartiness, the genial optimism, the rollicking humor, the pathetic appeal, the earnest conviction, . . . charmed and electrified the crowd, and certified the natural orator."[4] What appealed most strongly to the public was Beecher's apparent openness and sincerity. Unconventional of dress and careless of petty details, he spoke to each member of the audience as if he were addressing a personal friend.[5]

The apparent openness on the lecture platform stood in marked contrast to Beecher's private life. Though Beecher had many friends and wrote many letters, he kept his private emotions closely guarded. From the evidence that survives, it is extraordinarily difficult to ferret out his real feelings. In part, this difficulty arises from the formal conventions of the day that protected inner emotions by shielding them behind stereotypical reactions. In a larger measure, the difficulty in understanding the private man is a result of Beecher's own personality. He continually protected himself by destroying his more sensitive personal letters, including his early correspondence to his wife and much of the material relating to the suit for adultery later in his life. His autobiographical reminiscences, like those of his widely known sisters, Catharine Beecher and Harriet Beecher Stowe, were not always accurate.[6]

Critics of the man were quick to point out the discrepancy between Beecher's role on the lecture platform and his private life. Even his friends admitted that the Brooklyn preacher was unable to deal with the members of his own congregation on a personal basis. "He would not often visit the sick and dying, even among his best friends," wrote a close acquaintance. "He was a master in the art of public expression of all the range of human feelings when on the platform, dealing only

with generalities; but when he had to meet in private the case of an individual whom he loved, he lost control over his words and himself."[7]
Other commentators were more harsh. The New York *Tribune* complained that Beecher was often deceptive and that his sermons had a
tendency to degenerate into "vulgarity and gush."[8] And Paxton Hibben, his most recent biographer, has argued that Beecher was a hypocritical opportunist, a man driven by a hunger for love and a craving
for power.[9]

To some extent, Hibben and the other critics are correct in their
assessment of Beecher. Behind the charm and wit of his performance
on the lecture platform was an unpleasant streak of selfishness and
ambition. Yet, neither Beecher's critics nor his admirers, despite their
insights into the strengths and weaknesses of his character and speaking style, have recognized the basic source of his appeal. Beecher was
enormously popular, not simply because he was a great orator, but
because he articulated the attitudes and values of a new urban middle
class that emerged at mid-century to supply the organizational and
managerial skills for the expansion of industry and commerce.

Sensing the anxiety of the new middle class, Beecher appealed to its
members as a personal friend who understood the uneasiness aroused
by the growth of factories and the rise of cities and who longed for
the simpler and more natural virtues of a rural existence. He appealed
also as one who believed in the pre-Civil War moral ideals of individualism, democracy, self-help, and progress, and he sought to redefine
them so that they would be of more use in the Gilded Age. But he
appealed most of all because he offered Americans a new social ethos,
a system of beliefs and values that might best be labeled Victorian
because of its similarity to its better-known counterpart in England.
Beecher helped to define and popularize American Victorian culture.
Aided by the new middle class that was its most serious exponent,
Beecher publicized and spread the social ethos until it was embraced to
some degree by most of the American public. It was a system of
values that prompted compromise, defused discontent, and provided
the man on the street with a distinct identity and sense of achievement.

The new ethos was built around a core of religious beliefs that
might best be labeled romantic Christianity.[10] As espoused by Beecher, romantic Christianity was a religion of the heart, an appeal to the
feelings and emotions that replaced the cold, formalistic evangelical

theology of the previous generation and accepted the new theories of evolution and biblical criticism. Using the natural world as a source of inspiration, Beecher preached a new experiential Christianity that emphasized God's love for man and the availability of salvation for all. It was a cheerful and optimistic faith that gave people the confidence to attack vice and crime and encouraged them to work for a general reformation of society.

To this core of romantic Christianity, Beecher added a set of measures to reassure Americans that order and stability could be maintained in society. His favorite appeal, which derived from the revivalism of his father, was to extol the virtues of the inner-directed person, the individual who had developed the self-reliance and self-control necessary for surviving in the chaotic world of the nineteenth century. But where his father had stressed the importance of the conversion experience in instilling this perspective within the individual, Beecher argued that the family, the school, and the church were more effective instruments of social control because they would make the individual behave properly by force of habit.

The final element in Beecher's social ethos was his belief in Darwinism. Discarding the more brutal aspects of evolutionary theory, which emphasized the struggle for existence and the destruction of the less fit, Beecher extracted a scientific commitment to a belief in progress and fixed moral laws. The hand of God still ruled the natural world. Ethics were sanctioned by the laws of Nature.

Using these arguments, Beecher was able to reinforce central tenets of the Victorian middle-class outlook—the belief in fixed moral laws, the emphasis on individual self-reliance, the faith in education and high culture, and the stress on economic security and social control. An eloquent speaker who never lost an opportunity to become involved in a new social reform, Beecher came to articulate the ideals of his vast following.

Beecher's life thus provides a new insight into the relationship between religion and Victorian culture in America during the crucial middle decades of the nineteenth century. The story begins with the breakdown of the homogeneity of New England life in the early years of the nineteenth century and the resultant search for new forms of social control that led to the development of revivalism, the rise of the common school, and the beginnings of the temperance movement. It then moves to the city of Brooklyn, where the search for social stability finds expression in new conceptions of the social role of the ministry and the family, leading to Beecher's involvement in the antislavery and the women's rights crusades. The story ends with Beecher's attempt on a popular level to redefine the traditional American values of individualism and success so that they would be more compatible with the social realities of the Gilded Age. Beecher's career, in sum, touches on most of the major reform movements of the period and documents the changing nature of Protestantism in Victorian America at mid-century.

NOTES

1. *The Nation*, March 10, 1887; *Harper's Weekly*, March 19, 1887.

2. The term culture is used here in an anthropological sense as a "distinctive heritage of ideas and values, providing people with non-material resources to cope with life and a world view to make sense of it." See Daniel W. Howe, "American Victorianism as a Culture," *American Quarterly*, XXVII (Dec., 1975), 509. In addition to the influence of Howe's excellent article, my thinking about culture has been shaped by Clifford Geertz, *The Interpretation of Cultures* (New York, 1973) and William A. Muraskin, "The Social-Control Theory in American History: A Critique," *Journal of Social History*, IX (Summer, 1976), 559–69.

3. *The Nation*, March 17, 1887; New York *Tribune*, March 19, 1887.

4. *The Nation*, March 17, 1887.

5. *Harper's Weekly*, March 19, 1887.

6. Harriet was the greatest offender in this respect. After the publication of *Uncle Tom's Cabin*, she came to view much of her early life from an abolitionist perspective.

7. Thomas G. Shearman, *The Christian Union*, March 17, 1887.

8. New York *Tribune*, March 9, 1889.

9. Paxton Hibben, *Henry Ward Beecher: An American Portrait* (New York, 1927), 286.

10. For two recent important studies of popular Protestantism, see William G. McLoughlin, *The Meaning of Henry Ward Beecher* (New York, 1970) and Sydney E. Ahlstrom, *A Religious History of the American People* (New Haven, 1972).

1

The New England Way

"My boyhood was passed in a shadow," reminisced Henry Ward Beecher after the Civil War. "I never heard that Litchfield bell toll on a week day that I did not shake as if the judgment was upon me. . . . Until I was fifteen years old the whole air to me was filled with mirk and gloom. I was not a Christian, and therefore I had no God. Not being a Christian, I was under condemnation and wrath."[1] To the younger members of Beecher's congregation, this remark must have been hard to believe. For the preacher standing before them was a picture of self-confidence and assurance. Tall, with light blue eyes and long grey hair brushed carelessly behind his ears, Beecher was to them, as to many urban Americans, a symbol of the promise of American life. Wealthy and successful, he mirrored the optimism of the post–Civil War era.

Yet Beecher was not exaggerating when he spoke about his youth. His childhood and early adult life were dominated by an agonized search for a religious faith—a search that was shaped and molded by the community in which he lived, the intense personality of his father, and the changes taking place within the Congregational church. Unknowingly and without design, Beecher's own religious odyssey paralleled the changes taking place in Protestantism as the churches struggled to accommodate their outlook to the democratic and equalitarian doctrines that became popular after 1810. While the churches shifted from a strict Calvinism, with an emphasis on depravity, damnation, and divine authority, to a more open doctrine that permitted the individual to play a greater role in his own salvation, Henry Ward Beecher wrestled with the expectations of his father and the changing Congregational theology until he had developed his own personal faith. Drawing upon elements of the community ideals and his father's theology, he laid the groundwork for what was to become a distinctive faith.

The town of Litchfield, where Beecher was born on June 24, 1813, was one of the oldest and most prosperous communities in Connecticut. Situated in the rolling hills of the western part of the state, it was known for its astute politicians and excellent law school. What particularly distinguished the town was the social outlook of its inhabitants. Litchfield was a bastion of strict Congregationalism, a place where the townspeople firmly believed that man was depraved by nature and needed to be controlled. "Our fathers were not fools . . . ," declared the town minister a year before Beecher was born. "Their fundamental maxim was that man is desperately wicked, and cannot be qualified for good membership in society without the influence of moral restraint." [2] Tightly organized by a persuasive group of articulate, disciplined leaders, the town stressed uniformity of religious beliefs and strict social control.

Following these procedures, Litchfield had become unusually stable and prosperous. [3] In 1813, however, the townspeople were becoming uneasy. To many of them it seemed as if the achievements and prosperity of past years were being undermined. The Federalist party to which they belonged was losing power and they distrusted the Jeffersonian Republicans who now controlled the federal government. The townspeople were worried, too, by the number of residents who were leaving to settle in the West. But most upsetting of all was the apparent growth of atheism and immorality. Since religion was the keystone of their heritage, the town leaders envisioned the destruction of their religious and civic institutions. The Calvinist Congregational-Presbyterian tradition, which had been so strong in the past, was being passed by and neglected.

To meet the crisis provoked by the spread of atheism and infidelity, Lyman Beecher, the father of Henry Ward, was called to the Congregational Church in Litchfield in 1810. An intense and energetic man who often shoveled sand from one side of the cellar to another just to burn off energy, Lyman Beecher immediately organized a campaign to rebuild the town's religious faith. He began by starting a revival and urging the townspeople to support the laws of the commonwealth against immorality. "Much may be done in the way of prevention," he told his congregation, "but, in a free government, moral suasion and coercion must be united. If the children be not religiously educated and accustomed in early life to subordination, the laws will fail. . . ."[4] Lyman Beecher's approach, which combined revivals based on intense peer-group pressure with the indoctrination of children, was well-adapted to the emerging democratic ideals of the period. The stress on individual choice, moral self-discipline, and the instruction of children foreshadowed similar ideals that were to flower in the Jacksonian era.

Lyman Beecher's revival, supported by local voluntary associations, soon was in full swing. As he later admitted, "I read . . . the signs of the times. I felt as if the conversion of the world to Christ was near. . . . It is this that has widened the scope of my activities beyond the common sphere of pastoral labor. For I soon found myself harnessed to the Chariot of Christ, whose wheels of fire have rolled onward, high and dreadful to his foes and glorious to his friends. *I could not stop.*" In sermon after sermon, he painted a gruesome picture of impending disaster and urged the sinful minority of the town to mend their ways. He then offered them the promise of life everlasting if they would repent and dedicate their lives to Christ. Beecher's efforts were overwhelmingly successful and hundreds of new converts joined the local churches. Eventually the rest of the state was swept by a general awakening of religion.[5]

Lyman Beecher's spectacular success as a revivalist derived from his unusually astute assessment of the plight of the Protestant churches in 1810. He realized that the decline of religious enthusiasm in New England had resulted in part from the Congregational church's stern and uncompromising attitude toward original sin. Modifying the position held by his predecessors in Litchfield, he supported the position developed by his friend Nathaniel W. Taylor and argued that man was not depraved by nature, but sinned from choice. Since each individual was responsible for his own actions, every man had a moral obligation to work for his own salvation. By placing the stress on the individual as a free agent without denying the supremacy of God, Lyman Beecher helped to provide the evangelical movement with a dynamic impulse that turned it into a far-reaching moral crusade.[6]

In addition to recognizing the theological problems that beset the Congregational church, Lyman Beecher realized that the effectiveness of religion as an instrument of social control in America was closely related to its ability to influence public opinion. He saw, as Alexis de Tocqueville was later to see, that public opinion exercised an enormous power over individual behavior in a democratic society where the traditions of rank, profession, and birth were weak or entirely lacking. He therefore set out to control public opinion by the use of voluntary societies and revivals. As he continually argued to the people of Litchfield, "the friends of good morals and good government, have it yet in their power to create a public opinion, which nothing can resist."[7] All that was needed was to organize the citizens and spur them to action.

Lyman Beecher was not only an unusually effective organizer, he had great skill at making his doctrinal and organizational innovations appear to be essentially conservative. His campaign to spread revivals, though new as a technique, had as its end the restoration of order and the perpetuation of social stability. "It is not as if we were called upon to make new laws, and establish usages unknown before," he explained to the townspeople. "We make no innovations. We embark on no novel experiment. We set up no new standard of morals. . . . We stand on the defensive merely. We contend for our altars and our firesides. We rally around the standard which our fathers reared; and our motto is, '*the inheritance which they bequeathed no man shall take from us.*'"[8]

Because Lyman Beecher stressed the effectiveness of religion as an instrument of social control at a time when the New England states were being torn apart by rapid westward expansion and unprecedented economic growth, his campaign to spread revivals was enormously successful. Massive awakenings took place in 1812, 1815, and 1820, and thousands of new converts were added to the churches. Yet, as far as his own family was concerned, Lyman Beecher considered himself a failure. "My heart sinks within me," he wrote despairingly to his oldest son in 1819, "at the thought that every one of my own dear children are without God in the world and without Christ, and without hope. . . ."[9] Beecher was particularly upset because he believed that the second coming of Christ was near. He wanted more than anything to have his children undergo a conversion experience—that quasi-mystical dedication of the self to God—and join the church as full members.

To convert his children, Lyman Beecher followed the same tactics that he used on his congregation. He first would scare them by painting vivid pictures of hell and then would point out how easy it was to join the cause of Christ. "Do you not know . . . ," his daughter Harriet Beecher Stowe remembered his saying, "that you cannot love, and be examining your love at the same time? Some people, instead of getting evidence by *running* in the way of life, take a dark lantern, and get down on their knees, and crawl on the boundary up and down, to make sure they have crossed it. If you want to make sure, *run*, and when you come in sight of the celestial city, and hear the songs of the angels, then you'll know you're across."[10]

Like his brothers and sisters, Henry Ward Beecher, the ninth of Lyman and Roxana Foote Beecher's children, at first showed little interest in revivalism. His world instead was preoccupied by the everyday affairs of the large and busy household on North Street. As one of the youngest members of the family, he frequently was neglected and left on his own. Compared to Edward, George, and William, who were soon to enter Yale College, and Catharine and Mary, who were star pupils at Miss Pierce's academy, Henry was little noticed. Too young to understand the intense theological and educational debates that preoccupied Lyman Beecher and his older children, Henry played instead with Harriet, two years his senior, and the baby Charles.[11]

Living in such a large and intense family impressed upon Henry a sense of his own personal insignificance. This sense of insignificance was intensified by the death of his mother when Henry was three. Roxana Beecher was a sensitive and articulate woman, well-educated and devoutly religious. When she died, Aunt Esther Beecher, Lyman's stepsister, moved in and became, as one of the sons later wrote, a kind of brevet mother to the family. Aunt Esther was the one who washed and dressed the children, saw to it that they were catechised each morning and did their chores. Brought up under a strict system of rules, she passed them on to the children along with her "habits of extreme neatness and order." [12]

Though his father, who was busy leading revivals throughout the state, played a small role in the daily affairs of the family, he nevertheless was careful to stress the religious education of his children. Prayers and readings from the Bible were an important part of everyday life and Lyman often talked to all the children about their beliefs.

The death of his mother and neglect by the older family members, combined as they were with the father's high expectations about his religious faith, all left their mark on young Henry Ward. He was bashful and shy as a child and loved to be alone so that he could walk through the countryside and enjoy its views. "There," he later wrote, "we went wandering up and down forest edges and along crooked brooks, in flower-pied meadows, dreaming about things not to be found in any catechism." [13]

Later, when he went to school, Henry Ward Beecher's insecurity grew when he failed to do well. His worst experience came when he was ten years old and was enrolled in Miss Sarah Pierce's Female Academy. George, Mary, and Edward Beecher had been sent there earlier by virtue of an arrangement by which Lyman Beecher taught the Saturday Bible Class in exchange for free tuition. But where the older children had been successful, Henry ran into difficulty. Lacking the competitiveness of his brothers and sisters, he grew restless during the long recitation periods and paid little attention to what was going on in class. As a result, he fell behind in his studies and failed to obtain an adequate knowledge of Latin and Greek.

To remedy this deficiency, his father considered sending him to a new female academy that his sister Catharine recently had opened in Hartford, Connecticut. Catharine was confident that she could prepare her brother for college and welcomed the chance of having another student in her school. But Lyman was not sure that he could afford the additional expense of having his son live in Hartford. "If Henry can have board and washing anywhere in a good family at 2 dollars," he wrote to Catharine, "you may remove him but if not we must think a little before we remove him as 25 cents [for board] and washing besides, will amount to 25 to 30 dollars a year, a great hole in a salary of 800. . . ." [14] Despite his strong desire to see all his children well educated, financial considerations still came first. If Lyman Beecher did not have enough time to oversee the religious education of his youngest children, perhaps Catharine, who already had demonstrated her keen mind, would have a better chance.

Eventually Lyman agreed that Henry should go to Catharine's academy in Hartford. But after spending six months at his sister's school, he was sent back to Litchfield. Tired of her brother's jokes and pranks, Catharine returned him to her father with the recommendation that he be placed in the care of someone who could make him apply himself. Lyman was in fact happy to have his son back; for in addition to worrying about the expense involved in sending Henry away to school, he was deeply concerned about his son's spiritual condition. Now that Henry was home again, Lyman began to work in earnest to convert him. For more than a year thereafter the elder Beecher labored to save his son's soul and, in the winter of 1825, his efforts finally showed signs of success. A few weeks before Christmas that year the twelve-year-old boy began to struggle over his religious beliefs. Gradually, he became more and more upset. Unsure and confused, he at last turned to his brother George for advice. "Dear Brother," he began, "I write to you this evening to tell you how I feel. I suppose that you have heard that I was serious. I have been seeking after God but have not found him as yet. . . . I have been a little wretched before but never felt my lost condition [so strongly]. . . . I can't write you much this evening but at a more convenient season I hope I shall have some more important news about my soul."[15]

Henry wrote to his brother because George had undergone the struggle and despair of the conversion experience the year before. He was afraid, moreover, that his father might not understand his feelings. He had been pressured for so long to commit his life to the service of Christ that he hesitated about revealing his feelings before he had come to a more definite decision.

Eventually, of course, Lyman Beecher learned of the spiritual struggles of his son. He was encouraged by Henry's progress, yet he refused to let up the pressure. "It is like the wind upon the willow, which rises as soon as it is passed over," he confided to his eldest son. "It does not grapple, but the effect is good in giving power to conscience and moral principle, producing amendment in conduct."[16]

The more Henry worried about his religious faith, the more hopeless his chances of conversion seemed and the more depressed he became, to the dismay of his father. Depression was precisely the attitude that Lyman had warned against when he wrote to Catharine a few years earlier that "the state of feeling to be cultivated in those who superintend a revival is a mild, but constant and intense desire of the heart for the awakening and conversion of sinners." Excesses of feeling and symptoms of depression were to be avoided if possible. "We can neither carry the world on our shoulders nor govern it," he cautioned.[17]

Despite the warnings from his father and the advice from his brothers and sisters, Henry remained depressed. Confused and upset, he began to doubt whether he would ever be converted. To restore his son's confidence and shore up his religious faith, Lyman Beecher, in the fall of 1827, decided to send him to the Mount Pleasant Classical Institution in Amherst, Massachusetts—a school dedicated to providing "that moral and religious influence which contributes to fit a man for the high purposes of existence." Mount Pleasant had attracted Lyman Beecher's eye because the directors of the school shared his social views. Like Beecher, they wanted the school to be a protected community, "with its own public sentiment and its own atmosphere of moral feelings." Furthermore, they insisted that the school stand *in loco parentis*. "No other, than the guardian spirit of parental influence," they argued in the catalogue, "extending its vigilant, yet affectionate supervision to the whole history of sentiment and action, bending its holier sympathies at the altar of the *common Father*, . . . can successfully regulate and chasten the elastic and buoyant temperament of youth."[18] Such a school, Lyman Beecher hoped, might revive his son's depressed spirits and prepare him for college.

In accordance with his father's decision, Henry traveled to Amherst in September and entered the academy. Although at first he was not eager to attend a school that required the students to rise at five-thirty and attend chapel twice a day, he soon grew to like Mount Pleasant and eventually made many friends. One of his closest companions was Constantine Fondolaik, a refugee from the Greek uprising of 1821 who had been adopted by a Massachusetts family. In a secret meeting, the two boys drew up an elaborate code and pledged to defend each other if either were attacked. So close in fact was the friendship that Beecher adopted Fondolaik's first name as his middle initial and for several years thereafter signed his name H. C. Beecher.[19] Henry's friendship with Fondolaik, with its ritual and idealistic code, was in effect the searching out of two youths in a strange land who found a kinship with each other because of their sense of alienation. Because each boy understood the fears of the other so well, the friendship helped to restore each's faith and confidence in himself. Thus, after almost a year at the academy, Beecher at last felt secure enough to renew his questions about his father's religion.

In letter after letter to his family, he criticized the "remarkably low" state of religious faith at the academy and commented on his own attitudes toward God. "I do not like to read the Bible as well as I do to pray," he wrote confidentially to his sister Harriet, "but I suppose it is the same as it is with a lover who loves to talk with his mistress in person, better than to write when she is far off." Henry wrote to Harriet because she was his favorite sister and understood his yearnings for a new faith. To the older members of his family, he was less candid about his feelings. Dutifully, as if he were being watched, he explained to his brother Edward, then a tutor at Yale, that "I expect father received a letter from me about the same time that you did this one, in which I asked him to explain some things from the Bible to me. But if he is so much engaged in preparing his lectures for the press, that he cannot attend to it, will you answer them and some others which I intend to ask in this letter?" [20]

As Beecher's letter to his sister revealed, he was reluctant to communicate with his father. Overwhelmed by his father's strong personality and hesitant to intrude on his busy schedule, he tested his ideas first on Harriet. Slowly, after much searching, he began to find a set of beliefs that restored his confidence in himself and gave his life a sense of meaning. "I have such thoughts, such views of God, and of his love and mercy," he confided to his sister, "that my heart would burst through the corrupt body of this world and soar with the angels. . . . I believe that if I had not some where to lay my troubles, if Christ had not invited all those that are 'weary and heavy laden' to come unto him, that I should have been long since discouraged. . . ." [21]

As he worried about his studies and dreamed of his future work in the ministry, Beecher gradually came to the conclusion that he had been saved. At last, so it seemed, he had been converted and could become a member of the church. Convinced that he had been awakened, he returned home during his vacation and, after an examination by the elders of his father's church, was admitted to the congregation.

In later life, when he recalled the event, it was with a deep sense of disillusionment. For Beecher realized that, despite his wish, he had not had a real awakening. "I do not know how or why I was converted," he wrote. "I only know I was in a sort of day-dream, in which I hoped I had given myself to Christ."[22]

Beecher's comment was perceptive. Unlike many of the other evangelical leaders, he was born into the ministry rather than converted to it. Dominated by the strong personality of his father, he learned to accept the role for which his father had prepared him.[23] Conversion for Henry thus meant more than simply becoming a member of the church. It meant an identification with an outlook that placed an enormous emphasis on the maintenance of stability and the preservation of order within society. It meant, in final analysis, that his life would now have a new meaning and purpose, a commitment to the values and traditions of the New England way of life.

Lyman Beecher was pleased by Henry's apparent conversion. Nevertheless, he remained skeptical about the strength of his son's religious convictions. After all, Henry was young and imaginative and might easily change his mind. So later in the year when the question of a college education was raised, Lyman decided to send his son to Amherst College rather than to his own alma mater, Yale. The classes were smaller at Amherst and Henry stood a better chance there of making up his deficiencies in the classics. The students at Amherst, moreover, were supervised more carefully than those at Yale, and Henry would have less chance of becoming involved in wild parties or campus pranks. "Though I have good hope of his piety," wrote Lyman to the president of Amherst, "yet his temperament and spirit is of a kind which would make him susceptible to Southern influence, assailing him in the side of honor and spirit. So far as I know his conduct has been circumspect. But on the whole I shall regard his safety as greater in Amherst than in New Haven. . . ."[24] Following his father's suggestion, Henry enrolled in the freshman class at Amherst College.

When Henry arrived at Amherst in the fall of 1830, the small college was prosperous and rapidly expanding. Nine years earlier it had been founded by the farmers of western Massachusetts to check the spread of the Unitarian heresy at Harvard. Feeding on the revivals that swept through the state in the 1820s, Amherst grew so rapidly it soon be-

came the second largest college in New England. A fortress of orthodoxy, designed with the training of ministers specifically in mind, it
was the ideal place for educating a minister's son. Since Henry Ward
Beecher was familiar with the town of Amherst, having attended the
academy there, going to college there required little adjustment. Seventeen years old and idealistic, he entered upon his studies with a sense
of determination. "I am beginning to learn to *think*, *write*, and *debate*," he wrote confidentially to his sister Harriet. "I never shall be
much of a linguist or mathematician. But if I can excell in moral rea-
soning, . . . I can do as much as if I were thoroughly versed in the
Classics."[25]

Two forces worked to shape Beecher's education at Amherst. One
was the teaching of Heman Humphrey, the president of the college; the
other was Beecher's membership in the Athenian and Natural History
societies. President Humphrey was a passionate and inspiring preacher
who combined a belief in social control with an intense desire to
strengthen the ministry. The function of a college education, in his
view, was to provide the restraint and discipline that would curb the
passions, mold the affections, and inspire the consciences of his students.[26]

Henry Ward Beecher admired Humphrey's concern for social stability and was inspired by his vision of the ministry, but he substituted a
beneficent view of God for Humphrey's stern God of justice. As he
wrote to his brother, "more and more I am led by the goodness of
God to dedicate myself to Him. Oh his service *is* joy. Let us brother,
be faithful, 'tis such an honor to *live* under him—but to be a minister!
Oh we have never appreciated the glory of it. How beautiful on the
mountains of God will be the feet of those in Heaven who have brought
home souls to glory."[27] Romantic and idealistic, he yearned to finish
his studies and begin work in the field.

But the studies themselves presented a problem. Never much interested in academic subjects, Beecher did only enough work to get by.
Despite his assertion to his sister that he was "fast losing the habit of
practical fun . . . and with becoming sobriety and decency . . . [was]
studying the weightier matters of the law, debating, composition—the
philosophy of the mind, particularly of the *heart*, in which I make
the most laudable advances," Henry did not do well in his classwork.
His real interest lay not in his regular courses, but rather in his mem-

bership in the Athenian Society, which had been founded by the students in 1821 to provide a forum for "original declamations, compositions, criticisms, and extemporaneous discussions." The Athenian Society possessed an excellent library and encouraged the study of social and political subjects that were not discussed in class. Debates were held each Wednesday evening on topics that ranged in subject from current public questions such as whether Congress ought "to grant the petition lately presented to that body for the abolition of Slavery in the District of Columbia" to more light-hearted inquiries such as whether it was "desirable for students in college to enjoy female society."[28] After each debate, a vote was taken and the results recorded.

Beecher played an active part in the functions of the Athenian Society, serving first as librarian, then as orator, and eventually as president. He also spoke frequently in debates on such topics as "the importance of the three professions: medicine, law, and theology," and "the tendencies of society toward perfection."[29] But his favorite topic was the newly discovered science of phrenology, a subject later popularized by his friend and classmate Orson Squire Fowler.

Beecher's interest in phrenology, the "science" that held that man's character traits could be determined by the shape of his skull, was supported by his love of nature and his belief that a knowledge of the natural world would strengthen his faith in God. As he wrote to his sister Harriet:

> I am delighted in studying the doctrines lately—that is, within a year or two—and, in reading in science, in nature. I am searching for comparisons and analogies and similar principles to unfold, explain, and confirm the various truths of Scripture. It seems at times as tho' the most confirmed sceptic would give up—but my pride is a little humbled when I think that my great things are too small to be as first principles with father. I mean to continue, for by such labor the subject is to my own mind expanded and made plain.[30]

The juxtaposition of the references to nature with comments about his father was not fortuitous. Unwilling and perhaps unable to understand the fine distinctions within his father's theology, Beecher was searching for a new authority on which to rest his faith. Phrenology, which taught that the mind was composed of thirty-seven faculties, provided such an authority. By teaching that mental phenomena had physiological origins and that a person's mental capacity could be altered and molded, phrenology encouraged Beecher to believe in progress and the possibility of the perfection of the individual. Phrenology not only offered an alternative to metaphysical explanations of human behavior, it also seemed to point the way to a new understanding of the laws of nature. Convinced of the usefulness of this new science, Beecher began to build his own library on the subject and frequently presented the latest developments in the field to the other members of the Athenian and Natural History societies. As the secretary of the Natural History Society recorded, "the Society then listened with much interest to an able lecture on *Phrenology* by the President, Mr. Beecher. The object of this discourse was, 1st, to expose the futility of the objections offered against this science; and 2ndly, to exhibit and defend its *fundamental principles.*" [31]

In addition to these interests at school, Beecher used his vacations to further his education. Like the other members of his family, he had a sense of social obligation that occasionally bordered upon self-righteousness. Writing to his sister Harriet about his plans, Henry declared, "I mean to attach myself as some kind of agent to the Bible or Tract or Education or some other society wherever I can and travel round to the small towns at a distance and collect funds or distribute Bibles or Tracts or something like that." [32] But these plans proved to be overly ambitious. Unable to convince the trustees of the societies that he would be useful, Beecher was forced to settle for a position teaching school.

During his years at Amherst, Beecher became known among the other students for his humor, wit, and playfulness. He often engaged in friendly discussions and debates, neglecting the assignments he should have been doing. His casual study habits were matched by carelessness in picking up his room. As his roommate commented, he "had a place for everything and *everything* was in its place—that is, on the table." [33]

In the fall of his sophomore year, he encountered a new distraction. Henry spent his Thanksgiving vacation at his roommate's house and fell in love with his roommate's sister. In a letter to his own family, he humorously explained his feelings. The girl who most impressed him was named Mindwell Gould. "*Dear Mindwell*, Mrs. *Mindwell* Beecher!! How would that sound?" he wrote. "I wish it had been

Patience or *Prudence* or Experience. . . ." Although he was quite
taken by the young lady, Beecher decided to follow the advice of President Humphrey of the college on the matter—that "if a man is going
through a woods, and sees a good young *sapling*, he may *mark* it and
come back afterward and get it—if he *can*." Thinking that he should
wait until he was a senior before he began to consider marriage,
Beecher decided simply "to mark her" and come back later.

The visit to his roommate's house was important, for there Beecher
realized how bashful and shy he was with girls. The awkwardness
and insecurity that had characterized his childhood now reappeared as
it would occasionally during the rest of his life. As he confided to
Harriet after his visit, "I used to think that I knew a great deal of
human nature and was experienced, but every day shows me that I
was a fool, and I find myself often in lamentable straits."[34]

Beecher's plan of keeping in touch with Mindwell Gould, so artfully
conceived, was never fulfilled. During the spring vacation of the same
year, he visited the house of another friend, Ebenezer Bullard, and
fell in love with Ebenezer's sister, Eunice. Eunice Bullard was not a
pretty girl, but her affectionate nature and pleasant personality were
attractive to Henry. Well educated and interested in religion, she appealed to his idolizing view of his own mother. As he wrote to Harriet,
"she is as I should think mother was—and in some respects like
Mary," his older sister. Eunice, in turn, admired Henry's quick sense
of humor and good nature.[35]

The first visit to the Bullard household was followed by others and
soon Henry was convinced that he was in love. When Eunice began to
teach school during the following summer, Henry managed to stop by
and see her frequently. At Christmas time, he obtained a position as
a teacher in a nearby town and on January 2, 1832, they became
engaged.[36]

Though Beecher was only eighteen at the time, the decision to become engaged was made after much questioning about his future.
Several years earlier his father had become concerned with missionary
activities in the West, then the Ohio River valley, and had commu-
nicated this concern to the rest of his family. He was particularly worried about the numbers of new converts that the Catholics and Methodists were making in that area. Characteristically, Lyman Beecher
painted the problem in life and death terms. "I have thought seriously

of going over to Cincinnati, the London of the West," he wrote to one of his children, "to spend the remnant of my days in that great conflict, and in consecrating all my children to God in that region who are willing to go. If we gain the West, all is safe; if we lose it, all is lost." Although his father's plans remained uncertain, Henry eagerly took up the cause and began to think about his own future. "I cannot think of laboring in the West or any other place," he wrote to Harriet in 1831, "without thinking of whosoever shall labor with me and I am thinking much of laboring there and making plans. . . ."[37]

Like his father, Henry identified the destiny of the church with that of the state and worried that if the Methodists and Catholics gained control of the Ohio River valley, the political institutions of the nation might be endangered. This concern with the future development of the West was not limited to the Beecher family but was rather a question of national concern in the 1830s. The passage of the Missouri Compromise in 1820, the opening of the Erie Canal in 1825, and the rapid growth of manufacturing and trade gave many Americans the sense that the West was to be the cradle or grave of American democracy. The religious and educational institutions established there, so it seemed at the time, would determine the growth of the nation.[38]

The revivalists, led by Lyman Beecher and Charles G. Finney, were particularly concerned with the future of the West. Upset by the rapid changes in the economy and fearing a decline in the influence of the churches, they were eager to preserve the traditional power of the religious and educational institutions. By defining sin as selfishness and stressing the social responsibility of Christians, they hoped not only to convert the individual but also to remake society.[39] The East was ablaze with revivals; it was time to spread them to the West.

Among those infected by this intense desire to protect the spiritual welfare of the western settlers were two brothers, Arthur and Lewis Tappan, prosperous merchants in New York City. While Lewis Tappan looked after the family silk business, Arthur Tappan devoted most of his energy to furthering missionary and benevolent activities. Intense and dedicated, Arthur Tappan in 1831 decided to establish a "great national Seminary on the Manual Labor Plan" in the West; he chose Theodore Weld, a young and dedicated convert of Finney, to select the site. By coincidence, sixty acres of farm land and a charter for a seminary near Cincinnati, Ohio, had been donated two years earlier. The agent for this seminary brought it to the attention of the Tappans and after conferring with Weld, they consented to back it. Weld had been considering Rochester, New York, as a site and decided in favor of Cincinnati only after hearing the opinions of his friends. As one of them wrote to him, "I doubt not that Rochester may have some facilities which are not possessed by Cincinnati . . . .[But] if this is to be the great battle field between the powers of light and darkness, why not train the soldiers of the Cross within sight of the enemies' camp?"[40]

To place the seminary on a firm foundation, Tappan coupled his pledge of ten thousand dollars with the condition that Lyman Beecher be engaged to head the institution and additional funds be obtained for other professorships and buildings. Tappan wanted Beecher because Beecher's prestige would draw students and his organizational abilities would help to further the missionary movement. But Lyman Beecher was reluctant to accept the offer. Despite his interest in the West, he felt committed to serving his own congregation and therefore postponed his decision for a year.[41]

Tappan's offer to Lyman Beecher and the prospect of moving to the West were in the back of Henry's mind in the winter of 1832 when he became engaged to Eunice Bullard. Two years earlier his brother Edward had left Boston to assume the presidency of Illinois College and Henry was convinced that he, too, eventually would go to the West as a missionary. Since they did not want to be married until he was financially self-supporting, both Henry and Eunice realized that their engagement would be a long one and they eagerly awaited Lyman Beecher's decision.

In the spring of 1832, Lyman Beecher received a second offer and decided to travel to Cincinnati to see what the city and new seminary were like. Neither his congregation nor his children were sure what would happen. "Now for the West," wrote Henry to Harriet. "Do you think that father and family will go? Do you not think that he has gone out to prepare for our family? . . . I do trust, hope, and pray that he will *go*, and that Charles and myself shall go with him. I shall however be satisfied to wait two years more till my term is out." In the meantime, he resolved to spend his time "studying, writing, and trying to do good."[42]

The trip to Cincinnati more than convinced Lyman Beecher that he was needed and could be of use in the West. Instead of a rough frontier town, he found a thriving city of thirty thousand people, with twenty-three churches and numerous public schools. The upper part of the city, with its wide streets, brick houses, and view of the Ohio River, created a sense of permanency and industriousness. With many friends and relatives in the city, Lyman and his daughter Catharine felt completely at home. "Indeed," wrote Catharine to Harriet, "this is a New England city in all its habits, and its inhabitants are more than half from New England." [43]

The location of the seminary on a beautiful farm two miles from the city impressed Lyman Beecher with its possibilities as a site for a school. A call to be the minister of the Second Presbyterian Church in the city further demonstrated the need for him. But what really made him decide to go West was the growing conflict among the revivalists in the East. A dispute had arisen between the followers of the "New School" theology of Nathaniel W. Taylor, who modified the doctrines of original sin and election by arguing that the individual had the duty to work for his own salvation, and the followers of Dr. Bennet Tyler, who supported the older view that man was depraved by nature. After trying in vain to bring the two sides together, Beecher decided to go to the West where he could be of more use. As he told his Boston congregation, "against the enemies of the Lord I can lift up the spear with good will, but with the friends of Jesus Christ I cannot find it in my heart to enter into controversy. No, I cannot do it!" [44]

No sooner had Lyman Beecher rid himself of one controversy than he became enmeshed in another. During the second year of Lane Seminary, so named for one of its benefactors, the students began to work with black residents of the city. Though Lyman Beecher was not opposed to these activities and admitted students regardless of color, living in a city where much of the population sympathized with the South, he was wary of agitating for the slavery issue. When Arthur Tappan wrote to him inquiring whether he favored the abolitionist or colonization movement, Lyman Beecher was careful, as he had been during the theological controversies, to present a compromise position. "I would press the consciences, so far as they have any, of the Southerners, and shake their fears," he replied to Tappan, "and press their interests, as the Abolitionists are doing; but then, that the pressure might avail, I would not hermetically seal their hearts by cutting off the facilities of emancipation, and tempt them to delay it till insurrection might do the work, but offer them an easy, practicable way of doing their duty, as the Colonizationists are doing. . . ."[45]

To the students, however, this compromise was unsatisfactory. Led by Theodore Weld and Henry B. Stanton, they held a series of debates in the spring of 1834 and became dedicated converts to the abolitionist movement. In taking this step, they built upon the perfectionist impulse within Beecher's own theology. If the individual had the ability, with God's help, to save himself, then he had the duty to live a more nearly perfect life. Conversion was thus expected to bring with it a strong sense of social responsibility. Where Beecher emphasized the conversion of sinners as his foremost object and viewed social reform as of secondary importance, Weld and the students did not separate the two. Conversion for them brought with it a direct commitment to action. Thus, in the fall of 1834, when the Lane trustees, many of them with interests in the South, voted to abolish all societies not pertaining to academic work, fifty-three of the students left Lane and moved to the new college of Oberlin.[46]

Though defeated by the students, Lyman Beecher was not willing to give up so easily in his efforts to convert the people of the West. He realized that in order to make the seminary a success he would have to raise funds in the East. Ignoring the debate over slavery, he seized on an issue that appealed to both Easterners and Westerners—the fear of Catholicism—and wrote an astute and clever pamphlet entitled *A Plea for the West*. "A tenth part of the suffrage of the nation," he warned, "thus condensed and wielded by the Catholic powers of Europe, might decide our elections, perplex our policy, inflame and divide the nation, break the bond of our union, and throw down our free institutions."[47] By appealing to Eastern fears of the increasing number of Catholic immigrants, Lyman Beecher equated religion with the political destiny of the nation and thereby was able, for at least a decade, to obtain the needed support for his enterprise.

During the controversy at Lane, Henry, who was completing his studies at Amherst, closely watched the developments in the West. He, too, was interested in the problem of slavery and had frequently debated the subject at Amherst. When, in July, 1833, a group of students broke away from the college Colonization Society and created their own antislavery society, Henry Ward Beecher became a charter member. When the society sent delegates to speak at an antislavery convention in Boston, however, the faculty shut it down on the grounds that it might split the student body into opposing factions. Thereafter, Henry became more cautious about expressing his views on controversial subjects. Sensitive to criticism and eager to create a good impression before his peers, he resolved to follow his father's suggestion that "true wisdom consists in advocating a course *only so far as the community will* sustain the reformer." Thus he limited his antislavery activities to working with the black people in the Amherst area.[48]

By the end of his senior year, Henry Ward Beecher was one of the most popular students in his class at Amherst. He was noted for his interest in phrenology and natural science and had been elected president of two of the college's most prestigious societies. Gregarious and outgoing, he seemed to be relaxed, confident, and well adjusted. Yet, beneath the jovial facade, Henry remained troubled and insecure. He had not done well academically during his four years at Amherst and he worried about the impression that his poor record would make on his family. As he confided to his sister Harriet:

> Dear Sister in sober truth, I find no place with so little sympathy as home and I must say it—I almost always feel that my friends despise me. I know I don't deserve it—tho' they think I do. I don't—for I am not deceitful as mother has said. I *am careless* and I never found freedom in telling my plans. I shrink from my own kindred for it always seemed they looked coldly upon me. I ought not to have written this—but I could not help it, for it swelled as it often does till it seems as tho' my heart would burst. I never tell Eunice of it. . . . Don't you show this to *anybody*. I don't want father to know I feel bad, ever, for he is *always* kind to me—but I think he feels a *sorrowful* kindness and that is what *cuts* me more keenly.[49]

Beecher's insecurity derived in part from a conflict that had developed between his approach to religion and his father's. Soft-hearted and idealistic, Henry preferred to emphasize God's goodness and mercy rather than his power and omnipotence. Unlike his father, moreover, Henry believed that the majesty and splendor of God were exhibited far better in the world of nature than in the Bible. As he later recollected, "the first distinct religious feelings I had were in connection with nature. Although I was born, as far as any one can be born so, a Calvinist, . . . yet, as I look back, I see that the only religious feelings or impressions I had were those which were excited in my mind through the unconscious influence of God through nature."[50] Thus, unlike his father, who supported his faith with the rational, empirical arguments of John Locke, William Paley, and the Scottish Common Sense philosophers, Henry grounded his own beliefs on an emotional and intuitive approach that glorified the wonder and beauty of the natural world.

Nevertheless, though he rejected the philosophical basis on which his father's beliefs rested, Henry was afraid to express his views openly to any member of his family other than Harriet. Forced to hide his real beliefs, he became uneasy about discussing theological questions with his parents. This guilt, when added to the chagrin that he felt about his poor grades, often made him troubled and upset.

To relieve his conscience and to restore his family's faith in himself, Henry began to stress certain elements in his father's religious beliefs. He was particularly enthusiastic about the idea that his mission was to defend the word of Christ against the perversions preached by the Unitarians and the Catholics. As he wrote to his brother from Hopkinton, Massachusetts, where he was teaching school, "I hear that the Unitarians and enemies are watching [my] every word and action and I need help to be able to leave the honor of the blessed cause unspotted. . . ." Yet, he was optimistic about his chances of overcoming the opposition:

> Dear Brother to look forward upon the coming blessedness of Zion when she shall arise and shine, her light being come and the glory of the Lord being risen upon her, is enough to cheer despair itself and nerve the arm in the hardest labors. 'Tis enough to know that God *reigns* and *will do right*—and then tho' located in the wilderness, and able to bring in no sheaves, golden ripe, we can rejoice in the coming glories of Christ's Kingdom. Earth friends, yes the *dearest* of friends, myself and *all* seem nothing to His glory. And that we may mingle in his train—each one as near Him as he may wish, is rapturous. Pray for me again, I ask.[51]

As is evident from this letter, Beecher found a way around the more troubling elements of his father's theology by creating his own romantic conception of his future role in the church. He would become a social leader, a crusader against evil and sin who by his words and actions would help to pave the way for the second coming of the Kingdom of Christ.

By the end of his senior year in college, Beecher thus managed to mask the differences that existed between himself and his father by channeling his energies and enthusiasm toward socially conservative ends. Brought up and schooled in a tradition which combined an emphasis on discipline and social control with a commitment to furthering the cause of Christ, Henry Ward Beecher accepted his calling and resolved to devote all his attention to strengthening the Presbyterian church in the West. When commencement day at last arrived, he eagerly accepted his diploma and began to prepare himself for the ministry.

NOTES

1. H. W. Beecher, "Lecture Room Talk," Jan. 28, 1887 (typed copy), Beecher Family Papers, Yale University Library, hereafter cited as Yale MSS.

2. Lyman Beecher, *A Reformation of Morals Practicable and Indispensable*, pamphlet (New London, 1814), 16.

3. *Ibid.*, 16.

4. *Ibid.*, 16–17.

5. Lyman Beecher, *The Autobiography of Lyman Beecher*, ed. Barbara M. Cross (Cambridge, Mass., 1961), I, 46, emphasis added; Charles R. Keller *The Second Great Awakening in Connecticut* (New Haven, 1942), 42–44.

6. Timothy L. Smith, *Revivalism and Social Reform in Mid-Nineteenth Century America* (New York, 1957), 83, 87; Sidney E. Mead, *Nathaniel William Taylor, 1786–1858, a Connecticut Liberal* (Chicago, 1942), 125–26.

7. Alexis de Tocqueville, *Democracy in America*, trans. Henry Reeve and ed. Philips Bradley (New York, 1945), II, 17; Lyman Beecher, *A Reformation of Morals*, 26.

8. Lyman Beecher, *A Reformation of Morals*, 26.

9. Keller, *The Second Great Awakening*, 42; Lyman Beecher, *Autobiography*, I, 288; Lyman Beecher, *Sermons* (Boston, 1828), 265.

10. Lyman Beecher, *Autobiography*, I, 48.

11. Harriet Beecher Stowe, *Men of Our Time* (Hartford, 1868), 506.

12. Charles Beecher, letter in *Plymouth Chimes*, XX (March, 1897), 2: Catharine Beecher, *Educational Reminiscences and Suggestions* (New York, 1874), 16.

13. Frank S. Child, *The Boyhood of Henry Ward Beecher* (n.p., 1887), 23.

14. Forrest Wilson, *Crusader in Crinoline: The Life of Harriet Beecher Stowe* (Philadelphia, 1941), Chap. 2; Catharine Beecher to Mary Hillhouse, Nov. 2, 1824, Hillhouse Papers, Yale University Library. Catharine wrote that "Henry, whom I

mean to fit for college if circumstances will favor," was going to her school in Hartford during the following week.

15. H. W. Beecher to George Beecher, Dec. 2, 1825, Yale MSS.

16. Lyman Beecher to William Beecher, Nov. 9, 1825, quoted in Lyman Beecher, *Autobiography*, II, 19.

17. Lyman Beecher, *Autobiography*, I, 44–45.

18. *The Catalogue of the Mount Pleasant Classical Institution* (Amherst, 1828), 9, 15–16.

19. William C. Beecher and Samuel Scoville, *A Biography of Rev. Henry Ward Beecher* (New York, 1888), 104–5. This is the only biography of Beecher that has made use of the family papers.

20. H. W. Beecher to Harriet Beecher, Dec. 24, 1828 (typed copy); H. W. Beecher to Edward Beecher, 1829, Yale MSS.

21. H. W. Beecher to Harriet Beecher, Nov. 1829, Yale MSS.

22. Beecher and Scoville, *Biography*, 98.

23. Lyman Beecher continually pressured his other children to enter the ministry and to dedicate their lives to public service. As he wrote to Edward Beecher, "It is my hope that God has raised you up to promote revivals in colleges and Catharine to promote them in female schools." Lyman to Edward Beecher, July, 1826, Mt. Holyoke Library.

24. Lyman Beecher to Heman Humphrey, Sept. 30, 1830, Amherst College Archives; see also Thomas Le Duc, *Piety and Intellect at Amherst College, 1865–1912* (New York, 1946), chap. 1.

25. H. W. Beecher to Harriet Beecher, March 8, 1832 (typed copy), Yale MSS.

26. Heman Humphrey, "Inaugural Address," in his *Discourses and Reviews* (Amherst, 1884), 245.

27. H. W. Beecher to ?, 1832 (typed copy), Yale MSS.

28. H. W. Beecher to Harriet Beecher, April 5, 1832, Yale MSS; Athenian Society, Records, vol. 3, March 30, 1834, April 23, 1834 (both decided in the affirmative), Amherst College Archives.

29. Athenian Society, Records, vol. 3, Nov. 7, 1832, Feb. 20, July 3, June 5, 1833, April 30, 1834.

30. H. W. Beecher to Harriet Beecher, March 28, 1833, Amherst College Archives.

31. John D. Davies, *Phrenology: Fad and Science* (New Haven, 1955), 4, 5, 168, 169; Society of Natural History, *Album*, Oct. 14, 1833, Feb. 10, 1834, Amherst College Archives.

32. Like most other colleges at this time, Amherst had a three-term year. The first term was from September to December. This was followed by a long winter vacation that enabled the students to earn money by teaching school. The second term ran from February to June and the third from June to September; see, for example, Catharine Beecher to George Beecher, April 25, 1826 (Mt. Holyoke Library), where she writes, "especially tell me if your soul is in health and prospers and what opportunities you find for doing good to your fellow men"; H. W. Beecher to Harriet Beecher, Feb. 15 (no year), Yale MSS.

33. H. W. Beecher to Harriet Beecher, March 8, 1832, Yale MSS.

34. H. W. Beecher to Harriet Beecher, Dec. 5, 1831, Yale MSS.

35. H. W. Beecher to Harriet Beecher, April 5, 1832, Yale MSS; Mrs. Henry Ward

Beecher, "Mr. Beecher as I Knew Him," *Ladies Home Journal* (Oct. 1891), 3.

36. Beecher and Scoville, *Biography*, 125.

37. Lyman Beecher to Catharine Beecher, July 8, 1830, quoted in his *Autobiography*, II, 167; H. W. Beecher to Harriet Beecher, Dec. 5, 1831, Yale MSS.

38. For a description of the intense concern for this area see Arthur E. Bestor, "Patent-Office Models of the Good Society: Some Relationships between Social Reform and Western Expansion," *American Historical Review*, LVII (April, 1953), 505–26.

39. Winthrop Hudson, *Religion in America* (New York, 1965), 151–52.

40. Gilbert H. Barnes, *The Anti-Slavery Impulse, 1830–1844* (New York, 1933), 41; J. L. Tracy to T. Weld, Nov. 24, 1831, quoted in G. H. Barnes and D. L. Dumond, eds., *Letters of Theodore Dwight Weld, Angelina Grimké Weld and Sarah Grimké* (New York, 1934), II, 57.

41. Lyman Beecher, *Autobiography*, II, chap. 24.

42. H. W. Beecher to Harriet Beecher, April 5, 1832, Yale MSS.

43. Catharine Beecher to Harriet Beecher, April 1, 1832, quoted in Lyman Beecher, *Autobiography*, II, 199.

44. Theodore Bacon, *Leonard Bacon, A Statesman of the Church* (New Haven, 1931), 117–43; Mead, *Nathaniel W. Taylor*, 226; Lyman Beecher, *Autobiography*, II, 252.

45. The American Colonization Society, established in 1817, proposed to resettle the Negroes in Africa. In 1826, Lyman Beecher had joined this movement and worked to obtain a physician for the colony of Liberia. See Lyman Beecher to Edward Beecher, March 8, 1826, Mt. Holyoke Library; Lyman Beecher, *Autobiography*, II, 242; see also J. Earl Thompson, Jr., "Lyman Beecher's Long Road to Conservative Abolitionism," *Church History*, 49 (March, 1973), 89–109.

46. For a close examination of the relationship between revivalism and the antislavery movement, see Anne C. Loveland, "Evangelicalism and Immediate Emancipation in American Antislavery Thought," *Journal of Southern History*, XXXII (May, 1966), 172–88; Barnes, *The Anti-Slavery Impulse*, 74; Lyman Beecher, *Autobiography*, II, 245–49; see also "Report on the Subject of Slavery" by the executive committee of the Trustees, *Lane Seminary Papers*, Folder 15, roll 3, McCormick Theological Seminary, Chicago.

47. Lyman Beecher, *A Plea for the West* (Cincinnati, 1835), 62–63.

48. Athenian Society, Records, vol. 3, June 20, 1832, June 25, July 10, 1833, March 20, 1834, Amherst College Archives; Amherst College Auxiliary Anti-Slavery Society, Records, vol. I, Amherst College Archives. Looking back on the abolitionist agitation in 1835, Henry was afraid that the abolitionists "have produced [a] complete *reaction*, and far from aiding the cause, *convincing* the South, they have *driven* them throu' every middle ground onto the extreme of holding broadly and entirely that slavery is *right*, sanctioned by religion, ordained by nature, and essential to the successful progress of a republic." H. W. Beecher, Journal, Dec. 16, 1835, Yale MSS. See also Lewis Tappan, *The Life of Arthur Tappan* (New York, 1870), 233, and H. W. Beecher to Harriet Beecher, April 5, 1832, Yale MSS.

49. H. W. Beecher to Harriet Beecher, March 28, 1833, Amherst College Archives.

50. Beecher and Scoville, *Biography*, 77.

51. H. W. Beecher to ?, Friday evening, 1832, Yale MSS.

2

A Western Ministry

With considerable excitement and anticipation Henry Ward Beecher packed his bags after the Amherst commencement exercises and prepared to leave for Cincinnati. At last he was going to enter theological seminary and rejoin his brothers and sisters, whom he had seen infrequently during his college years. With the exception of Mary, who now was married and living in Hartford, the entire Beecher family had moved to the West. Edward was president of Illinois College, William and George were ministers in Putnam and Batavia, Ohio, and Catharine and Harriet were busy running the Western Female Institute in Cincinnati.[1] With Henry and Charles entering Lane, Lyman Beecher's dream of seeing his children laboring for the Lord in the West seemed about to be fulfilled.

The years at Lane Seminary were to be crucially important for Beecher. Though he was not naturally talented as a speaker and had a speech defect as a child, Henry spent hours and hours at Lane studying popular orators and began to develop his own distinctive preaching style. Under the close supervision of his father, he also learned to thread his way through the theological debates that were convulsing the Presbyterian church. But what was more important, Beecher established his own cautiously liberal stand in opposition to slavery. Buffeted by intense partisans on either side of the debate, he learned to judge the limits of public toleration for criticism and social reform.

When Henry arrived at Lane in July, 1834, he found the seminary moderately prosperous despite the loss of students after the antislavery debates the previous spring. In addition to his father's two-story brick house, there was a classroom building, a dormitory, a steward's house, and two faculty residences.[2] The seminary also boasted a new library that had been recently obtained in Europe by Professor Calvin Stowe.

From the start, Beecher's education at Lane was somewhat unconventional. Although he studied theology with the other students and even taught a Bible class at his father's church in Cincinnati, he spent most of his time reading the popular literature and poetry of the day in an attempt to discover why it appealed to the public. Once he had finished a book, he would write an assessment of it in his private journal. In his efforts to acquire a broad background in current literature, he began to buy books. By the end of his second year, he had collected 147 volumes of his own, including a complete set of Sir Walter Scott's works, two volumes of Shakespeare and Milton, Samuel Johnson's works, six volumes of Edmund Burke's and Noah Webster's speeches, and seven volumes on phrenology.[3]

Beecher's favorite writers were Sir Walter Scott and Robert Burns. Both authors, he noted in his journal, had acquired a mass following because they were able to provide moral instruction that appealed to the emotions of the common people. "He is sure of popularity," Beecher noted after reading a biography of Burns, "who can come down among the people and address to them in their own homely way and with broad humor—and at the same time has an upper current of taste and chaste expression and condensed vigor."[4] Later he commented, "those are to be esteemed the finest writers who can say the shrewdest, liveliest, *witiest* [sic] things and who can impart the greatest instruction without the *formalities* of learning, and who infuses alike through wit and learning a generous glow of feeling."[5]

These comments are revealing because they unconsciously displayed some of the mixed motives behind Beecher's devotion to revivalism. Personal ambition was inextricably combined with an altruistic desire to further the cause of Christ. Like the classical economic theory of his time, which identified self-interest with the good of the community,

Beecher's dedication to revivalism combined a quest for personal popularity with a desire to serve the Lord. Beecher's comments were also strongly elitist, for implicit in his remarks was the assumption that only those of superior intelligence and virtue could speak to the mass of men. Like the early leaders of New England who divided the world into those who were saved and those who were damned, Beecher distinguished between those individuals who were educated and refined and those who were dull and prosaic. He, of course, was one of the former.

Beneath the elitism and egotism implicit in Beecher's comments, there was a perceptive insight. Writers and poets who appealed to the emotions and the heart, who emphasized intuition and feelings, hit a responsive chord in the public mind. Beecher found the poetry of Byron, Coleridge, and Wordsworth particularly appealing in this respect and wrote long critiques of it in his journal. As he noted for his own use, "I admire the German way of going into the motive and spirit of a poem, and discussing the principles and source of feeling."[6] Like the American transcendentalists, though in a more crude and unsophisticated manner, Beecher found a new inspiration in the poetry of the English and German romantics.

In his study of poetry, Beecher liked to compare the German romantic poets—Jacobi, Goethe, and Lessing—to the New England transcendentalists. "It is to be remembered in respect to the Idealism or the *inwardism* of Germany," he noted in his journal, ". . . that it is directly the result of an unnatural *state*—there they are all shut up from all outward action and enterprise. . . . Those who are not *compelled* inwardly, . . . [the] N. England Transcendentalists, only make a mockery of their German brethren. . . . We doubtless tend to the other extreme. There is a development of the exterior, a call for labor and enterprise which draws us to the physical too much—but as this subsides, and it will as wealth enables more [men] to study, I think the American mind will hit the first medium."[7] Although Beecher admired the German notion that true knowledge comes only from an appeal to feelings and emotions, he insisted that the achievement of a higher spiritual understanding be followed by socially beneficent action.

Using the insights he gained from his reading, Beecher began to build his own distinctive style of preaching. Having studied "the power and beauty of language," he now tried to write sermons that any person could understand. "What are called *practical sermons*," he noted in his journal, "should be simple and plain. There is no excuse for *obscurity*—since all that is sought after by a sermon is *lost* if it be not exceedingly simple."[8] Beecher was tired of listening to long, abstract, tedious sermons. What he wanted to develop was a new approach that would touch the emotions of the congregation and instill in them a new commitment to the cause of Christ. The works of Wordsworth, Burns, Coleridge, and Sir Walter Scott, by emphasizing the feelings and finding inspiration in the world of nature, pointed toward a more romantic conception of Christianity, and Beecher slowly began to reshape his religious views to take into account their insights.

In addition to his study of preaching at Lane, Beecher resolved to excel in "instructive, entertaining conversation" so that he would be able to meet people more easily. "Nor will I allow hard study to drive me from *social* habits," he asserted, "and if possible will reserve my afternoons to visits, being studious of gentlemanly manners."[9] Through his activities in the church choir and Bible class he soon became acquainted with many of the most prominent families in Cincinnati. Tall and well built, Beecher possessed an infectious sense of humor that immediately made him popular. A typical example of his playful style was a note he wrote to a friend in 1835:

> The medical authorities of the family, having ordered me up for inspection have decided I was not seaworthy, but have, in view of past services, ordered me into dock to be a receiving ship, and there to undergo thorough repairs. I am quietly riding in the dock without mast or rigging. They have sent aboard two sets of workmen this morning, under the care of Messrs. Calomel and Aloes; and these are to remove all my cargo, ballast, etc., after which I am to be new rigged and furnished and sent out on a new cruise. This is well. I have sailed very dully for some time and came near to floundering once or twice.
>
> Yours truly,
> "Old Constitution"[10]

Beecher's warm-hearted nature and lively sense of humor made him popular with women. Even though he was engaged, he formed a number of strong and lasting friendships. At the same time, in accordance with the strict moral code of the period, he took a stern attitude toward anything having to do with sex. Classical art that revealed "specifics" he criticized as destroying "female delicacy," and dancing he considered unrefined and vulgar. To save his conscience, Beecher carefully recorded his thoughts about his female friends in the journal, which he intended his fiancée to read. The sentimental and idealistic comments were frequently apologetic. Typical was his statement that "Margaret Grosbeck has returned and right glad am I for I love her tho' I am not '*in love* with her.' As a wife, I should hardly select her . . . but I enjoy her society exceedingly. . . . Nothing I have ever dreamed of could better my real choice."[11]

Margaret Grosbeck, Mary Wright, and Catherine Dickinson were articulate and well-educated women with whom Beecher formed close friendships. Observant and sometimes critical, they forced him to think about the impression he made on other people. When Margaret Grosbeck teased him about being "a careless, shallow, flippant trifler," Beecher went out of his way to defend himself. "There are, in fact," he wrote to her, "three classes of divines—the ascetic, the neuter, and the sunshiny: the first conceive the chief end of man to consist in a long face, upturned eyes, a profoundly sanctimonious look. . . . The second class I call neuter because they (like the Chinese leaf by which character is told) quirl [sic] and roll just according to the party with which they are. . . . Now for the third class. I envy them, I emulate them. . . . While they labor hard, think and write, preach and visit, weeping with those who weep, they conceive by the same authority that they may unbend and refresh the mind by laughing with those who laugh. . . ."[12] The fact that a passing comment provoked a two-page letter reveals a degree of insecurity that Beecher was never able to hide. Though at times he gave others the impression that he was self-confident and carefree, he remained sensitive to criticism all his life.

Beecher's outgoing nature and friendliness made him attractive to a number of young women in the city and some of them began to take a serious interest in him, much to his embarrassment. It was only natural that they should become interested, despite his engagement, for then as now, engagements that last five years seem fated to break up. His sister Harriet discovered one case where a young girl had developed a crush on him and advised him to stay away from her. This took Beecher completely by surprise as the girl was some years younger than he was, and he quietly ended the friendship. A second case several months later was even more embarrassing. Beecher was flattered that the girl seemed interested in him, but was mortified that she might be thinking of becoming seriously "involved." In his own naïve way, he was curious about what it was that attracted her. "I must either express too freely my views in her company or my admiration of her unusual maturity and richness of mind," he confided to his journal. Regardless of the cause, he resolved to stay away from her in the future.[13]

This naïve attitude toward women was characteristic of Beecher. Because of his closeness to his sisters and the friendships formed at Lane, he tended to confide his thoughts to women more readily than to men. Moreover, in accordance with the sentimental outlook of the day, he always looked upon women as creatures of purity and refinement and thus was shocked when at times they acted in a more down-to-earth manner.

In the fall of 1835, Beecher's theological studies were disrupted by the heresy trial of his father. The trial was part of the Old School–New School controversy within the Presbyterian church that Lyman Beecher had tried to avoid when he moved to Lane. The dispute developed around the Old School's assertion that man was not a "Free Agent," capable of choosing between good and evil, but was "depraved by nature." Nathaniel S. Beman of the New School summarized the controversy with a parody of the New England *Primer* about the Old School leader Ashbel Green that went as follows:

> In Adam's fall
> We sinned all;
> In Cain's murder,
> We sinned furder;
> By Dr. Green,
> Our sin is seen.

The charges were brought against Lyman Beecher by Joshua L. Wilson, pastor of the First Presbyterian Church of Cincinnati, who was jealous of Beecher's influence in the city. Convinced that the weakened condition of the seminary after the loss of most of the students gave him a better chance for success, he filed a formal complaint against Beecher with the Presbytery. The charges were:

"1. Heresy on the subject of ability, original sin, and Christian perfection.

2. Hypocrisy in claiming belief in the confession of faith.

3. Slander in claiming his opinions are those of the evangelical church in all ages."

The trial was held first in Beecher's church in Cincinnati where Lyman, his books and tracts gathered about him, successfully defended himself against all charges. Unconvinced by the verdict, Wilson appealed to the church synod and a second trial was arranged for October, 1835.[14]

The synod was to be held in Dayton, Ohio, and the defense became a family affair. Supremely confident of his ability to exonerate himself, Lyman Beecher did not begin to prepare his defense until the day before the trial, when he abruptly decided on his approach while clearing a field of stumps and rushed to his study to write down his ideas. Later in the day he drew up a series of resolutions, which he showed to his sons for approval. Henry was particularly impressed by the one that vowed to avoid "the shortlived gratification of retaliation" and "to say nothing in anger or retort or invective and nothing but as made necessary to my sober defense."[15]

On the following day, after a frantic search for the necessary books and papers, Lyman and Henry left for Dayton by canal boat. They arrived in the city after a short trip to find it filled with clergymen and elders who were busy preparing for the trial. Neither Beecher was impressed by the gathering. "I never saw so many faces of clergymen and so few of them intelligent faces," wrote Henry to the rest of the family in Cincinnati. After the first few days, which were devoted to missionary and other matters, Henry was forced to agree with his father that "nothing laid such a tax on a man's patience, whether personally interested or not, as ecclesiastical judicial proceedings."[16]

The trial itself lasted nearly a week as Wilson tried his best to get Lyman Beecher to acknowledge that he had erred. Though Beecher admitted he had used "terms and phrases, and modes of illustration" that might have been misleading, he was so skilled in the fine points of the theology that Wilson and the Old School could not convict him of heresy. When the synod ended, they were forced to be satisfied with a resolution of warning and a demand that Beecher publish a precise statement of his views in pamphlet form. Neither side was happy about the result. Wilson threatened to appeal the issue to the coming session of the General Assembly and Beecher intimated that he himself might press countercharges.[17]

The continuing controversy upset the Beecher family. Both Henry and Charles were disillusioned by the sectarian bickering, the petty squabbles over theological minutiae, and the bitter personal invective brought out by the trial. Much to the dismay of the family, Charles decided to leave the ministry and become a musician. He dropped out of the seminary and went to New Orleans, where he became a clerk for a cotton merchant and the organist for a Presbyterian church. Henry, too, was profoundly disturbed by the trial. Never much interested in the fine points of theology, such as the debates over free will and original sin, he now boldly vowed to concentrate on perfecting his preaching style and to avoid all theological disputes. He would never, he asserted, join any sectarian movement or become the spokesman for any faction or clique.[18]

Shortly after his father's heresy trial, Henry began to clarify his thoughts on the abolitionist and colonization movements. His attention was drawn to this issue by the increasingly frequent outbreaks of mob violence in Ohio. A few days after Lyman Beecher's trial, James Thome, an abolitionist lecturing near Granville, was driven out of town and the building he used was burned to the ground. In the following year, there were at least eleven incidents of mob violence in the state's towns.[19]

Like his father, Henry was sympathetic to the colonization movement and had commented in his journal that the abolitionists had driven the southerners to the extreme of "holding broadly and entirely that slavery is *right*, sanctioned by religion, ordained by nature, and essential to the progress of a republic." He shared, moreover, his father's preoccupation with order and social control. Thus, the frequent outbreaks of violence particularly upset him. "Mobs," he wrote, "confused things of dregs," were the work of the Devil. They could never accomplish anything positive.[20]

In July, 1836, the Birney riots broke out in Cincinnati, giving Beecher his first direct contact with mob violence. Cincinnati in those years was very much a southern city on free soil. A market in which southerners bought many of their manufactured supplies and a center for the shipment of pork, it remained sympathetic to southern interests despite a sizable northern population. Thus, when James G. Birney moved his antislavery paper, *The Philanthropist*, into town in April, he was immediately confronted by a hostile public.[21]

One of the few townspeople interested in Birney's paper was Henry Ward Beecher. A month before Birney arrived, Beecher had become the temporary editor of a local publication, *The Journal and Western Luminary*, for which he received a much-needed forty dollars a month. Shortly thereafter, Beecher used the paper to attack abolitionists of Garrison's stamp, contrasting them with the "courteous, calm, and able" Birney. "We," he quickly added, "are partisans with neither side."[22]

Hostility to *The Philanthropist* increased throughout the spring, and on July 12, during the semiannual influx of southern buyers, a mob entered the building where Birney published his paper, wrecked his type, and destroyed his ink and paper. Beecher responded with a ringing editorial in the *Journal and Western Luminary* entitled the "Spirit of Our Times."[23] This editorial revealed an attitude toward mob violence that Beecher had developed during the preceding year. The basis for this attitude was Beecher's belief in majority government. Mobs could never be legitimate. The only protection for the rights of the minority, he wrote in his journal, was the "religious obligation in obedience to Justice which God enjoins." If the minority took the law into its own hands, it would become a mob, acting without fear, conscience, or the restraint of public opinion. Once the mob became accustomed to judge, condemn, and execute, it would treat all laws with contempt and would destroy the fabric of society.[24]

Beecher supplemented his views about majority rule with the theory that the riots were the result of a conspiracy to overthrow society led by the utopian socialists. These outbreaks of violence, he declared, are "the foreseen results of well-applied, carefully prepared means. The Owens, Wrights, and Kneelands are laboring to convince the people that they are oppressed and abused, that law is a mere farce," and that society must be turned upside down. This statement, which was without factual basis, was similar to his father's argument that the Catholics were conspiring to take over the West. It rested upon the belief, held by many Americans in the nineteenth century, that a democracy was particularly vulnerable to subversive tactics because of its openness. Since the country lacked strong military or police forces, it was vitally important to prevent small.factions from disrupting society and seizing the reins of power.[25]

The worst aspect of the riots, Beecher continued, was that they denied a fundamental right—"the first, the highest, the most sacred, the last deserted right of freedmen, the right of free discussion." If freedom of speech were denied, Beecher argued, the foundation of a democratic society would be destroyed, for the moral restraint that protected American society rested upon an enlightened public opinion. Without the free and open discussion of all issues, the moral fiber of the nation would weaken and the country would be destroyed.

Beecher's editorial, though it did not sway public opinion, was courageous. Harriet thought it admirable and Birney himself, writing to Arthur Tappan on the day after the riots, mentioned it as part of a more favorable attitude in the city toward his paper. But when he began to publish it again, riots broke out a second time and Birney left the city.[26]

The most interesting aspect of Beecher's editorial was its strong similarity to his brother Edward's protest a year later against the Alton, Illinois, riots in which Elijah P. Lovejoy was murdered. Both riots were reactions against abolitionist editors and in both cases the key principle was that of freedom of speech. "Of this kind," wrote Edward Beecher, "are the events which preceded and led to the death of the Rev. Elijah P. Lovejoy, the first martyr in America to the great principle of freedom of speech and of the press."[27]

The similarity of position grew out of the emphasis of the New School theology on God's moral government, a concept that had played a central role in their father's theology. In his sermon "The Bible as a Code of Laws," Lyman Beecher had defined moral government as "the influence of law upon accountable creatures," which the Bible revealed and judgment day sanctioned. It was Edward, however, who best summed up the theory:

> Who can deny, that the tendency of the age is, to make one sublime and simple truth the regulating principle of all human society: —that in the very nature of the human mind, and in the relations of man to God, there is a foundation laid for certain immutable duties and rights; that the relations of the individual to God are higher and more sacred than any other

relations; and that, as God has made it the duty of every individual to live for him, so it is the immutable right of every human being to be free to do it.[28]

The concept of God's moral government not only placed a great emphasis on the principle of freedom of speech and of the press, it also gave a fillip to the crusade against slavery, for when carried to its logical conclusion, the concept meant that the slave as one of God's creatures had an immutable right to be treated as an equal. As Beecher acknowledged in one of his sermon books, "the radical sin of American Slavery is that it *denies* manhood to those on whom Christ bestowed it."[29]

As Beecher came to realize the logical implications of his views, he slowly modified his attitude toward the treatment of black people. The most noticeable change in outlook came in 1839, three years after the Birney riots. Only a year earlier Beecher had been an active member of the colonization society and had raised funds for that movement during a drive in July. At that time he had delivered a sermon based on the assumption that the two races, black and white, would not intermarry. Rather than having the races live as two distinct and separate peoples, which, he thought, would lead to one of them becoming superior and controlling the other, he had counseled removal of the Negroes.[30]

Reflecting upon his discourse a few months later, Beecher concluded that his assumption had been wrong. Intermarriage was possible and had actually taken place in history. His example was the Ethiopians, who had mingled with the lighter race of the Egyptians and had advanced civilization. Since blacks were not inferior—"they once gave civilization to the world by mingling"—they would marry mulattoes and eventually lighten in color until the prejudice against them disappeared.

After thinking further about the matter, Beecher also concluded that slavery was unprofitable and would eventually decline and die out. "The cotton and sugars of America," he wrote in his journal, "have drained Africa of her offspring for slavery and I think ere long the cottons and sugars of Africa and India will drain America of slavery." Soon, he believed, the peculiar institution would be undersold on the world market and this, rather than the hand of philanthropy or the word of justice, would destroy it.[31]

Beecher's new attitude toward slavery, though more liberal than his father's middle-of-the-road stand, was tempered by his dislike of violence and his concern for social stability. Although he now recognized that the colonization movement did not provide an acceptable solution for the problem of slavery, he still did not believe that the sinfulness of the peculiar institution, bad as it was, justified overturning the present social system. By arguing that slavery would die a natural death because it was becoming unprofitable, he thereby avoided the tougher moral issue which concerned the question of how to correct the present injustice.

The debate over slavery, together with the theological battle his father had just undergone, convinced Henry that he should in the future steer his way carefully through debates on moral issues. An opportunist like his father, he was convinced that the best course was to avoid if possible all theological and political controversies and to concentrate instead on winning new converts for the church. Thus, he confided to his journal during his last weeks at Lane, "Remember! you can gain more easily if you get around . . . [people's] *prejudices* and put truth in their minds. But *never* if you attack *prejudice*. Look well at this. . . ."[32]

Shortly before he left Lane in the spring of 1837, Beecher began to look for a church of his own. The year before, his sister Harriet had married Professor Calvin Stowe and in October she had given birth to twin girls. "One is the perfect image of Mr. Stowe," wrote Henry to his brother William, "except unfortunately it was not born with spectacles on—a singular event if we reflect on the habits of its parent —but so providence has ordered it." The marriage of his sister and the birth of her children made Beecher eager to have a family of his own, and he began to search for a position at a church so that he could return East and get married.[33]

Early in May, he visited the First Presbyterian Church in Lawrenceburg, Indiana, a small town of fewer than fifteen hundred people at the junction of the Ohio and Miami Rivers. Not many parishioners turned out at the small brick church to hear him preach and his first sermon did not seem well received. Beecher nevertheless remained optimistic about his chances of getting a call and commented in his journal that he was thinking "seriously of settling there—a desolate place indeed."

Beecher's second sermon several weeks later went better, and on June 15, 1837, he received a call from the church and an offer of a salary of $250 per year. The offer, though not large by the standards of the time, was nevertheless flattering, and Beecher quickly accepted it, vowing to secure a large congregation by preaching well and visiting widely.[34]

Beecher had originally planned to wait until he was ordained before getting married. But seven years was a long time to be engaged and so in July, shortly after he had explained his plans in a letter to his fiancée, he started for the East. The letter arrived on the twenty-ninth and Beecher appeared, much to the surprise of the Bullard family, on the afternoon of the same day. The wedding was held later that week, and the young couple left immediately for the West, traveling by boat from Boston to New York and then by train to Ohio, where they stopped to visit Beecher's father.[35]

Beecher and his new wife arrived in Lawrenceburg on October 17 and took up residence with one of the church elders while they looked for a place to live. After searching the town from top to bottom, Eunice finally found two rooms over a stable. Friends supplied sheets, a bedstead, and some old carpet, while George Beecher lent them a stove. Eunice sold her cloak to purchase the other necessities and together the couple cleaned and organized their quarters. About the only thing of value in the whole apartment was Beecher's small library, which he arranged in its packing cases on one side of the room.

Having set up the apartment, Beecher now turned his attention to the problems of his church. He sincerely believed, as his father had argued, that the destiny of the nation would be controlled by the religious development of the West, and he was eager to promote a revival. As he wrote to a friend, "May God give us all strength, in this twilight of [the] Millennium to labor . . . and conquer. Things look encouraging. Public sentiment is fast forming. It's the seed time."[36]

Despite his high expectations, Beecher's efforts to start a revival were at first marked by failure. His opening sermon, which was designed to show off his theological education, was too dry and abstract for the members of the congregation who were used to the vivid harangues of the local Methodist and Baptist preachers. Nor did Beecher have much success when he visited the members of the church at home and urged them to commit themselves to Christ. The usual conversion experience went through three stages. The individual first became convinced of his own sin and anxious about the future of his soul. Then he decided to repent of his sins and lead a new life. This decision was followed with an examination by the minister and church elders and then by communion. Beecher had a number of individuals in his congregation on the threshold of making the decision and yet was unable to get them to follow through. One member of the congregation whom Beecher visited numerous times and urged to repent replied that he was willing "to think, read, [and] pray, but [was] not *willing to give up the heart*." Beecher's response, which he recorded in one of his notebooks, was smug and self-righteous. "I then solemnly addressed him on his danger and left," he wrote.[37]

Beecher worried about his failure to interest his congregation in revivalism, and he began to have doubts about his ability as a preacher. To add to his troubles, his wife was upset by the rigors of frontier life. She disliked the isolation of Lawrenceburg and blamed her husband for spending his limited salary in a foolish manner. Henry had always been careless about his funds and even at Lane Seminary had only been made solvent by a gift of a hundred dollars from his stepmother. Now his careless habits and his passion for buying books threatened to bankrupt his family.[38]

Eunice was particularly concerned because she was expecting her first child and did not think that they would have enough money to live on. Fortunately, when on the morning of May 16, 1838, their first daughter was born, the members of the church helped out, contributing food and clothes so that Henry could proudly announce to his mother-in-law that "the whole preparation for this event has not cost us a single cent."[39]

Despite the difficulties Beecher encountered during the first year of his pastorate, he continued to work hard, and gradually his efforts showed signs of success. As he became more experienced, he modified his sermons, emphasizing the love of Christ and the evidence of God that could be found in the natural world. Instead of lecturing his congregation on "Avarice" and "Human Depravity," he now appealed to their emotions with sermons entitled "Ashamed of Christ" and "Put on the Armor of God." The new approach worked, and many members of the congregation were frequently reduced to tears. Soon more people were attending his services. In a note to his brother and sister-in-law, Henry confidently reviewed his progress. "The Methodists held a ten days meeting here about a fortnight ago," he commented, "and tho' they took in about 40 it is beyond doubt a decided failure and demonstrates that one year of clearly preached truth has done a great deal. My meetings are fuller than before and more of the intelligent of that church are gradually giving in to right views and feelings. . . ." [40]

A new problem arose for Beecher in the fall of his second year at Lawrenceburg when he went before the Oxford presbytery to be ordained. Since his father's heresy trial two years earlier, the conflict between the Old and New Schools of the Presbyterian church had been intensified by the introduction of the slavery issue. A crisis was reached in 1838 when the Old School gained control of the General Assembly and voted to remove four New School synods, which were theologically liberal and opposed to slavery. This, in turn, led to a general division within the church. [41]

Beecher's ordination examination before the Old School Oxford presbytery thus became a potential source of conflict. Beecher himself looked upon his examination as a challenge because he believed that the basis of the church dispute was organizational rather than doctrinal —that it was a conflict between Old School Scotch-Irish Presbyterians who wanted to place church power in the hands of the General Assembly and the New School members who wanted the power distributed among the presbyteries, as the federal power was distributed among the states. [42]

Thus, when Beecher appeared before the presbytery, he was prepared for a long and intensive examination.

"Will the man tell us in what relation Adam stood to his posterity?" asked the moderator.

"In the relation of a *federal head*," answered Beecher.

"What do you mean by federal head?" questioned the moderator.

"A head with whom God made a covenant for all posterity," was Beecher's reply. And so the meeting went. Like his father, Beecher was so well versed in the debate over original sin that he was able to answer all questions easily. When the examination ended and a vote was taken, the presbytery decided unanimously to ordain him. Before the presbytery took the final step, however, it passed a resolution that no one should be licensed or ordained who did not connect himself with the Old School Presbyterian church. Unable to accept this condition, Beecher returned home and spoke to his church. "I am unwilling to be hemmed in by the narrow lines of schools and parties," he explained, "but, standing as a freeman in God's Church, I look about to see who is *most loved of God*; and the holiest, humblest, and most useful man, is dearest to me, whether *in* or *out* of my particular church." Persuaded by Beecher's arguments, his church withdrew from the Oxford presbytery. On November 9, 1838, Beecher was ordained at his own church in a ceremony presided over, appropriately, by his father and led by Calvin Stowe. Despite his early struggles with his father's theology, Henry Ward Beecher entered the ministry exactly as his father had wished, as a spokesman for the New School theology.[43]

Although Beecher's church went along with his desire to join the New School, it took advantage of the incident to criticize him. One of the members of the church explained to Beecher that the congregation was dissatisfied with him on two grounds: he was too free in his use of credit and he had failed to visit his congregation frequently enough during the summer. Beecher accepted the criticism with humility, realizing that he had become "too much elated, and too independent." After thinking the matter over, he drew up a list of resolutions in his journal:

> 1. Take vigorous measures to liquidate all my debts.
> 2. I am *determined* never again to have credit or regular bills at stores in my affairs.
> 3. I shall visit more and labor more abundantly.
> 4. Strive to exercise a meek, forgiving softened spirit toward all.
> 5. *See to it*, that these things by the above course do not break me up from here at present. To church, to our cause at the West, and to my own character it would be eminently disasterous [*sic*]. . . .[44]

Beecher's resolutions reveal not only an awareness of his own shortcomings, but also a strong determination to succeed. Though he was vain and egotistical, he remained deeply committed to working for the cause of Christ by starting in the West. "In public and private," he noted in his journal, "I will give my life to bringing all Christians to [the] work of spreading the *true* power of the Gospel—the love of Christ."[45]

Still another problem that hindered his efforts to spread revivals was the general lawlessness of the town. An incident that took place in 1838 was not unusual. At one o'clock in the morning Beecher was called to the town's bank to see a man who was said to be shot through the head and dying. On the way over he speculated about what had happened and assumed that someone had tried to rob the bank. As things turned out, the wound was received in a house of ill fame, which the injured man's father visited and supported. Nine men had already left town to seize the girl who was responsible and bring her into custody. Since the town lacked a hospital, Beecher spent the night in the bank helping the local doctor. The entire event was vividly described in his journal.

> I helped in all proceedings. Two bullets extracted from upper vertebra—somewhat difficult. At noon, on dressing wound, a new wound was discovered. . . . This causes so much pain in arm. After ball extracted—pains began to commence and he begged the Dr. to kill him. After breakfast he was moved home—Ed Tate met us and burst into tears. . . .
>
> Afternoon not so well. Dr. very dubious. My expectation then is that this will do nothing toward a revival spirit. . . . The reason obvious, it produces in everyone an excitement and interest wh[ich] are not congenial to contemplation of religious subjects. In short, men all think of the accident and wholly direct their attention away from God.

Despite such interruptions, Beecher made some progress in promoting a revival, though no large additions were made to his church. What success he did have was the result of extremely hard work. Beecher wrote out all of his sermons and spent hours each week trying to improve them. He was not hesitant, moreover, to discuss his own mistakes in public as examples. As he wrote in his notebook in September, 1838, he preached on "Humility" because of the "general uneasiness of my Ch[urch] at not visiting and rumors getting abroad as to my pecuniary matters." This frank approach, together with Beecher's resolution to "preach better, visit more, and labor harder," gradually made him a more mature and effective minister.[46]

Because of his work at Lawrenceburg, Beecher, in the spring of 1839, came to the attention of Samuel Merrill, the treasurer of the state, who was visiting the town on business. Merrill was a deacon of the Second Presbyterian Church in Indianapolis, which was looking for a new minister. The church had already extended a call to two other clergymen and had been turned down. Now the congregation was becoming somewhat anxious. At Merrill's invitation, Beecher traveled to Indianapolis, delivered a trial sermon, and received a call. After some hesitation, he accepted the offer, explaining his reasons in a letter to his father. "Ohio and Illinois is [*sic*] safe," he wrote. "Indiana, a richer state than Illinois and determined to rise very high—is in *nobody's* hands. Her capital is her centre—geographically, commercially and *morally*. It is the key of the state. That held, will be an *advantage* not easily equalled at any other point in the state—the old school know it—are aiming at it. . . . The Churches are enterprising—will be wealthy—are influential—will *publish* what is well written—and from this point it can be diffused by Representatives and business men over whole surface of land." [47]

Beecher's comments were perceptive, for many of the leading merchants of the city, like Samuel Merrill, had migrated from New England and were eager to make Indianapolis into a show place that would set the standard for other cities within the state. They wanted an educated clergyman who would preserve the social values they had known in the East and who could give the town a sense of cultural refinement. They wanted a minister who hated the lawlessness and violence of the West and would work to instill within society the virtues of discipline and self-control. But they wanted, most of all, a man who not only would emphasize the virtues of the New England way of life, but who also knew how to communicate with a rough, provincial western audience. Because he possessed these qualifications, Henry Ward Beecher was an ideal choice for the Second Presbyterian Church.

During his five years in the West, Beecher's ideals had changed quite noticeably. Living on the frontier forced him to deemphasize some of his opinions and to stress others. Although Beecher never had been fond of the classics or interested in academic learning, he now deliberately erased all traces of formal study from his sermons and tried to make his arguments appear to be nothing more than simple common sense. In this fashion, he hoped to reach a western audience that distrusted the intellectual pretentiousness of many Presbyterian clergymen. If Beecher's interest in formal learning waned, however, his concern for the maintenance of law and order increased. Incensed by the destruction of property and the thoughtless violence that occurred during the attacks on the abolitionists, Beecher vowed to use all his ability to preserve order and stability within society. His concern for the maintenance of social control, in fact, now became a passion. "The tyranny of a multitude is much worse than [that] of the man," he confided to his journal. "The force and momentum of combined action is greater than individual. Tyrants may have conscience—a multitude has none. . . . [Tyrants] may be restrained by public opinion —a multitude is the public which judges of its own acting, and stands in no fear of itself." Beecher's reaction to western violence thus confirmed the intense concern for social control that had been one of the central features of his upbringing in New England. The experience in the West thereby reinforced the traditions of the East and provided a firm basis for his conservative stands on social issues.[48]

Because of his intense dislike of violence and conflict, Beecher also learned while in the West to steer clear of controversial subjects. For reasons that were both personal and pragmatic, he deliberately avoided becoming associated with a particular stand on social issues. Though he claimed that he adopted this tactic because it gave him greater freedom of expression, the fact was that it also allowed him to avoid taking sides until the controversy seemed headed toward a solution.

Beecher's pragmatic and conservative approach was in large part responsible for his success in Lawrenceburg. During his three years there, he had built up the membership of his church, organized Temperance and Sunday School societies, and sparked revivals in the neighboring areas. Lawrenceburg had been a proving ground where he had developed his preaching style and increased his self-confidence. Now that the church was on its feet, he felt less guilty about departing, because he knew that it could continue without him. Besides, the possibility of sparking a revival in the state capital was too great to pass up. Although Beecher was still an unknown backwoods preacher, he would at last have the opportunity to establish a reputation for himself. That opportunity could not be missed, and Beecher vowed to make the most of it.

NOTES

1. Forrest Wilson, *Crusader in Crinoline: The Life of Harriet Beecher Stowe* (Philadelphia, 1941), 147.

2. *Ibid.*, 149.

3. H. W. Beecher, Journal, Dec. 2, 1835, Yale MSS.

4. *Ibid.*, Oct. 17, 1835.

5. *Ibid.*, Nov. 15, 1835.

6. William G. Beecher and Samuel Scoville, *A Biography of Rev. Henry Ward Beecher* (New York, 1888), 146.

7. H. W. Beecher, Journal, n.d., p. 231; see also William G. McLoughlin, *The Meaning of Henry Ward Beecher* (New York, 1970).

8. H. W. Beecher, Journal, Jan. 5, 1836.

9. *Ibid.*, March 27, 1836.

10. *Ibid.*, Nov. 14, 1835.

11. *Ibid.*, Sept. 14, 18, Oct. 2, 1835.

12. *Ibid.*, Oct. 29, 1835; see also H. W. Beecher to Abbe Hall, May, 1837, White Collection, Stowe-Day Foundation.

13. H. W. Beecher, Journal, Dec. 7, 1835, March 26, 1836.

14. Henry B. Stanton, *Random Recollections* (New York, 1887), 29; Wilson, *Crusader in Crinoline*, 154; Lyman Beecher, *The Autobiography of Lyman Beecher*, ed. Barbara M. Cross (Cambridge, 1961), II, 265.

15. H. W. Beecher, Journal, Oct., 1835.

16. H. W. Beecher to family, Oct. 16, 1835, quoted in Lyman Beecher, *Autobiography*, II, 269: H. W. Beecher, Journal, Oct. 16, 1835.

17. Lyman Beecher, *Autobiography*, II, 271; Lyman Beecher, *Views in Theology* (Cincinnati, 1836).

18. H. W. Beecher, Journal, Oct. 9, 1835; Lyman Beecher Stowe, *Saints, Sinners, and Beechers*, 336ff; H. W. Beecher, Journal, Oct. 16, 1835; Dec., 1839. Under the "Plan of Union" of 1801, the Presbyterians and Congregationalists had agreed to join forces in their western missionary activities. The Beechers, who were Presbyterians and worked under this plan, were never entirely happy with it.

19. Russel B. Nye, *Fettered Freedom: Civil Liberties and the Slavery Controversy, 1830–1860* (East Lansing, 1949), 169.

20. H. W. Beecher, Journal, Dec. 16, 1835.

21. Benjamin P. Thomas, *Theodore Weld, Crusader for Freedom* (New Brunswick, N.J., 1950), 44.

22. H. W. Beecher, Journal, May 11, 1836; *The Journal and Western Luminary*, quoted in Wilson, *Crusader in Crinoline*, 182.

23. *The Journal and Western Luminary*, July 21, 1836.

24. H. W. Beecher, Journal, Sept. 26, 1835, July 10, 1839, March, 1840.

25. *The Journal and Western Luminary*, July 21, 1836.

26. H. B. Stowe to Calvin Stowe, n.d., Yale MSS; James G. Birney to Arthur Tappan, July 22, 1836, quoted in *Letters of James Gillespie Birney, 1831–1857*, ed. Dwight L. Dumond (New York, 1938), I, 346.

27. Edward Beecher, *Narrative of Riots at Alton in Connection with the Death of Rev. Elijah P. Lovejoy* (Alton, Ill., 1838), 114.

28. *Ibid.*, 2.

29. H. W. Beecher, Sermon Book, 1837, Yale MSS. William Ellery Channing took a similar position on the right of freedom of speech, in his book, *Slavery*, published in Boston in 1836.

30. H. W. Beecher, Journal, Jan. 2, 1839.

31. *Ibid.*, Jan. 2, 1839, Feb. 28, 1840.

32. *Ibid.*, May 4, 1837.

33. H. W. Beecher to William Beecher, Oct. 4, 1836, Beecher-Stowe Collection, Schlesinger Library.

34. H. W. Beecher, Journal, May 4, June 15, 1837.

35. Beecher and Scoville, *Biography*, 170–72; Mrs. Henry Ward Beecher, "Mr. Beecher as I Knew Him," *Ladies Home Journal* (Nov., 1891), 9.

36. H. W. Beecher to W. S. Tyler, May 2, 1835, Amherst College Archives. The best description of the Lawrenceburg years can be found in Jane Elsmere's *Henry Ward Beecher: The Indiana Years, 1837–1847* (Indianapolis, 1973).

37. Beecher and Scoville, *Biography*, First Sermon, in Appendix; L. C. Rudolph, *Hoosier Zion: The Presbyterians in Early Indiana* (New Haven, 1963), 26; H. W. Beecher, Notebook, March 12, 1838, Beecher Papers, Library of Congress.

38. H. W. Beecher, Journal, March 14, 1837.

39. H. W. Beecher to Lucy Bullard, May 17, 1838, Yale MSS.

40. Eunice Beecher to Ebenezer and Lucy Bullard, with a note from Henry Ward Beecher, June 25, 1838, Yale MSS; see also Sermon Book, 1838, and Notebook, 1838.

41. This point is made by C. Bruce Steiger, "Abolition and the Presbyterian Schism of 1837–1838," *Mississippi Valley Historical Review*, XXVI (1949–50), 391–414, and M. Brainerd, *Life of the Rev. Thomas Brainerd* (Philadelphia, 1870), 145, 169.

42. H. W. Beecher to John H. Thomas, Oct. 3, 1838, copied from Beecher's Journal, 154–62.

43. Beecher and Scoville, *Biography*, 161; H. W. Beecher, Journal, Sept. 27, 1838; John H. Thomas, *An Historical Sketch of the Presbyterian Church of Lawrenceburg, Indiana* (Lawrenceburg, 1887), 7; H. W. Beecher, Journal, Oct., 1838.

44. H. W. Beecher, Journal, Sept. 27, 1838.

45. *Ibid.*, Dec., 1839.

46. *Ibid.*, 1838; H. W. Beecher, Notebook, Sept. 30, 1838; H. W. Beecher, Journal, Oct. 22, 1838. During his first two years Beecher wrote more than a hundred sermons and most of them have been preserved at either the Yale Library or the Library of Congress.

47. H. W. Beecher to Lyman Beecher, May 18, 1839, Schlesinger Library.

48. H. W. Beecher, Journal, July 10, 1839.

3

Indianapolis

In the summer of 1839 Henry Ward Beecher began his pastorate at the Second Presbyterian Church in Indianapolis. It was an enormous success. During the next eight years his church became the largest Presbyterian parish in the state, and Beecher gained a much-deserved reputation as a dynamic and forceful preacher. Traveling to neighboring towns and cities, he helped lead a general awakening of major proportions. Unlike his father and his sister Catharine, who sometimes alienated western leaders with their insistence on eastern styles and standards, Henry adapted his approach to fit the interests of the western common man. Forced to compete with Baptists and Methodists, he was instrumental in transforming the elitist Presbyterian theology into a simplified doctrine that would appeal to a broad cross section of Jacksonian America.[1]

Beecher's success as a preacher was matched by his achievements as a reformer and his role as a spokesman for the new Victorian morality. Using the reform strategy he had developed at Lane Seminary and at Lawrenceburg, he adapted revivalist theology to the gospel of success, publishing a series of lectures to young men that were widely praised and reprinted. Because he sensed the contradictory public concerns for both individual freedom and social control, he adeptly combined the two ideals in his doctrine of the industrious, self-policing, inner-directed man—an individual who was on his own but was always responsive to peer-group pressure. Such an individual, following the older Calvinist preoccupation with inner faith and personal commitment, could now judge his own standards of behavior against a set of secular community-wide ideals. Drawing upon the tremendous sense of community and support that developed during a revival, Beecher offered his midwestern audience a set of personal standards that fused individual choice and social control—themes that lay at the heart of the revivalist tradition. Ignoring the contradictions in such a fusion, Beecher articulated a set of beliefs that were to be widely adopted by Victorian Americans in the next two decades.[2]

Energetic and forceful, yet deeply sensitive to the changing public mood, Beecher also modified the traditional conception of the minister's role. Where his father and the earlier generation of clerics had been looked upon as exponents of partisan causes—New School versus Old School—Federalist versus Jeffersonian—Henry Ward Beecher established through his cautious handling of the explosive abolitionist issue a new ministerial ideal: the disinterested, nonpartisan spokesman for the public good. Critical of both sides in the debate over slavery, he insisted that a new, fair-minded, committed position could be established. One could oppose slavery without identifying with either radicals or southerners. To the cautious, middle-class westerners, the ideal was enormously appealing, and they cheered his efforts. Though the ideal of nonpartisan public reform was as contradictory and as hard to achieve as the ideal of the totally free yet socially controlled citizen, it appealed to an audience that was impatient with theological fine points and eager for action.

When Henry Ward Beecher arrived in July, 1839, Indianapolis was a typical country village. Streets were unpaved and lined with stumps, and pastures existed at different places within the town. Yet even then Indianapolis showed signs of future development. In addition to the governor's house and a number of public buildings, the town boasted of a new three-story brick hotel, built at the cost of thirty thousand dollars. Conscious of its position in the state, its citizens had established a large number of educational institutions, including a benevolent society, a female institute, an academy, and a seminary. To the new arrivals, the town seemed to be a seedbed of new ideas and interests.

The Second Presbyterian Church, whose call Beecher accepted, had been established a year earlier by fifteen New School members who had broken away from the First Church. At that time the new church had secured the temporary services of a minister and the use of a school building for worship. Beecher's task, as the church's first full-time preacher, was to attract a larger congregation and to secure a new church building. The success of the New School Church in the city as well as the support of his family depended upon his efforts.

Although he was only twenty-six years old, Beecher looked forward to his new position without trepidation. The prospects for success were far brighter than they had been in Lawrenceburg. Although the congregation was small, it contained some wealthy individuals and had promised to pay Beecher a salary of six hundred dollars.[3] Living quarters, too, were cheaper and more available. Instead of an apartment, the family now rented a three-room house and had a small plot of land in which to plant a garden.

Despite the improved physical circumstances and the auspicious prospect of his new position, the first two years in Indianapolis were very difficult for Beecher and his family. The trouble began early when the Beechers came down with malaria, or the "chills and ague," as it was called. The boggy woods and swampy river valleys made the state an ideal breeding ground for mosquitoes, and sooner or later most people caught the disease. As Theodore Parker commented after traveling through the area, "I saw 300 or 400 children in the schools of Indianapolis—not one rosy cheek! The women are tall and bony, their faces thin and flabby-cheeked."[4]

After living in the town for only a few weeks, Beecher became so sick that he could not preach and had to remain in bed. As he had done on earlier occasions, he used the time to look back over his life and came to the conclusion that his illness was a form of divine chastisement. "During my confinement," he wrote in his journal, "I have been greatly profited. In looking back on my past life I find it wholly wrong—a wonderful deficiency of right feeling. . . . In God's help, I I am determined in future to make very serious and specific efforts for spiritual advancement."[5]

Eunice Beecher, who was expecting her second child, was even sicker than her husband, and for a time the neighbors had to look after her one-year-old daughter. In March, 1840, after three weeks of false labor pains, she gave birth to a dead son. That fall Beecher decided that his wife should spend the winter in the East and took her back to her parents' home in West Sutton, Massachusetts. Commenting on the trip, Samuel Merrill, the most prominent deacon of Beecher's church, wrote his brother that "Mr. Beecher is still popular but his wife is a great weight on him, whether from severe ill health of something else I cannot say."[6]

The following July, Beecher returned East to bring his wife and family back to Indianapolis. On the trip he took with him Julia Merrill and Elizabeth Bates, the daughters of two members of his congregation who wanted the children to visit the East while they were still under fourteen and could travel at half fare. Mrs. Beecher returned to Indianapolis that summer and later in the fall gave birth to a second son, who was named Henry Barton. The frequent pregnancies and periodic bouts with malaria gradually wore down Eunice's health and made Henry worry about her.

The problems created by malaria and sickness were compounded by worries over money. In addition to the money owed to doctors, Beecher owed one hundred dollars a year for his house, two hundred dollars for two extra lots and interest payments, and various smaller amounts to different creditors. Although his house was a tiny one-story frame structure just ten feet wide, his wife was forced to take in a boarder to increase their income.[7]

Despite the problems created by his wife's poor health, his unstable finances, and his own frequent illnesses, Beecher was from the start more successful as a minister in Indianapolis than he had been in Lawrenceburg. In part, this was because he was now preaching to a better-educated congregation, proud of their few cultural attainments and eager to improve themselves. In part, too, Beecher's success resulted from a change in his preaching style, which now combined graphic images drawn from nature with an intense personal appeal to specific members of the congregation. But more effective than anything else was the grueling routine that he followed. His average weekly schedule included daily prayer meetings, two sermons on Sunday in his own pulpit, and five additional sermons at other churches. In addition, he ran a Sunday School and served as clerk of the newly formed presbytery of Indianapolis. By the end of his second year, Beecher had succeeded in building a new church and had increased the size of his small congregation.[8]

But not until his third year was he able to start a major revival. Working first in Terre Haute and then in Indianapolis, he launched a major crusade. In the spring more than a hundred new members were added to his church. As he reported to his father in May, "prosperity and peace dwell with us. Our church is filled; our young converts run well, and already there is gathered in material for another revival of persons not wont to attend Church anymore. . . . The neighborhoods about town are also revived." Working at a hectic pace, Beecher was able to inform the General Assembly in 1843 that 210 new communicants had been added to his church. In only three years the Second Presbyterian Church had grown to be the largest in the state. In Indiana, where the usual condition of the Presbyterian churches was one of destitution, Beecher's church stood out as an exception and attracted the attention of religious leaders in the East.[9]

Once he became known as an effective revivalist, Beecher was called to visit other congregations in nearby cities and towns. Each year he traveled several hundred miles by horseback and spent weeks at a time promoting revivals. In Lafayette, Indiana, he was responsible for more than sixty conversions during a two-week stay in 1843. Aggressive, energetic, and good-natured, he gradually built a statewide reputation.[10]

In the midst of these revivalist activities, Beecher was informed that his brother Charles was about to lose his faith. Charles's belief in God had been weakened while he lived in New Orleans and by 1842 he was convinced that he never should become a minister. "I think you will agree with me," he wrote to his father, that "the constitution, physical and intellectual with which God has blessed me—and the course of his providence toward me—show clearly to my mind that he never intended that my field of action should be the gospel ministry." But Lyman Beecher was unwilling to accept his son's conclusion. After conferring with Henry and Catharine, he suggested that Henry invite Charles to come to Indianapolis and lead the music in his church. "Charles would be safe and happy," he wrote to Henry. "You are the only one who could do the needful 'take live and let alone' indispensable for his recovery." With his customary shrewdness, Lyman Beecher realized that Henry would not pressure his younger brother and that Charles would probably become involved with the revival that was sweeping Henry's church.[11]

Lyman Beecher's assumption proved correct. The revival had commenced in March and dozens of new members had been added to the Second Presbyterian Church. "My leading men seem to have come almost upon a new ground, and I never saw even an approximation, to the clearness and strength of Christian feeling, visible among my people," wrote Henry to his father a few months later. "But though you will rejoice in all this, God has been pleased to give us reason of greater joy—Charles has been very deeply affected—has most heartily dedicated himself to *Christ*, and tho' as yet he experiences no such *fullness* of intense personal love to Christ as he seeks for, his *will* is settled for Christ. . . . He will in about a week gather the young men of my congregation into a *Bible class*." In August, 1843, the presbytery of Indianapolis made Charles a licentiate and candidate for the ministry.[12]

During the rest of the year Charles remained at Henry's church as music leader and unofficial assistant pastor while his older brother searched for a church for him. During a two-week stay at Fort Wayne the following spring, Henry succeeded in raising a new congregation, and in July the Second Presbyterian Church of Fort Wayne extended a call to Charles to be its minister. But Charles soon ran into difficulty. The Old School members of the opposing First Presbyterian Church accused him of harboring sympathies for Unitarianism—a charge that threatened to alienate six New England families who had recently moved into town. If the dissidents were successful, the church would refuse to extend a call and Charles, who was soon to be ordained, would be left without a congregation. Henry wished to help, but Eunice was expecting her fourth child and he wanted to stay with her until the baby was born. Writing to his father, Henry urged him to leave for Fort Wayne immediately and take his place. "Your notoriety as an Eastern man will be very influential with all Eastern families," he explained, "whereas I am a *Western* man. . . . Nevertheless, if you cannot [go], I must. For I feel that some *leader* must be there *before* Synod [meets]. . . ."[13]

Lyman Beecher agreed to go and made plans to depart. Before he left, however, he wrote a letter to Charles to which Henry appended a note. "Preach little doctrine except what is of mouldy orthodoxy," encouraged Henry. "Keep all your improved breeds, your short-horned Durham, your Berkshires, etc., away off to pasture. They will get fatter, and nobody will be scared. Take hold of the most practical subjects; popularize your sermons. I do not ask you to change yourself; but, for a time, while captious critics are lurking, adapt your mode so as to insure that you shall be rightly understood."[14] It was the customary Beecher tactic of attacking problems cautiously and indirectly.

On October 18, Eunice Beecher gave birth to a healthy boy, George Lyman—named after Henry's brother George, who had accidentally shot and killed himself in 1843.[15] Since both the other children were sick and Eunice was slow to recover, Henry waited another week and a half before leaving for Fort Wayne. Lyman Beecher had arrived there the previous week, having ridden on horseback all Friday night and all Saturday to avoid traveling on the Sabbath. Henry was amazed that his seventy-year-old father not only made the journey, but also was able to preach two sermons on Sunday even though he had not slept the night before.

The combined efforts of Henry and his father soon won over the town. When the Fort Wayne presbytery met to examine Charles, Henry and Lyman were there as members of a sister presbytery. After some debate, Charles passed his examination. Henry then delivered the ordination sermon and Lyman followed by giving the candidate his charge. The crisis was solved and the wayward son was now a minister with his own congregation.[16] Lyman Beecher's dream of seeing his sons crusading for the Lord in the West was at last fulfilled.

As his church increased in size and became more popular, Henry Ward Beecher devoted more time to humanitarian efforts and social issues. In 1843, William Willard, a mute teacher from Ohio, set up a school for deaf mutes in Indianapolis. Beecher helped bring him to the attention of the legislature, and when the school was taken over by the state, Beecher became one of its trustees. In the following year Beecher lent his church to William H. Churchman for a demonstration by blind pupils from the Kentucky Asylum, and the legislature again followed Beecher's suggestion and established an asylum for the blind.[17]

Beecher also devoted a great deal of time to editing the *Indiana*

Farmer and Gardener. He took over the editorship of this magazine in the spring of 1845 and by the end of the year the journal had achieved a circulation of twelve hundred. "A work of love, an unfeigned desire to promote intelligence among the laboring classes; a strong sympathy with their pursuits; the hope of advancing the cause of popular education—these are my reasons for laboring in the vocation of an editor," wrote Beecher in the first issue.

Beecher's interest in the *Farmer and Gardener* was in keeping with his love of nature, his faith in the self-discipline that comes from hard work, and his belief in the virtues of rural life. As he wrote in his notebook:

> It is my deliberate conviction that physical labor is indispensable to intellectual and moral health; that the industrial and producing interests of society are powerfully conservative of morals; especially do I regard the tillage of the soil as conducive to life, health, morals, and manhood. I sympathize with the advance of society through practical physical labors more than I do through metaphysical speculations. . . . I have followed both inclinations and convictions [by] allying myself to the laboring classes.[18]

Beecher's services as editor further improved his stature in the community and brought him to the notice of an increasingly large audience. However, the event that attracted most attention during his pastorate at Indianapolis was a series of seven lectures to young men, which Beecher delivered in 1843 and subsequently published.

The *Lectures to Young Men* developed out of Beecher's concern with the unstable social and economic conditions in Indianapolis. Like many other settlers who wished to implant traditional social and religious ideals in the West, Beecher was upset by the fever of land speculation and the mania for railroads and canals that swept the nation in the 1830s and 1840s. The same boom psychology that attracted the new population threatened to destroy the social values many settlers were striving to maintain. The lectures, therefore, not only documented Beecher's own beliefs, but also reflected the outlook of many middle-class citizens who were conscious of their position in society and eager to preserve their respectability.

Beecher's two main themes in the lectures were the moral deterioration of youth, especially in the new western cities, and the "universal derangement of business" caused by speculation and gambling. Everyone, even those in rural districts, had need of these warnings, argued Beecher. "We are such a migratory, restless people, that our home is usually everywhere but at home; and almost every young man makes annual or biennial visits to famous cities," the dwelling place of that "flash class of men" who were the most dangerous.[19]

The lectures on moral dangers ranged in theme from a discussion of gambling and gamblers to a warning about the prostitute—"the strange woman." In effect, they were sermons rather than lectures, built around the exegesis of passages from the Bible. Following the approach that he had developed in his studies of preaching, Beecher simplified each question and presented it as a sketch of a character type —the wit, the libertine, the demagogue, and the party man. In each case he argued that once the first step was taken, the youth would be committed to a life of degeneracy and sin.

The lectures were immediately popular. Part of their appeal derived from Beecher's selection of topics. To introduce a lecture on prostitution required a great deal of courage and also a sense of tact. While Beecher condemned the "false modesty" and the "criminal fastidiousness of the community" that prevented a discussion of this subject, he was careful to present his lecture in the form of an allegory. Yet, though he avoided the coarser aspects of his subject, he compensated by using lurid language. Typical of his allegorical discussions was his description of one of the rooms in the house of prostitution—the ward of disease.

> Ye that look wistfully at the pleasant front of this terrific house, come with me now, and look long into the terror of this Ward; for here are the seeds of sin in their full harvest form! . . . Here a shuddering wretch is clawing at his breast, to tear away that worm which knaws [sic] his heart. By him is another, whose limbs are dropping from his ghastly trunk. Next, swelters another in reeking filth; his eyes rolling in bony sockets, every breath a pang, and every pang a groan. But yonder, on a pile of rags, lies one whose yells of frantic agony appall every ear. Clutching his rags with spasmodic grasp, his swoln [sic] tongue lolling from a blackened mouth, his bloodshot eyes glaring and rolling, he shrieks oaths; now blaspheming God, and now imploring him.[20]

The gruesomeness of this rhetoric, which was designed to deter a youth from entering a house of prostitution, had an attraction of its own for a western audience, for whom entertainment of any kind was scarce.

The greatest appeal of Beecher's lectures, however, derived not from his gruesome descriptions or from his strictures on moral dangers, but rather from his discussion of economic success. In an age when speculators, wildcat bankers, and gamblers seemed to be getting ahead most rapidly, Beecher reaffirmed the traditional view that success depended on industry, piety, and frugality. In doing so, he helped relieve the anxiety and insecurity of a generation troubled by rapid economic and social change.

As presented in these lectures, Beecher's version of the gospel of success was closely patterned after the major tenets of the New School evangelical faith. Central to his guide to success was his attitude toward human nature. Like the New School theologians, Beecher argued that although all men have a tendency to sin, they also have the ability, if they wish, to save themselves. "I do believe that man is corrupt enough," Beecher declared, "but something of good has survived the wreck."[21] This optimistic view of human nature, when carried over into the gospel of success, became the basis for Beecher's belief that anyone could become successful if only he worked at it. But Beecher also retained an element of the Old School view of original sin and argued that "the children of a sturdy thief, if taken from him at birth and reared by honest men, would, doubtless have to contend against a strongly dishonest inclination."[22]

Like the revivalist theology, Beecher's version of the gospel of success emphasized the individual, but not to the extent of ignoring his social responsibility. "Satisfaction," wrote Beecher, "is not the product of excess, or of indolence, or of riches; but of industry, temperance, and usefulness." He considered it essential that the individual contribute to the public good by "private usefulness" and a "record of public service." The individual was to be both self-reliant and socially responsible.

Success, like salvation, was the result of conscious choice, fervent dedication, and unremitting toil and effort. Like salvation, it was available to all. Beecher went out of his way to emphasize that luck had no influence. "A good character, good habits, and iron industry," he declared, "are impregnable to the assaults of all the ill luck that fools ever dreamed of." Success, like conversion, would bring with it other benefits. "Experience has shown," wrote Beecher, "that the other good qualities of veracity, frugality, and modesty are apt to be associated with industry."

Beecher further argued that the object of success, like that of conversion, was the development of character. Riches were more of a hindrance than an asset. Only if they were gained gradually as the result of hard work could they be considered as the "gift of God." As Beecher declared, "If the taste is refined, if the affections are pure, if conscience is honest, if charity listens to the needy, and generosity relieves them; if the public spirited hand fosters all that embellishes and all that ennobles society, then is the rich man happy."[23] Although this comment clearly links the notion of stewardship (the duty of the rich to help the poor, an ideal later to become a keystone in Andrew Carnegie's Gospel of Wealth) with Benjamin Franklin's emphasis on moral character, Beecher's objective, like that of the conversion theology, was to balance personal integrity against a commitment to socially benevolent action. Neither alternative by itself was acceptable. Both were needed. Later advocates of the gospel of success were to confuse material gain with moral worth in a way that was very different from Beecher's intention.[24]

Still another parallel between the conversion theology and the gospel of success was drawn by Beecher in his remarks on suffering and hardship. Just as tribulation and setbacks frequently made sinners aware of their faults and more willing to be converted, economic hardships were beneficial because they taught the value of thrift and frugality. "Adversity," wrote Beecher, "is the mint in which God stamps upon us his image and superscription."[25] Like his sister Catharine, Henry believed that suffering and sacrifice were important to individual self-knowledge.

It was natural for Beecher to use the basic tenets of revivalist theology to support his version of the gospel of success in this fashion because both sets of beliefs shared a common objective. Both were designed to develop self-reliant individuals who were motivated and controlled by internalized sets of beliefs rather than by legal or institutional forms of coercion. The object of revivalism, as seen in the act of conversion, was to internalize the religious beliefs of the individual so well that he would be able to maintain his faith at times and in areas where the church was poorly organized, feebly supported, and without a clerical hierarchy. Similarly, those who advocated the gospel of success wanted to internalize a sense of ethical norms so that individuals who participated in the open atmosphere of the marketplace would do so fairly and equitably. Both sets of beliefs were thus part of a rearguard action—a defensive move designed to strengthen the churches and improve the conduct of business during a period of western expansion and rapid economic growth.

By using the assumptions of revivalist theology to support his version of the gospel of success, Beecher helped to modify the conception of success that had been popularized by Benjamin Franklin. Franklin's image of the self-made man now became the image of the middle-class American whose goal in life was not the accumulation of wealth or the gain of social status, but rather the development of character. The other rewards might come to the responsible, self-reliant individual but they were never ends in themselves. Franklin's suggestion that proper behavior in public was more important than personal rectitude in private was in a similar fashion no longer considered adequate advice. "Moral dishonesties practised because the law allows them," argued Beecher, were still sins. To develop character, the individual had to adhere to the basic standards of Christian morality in both his public and private life.[26] Thus Beecher's concept of character fused self-discipline, moral purpose, and total honesty.

Beecher's interest in self-help and success, conversely, had an important influence on revivalist theology. By emphasizing ethical behavior rather than spiritual dedication, Beecher helped to blur the distinction between religious and secular issues and to change the focus of religion from the world-to-come to the present. By stressing the ability of the individual to save himself in both spiritual and economic terms, he also helped reduce the importance of the church to that of an outside adviser. And, by using the basic tenets of revivalism to support his version of the gospel of success, he created an internal dynamic within evangelical theology that helped to change it from a distinctive religious outlook into an apology for the status quo. In this way, Beecher contributed to the secularization of Christianity that was taking place in the pre–Civil War period.

The success of Beecher's lectures, together with large increases in his congregation, kept the Beecher family in good spirits. When Harriet Beecher Stowe visited them in the summer of 1844, she found the family healthy and happy. At the time, Harriet was herself depressed by the difficulties of raising her family and by her own poor health. "So many perplexities and trials and sicknesses have beset my way since my marriage," she wrote to Eunice Beecher, "I have found it almost impossible to keep any thing like a steady hold of a better world, and to set my affections on things that are above." Harriet's visit helped to restore her former confidence and spirit, even though she occasionally got into disputes with Eunice.[27]

These disputes developed from a clash of personalities. Harriet was domineering and possessive. At times, she acted as if her advice to her brother should overrule that of his wife. Eunice Beecher, for her part, was independently minded and willing to fight for her own rights. The result was that the two women on occasion got into fights. Looking back on her visit to her brother's house several years later, Harriet admitted her bias. "All these things I thought and turned over in my mind," she wrote to Eunice, "and thought also that tho' you were such a good for nothing saucy baggage, yet I could not help loving you, sins, sinner, and all, as I always did and do." The condescension apparent in this letter, which Henry Ward himself occasionally displayed, was enough to disrupt relations between the two families from time to time.[28]

When Harriet had visited Indianapolis in the summer of 1844, she had brought with her several ideas with which she had been toying. Denied entrance into the ministry, Harriet searched for substitutes and was usually unhappy unless she had a new cause to promote or a question to explore. The two interests she brought to Indianapolis were the advancement of female education in the West and mesmerism. Harriet shared her sister Catharine's dedication to women's education. They had collaborated on a geography textbook, and, for a while, they hoped to promote female education in the West with the profits from a series of school books. Just as Henry and his brothers were spreading the gospel through revivals, Catharine and Harriet sought to convert the nation through education. "Let the leading females of the country become well-educated, pious, and active," wrote Catharine to a friend, "and the salt is scattered throughout the land to purify and save." When Catharine had accused Harriet of helping herself to the funds of the Western Female Academy in 1838, the two sisters had parted ways, though they still retained their interest in education.[29]

Harriet's latest project was to set up a school in Indianapolis for the training of women, one similar to Mary Lyon's seminary at Mount Holyoke. She had found a young woman willing to take on the lower grades, or preparatory department as it was called, and she wanted Henry to send his daughter to school there. "You have received your first warning," Harriet wrote her brother, "and who will educate the Indiana mothers if you will not meet these Jesuits by Yankee women. I'll risk the combat—one bright well-trained free born Yankee girl is worth two dozen of your nuns who have grown up like potato sprouts in the shades of a convent." Since Beecher agreed with his sister about the crucial importance of education, he consented to send his daughter to Harriet's school. Later in the year, to emphasize further his interest in education, he became a trustee of Wabash College.[30]

Harriet's other major interest in the summer of 1844 was mesmerism. Like many other western settlers, she hoped that mesmerism would be a cure for nervous diseases—convulsions, hysteria, epilepsy, paralysis, and neuralgia in general. When she arrived in Indianapolis, Harriet decided to ask Henry to experiment with her. Like phrenology, mesmerism might also, she thought, be able to unlock the secrets of the mind.

The technique that Harriet had heard of was very simple. Two persons sat opposite each other with their eyes fixed and their thumbs in contact for a half hour. After trying this experiment, Harriet described the results in a letter to her husband. "The first session he succeeded in almost throwing me into convulsions—spasms and shocks of heat and prickly sensation ran all over me. My limbs were violently constricted and my head in dreadful commotion and I was so frightened that I called out for quarter." Harriet later came to the conclusion that "mesmeric passes" such as these would assuage "neuralgic pain." Eunice, whom Harriet urged to try her method, remained unconvinced, and Henry agreed with his wife that mesmerism was useless.[31]

Henry's experimentation with mesmerism was indicative of the extent to which he shared the nineteenth-century American preoccupation with health. At a time when medical knowledge was limited and families like Beecher's were often decimated by smallpox, diphtheria, and other diseases, he was ready to accept any technique or medicine which might offer relief. So strong, in fact, was Beecher's concern for health that he incorporated it into his version of the gospel of success. Sickness in his view became a sign of sinfulness, while good health was considered to be a reward for living an upright and moral life. It was an argument that many Americans found hard to resist, especially when vices like intemperance sometimes led to sickness and disease.

In addition to enabling Henry to experiment with mesmerism, Harriet's visit to the Beecher family allowed brother and sister to renew their old ties. Together they played with the children, drank spruce beer, and stayed up late into the night discussing their hopes and ideals. "I have had such a delightful visit with Henry this summer," wrote Harriet to her husband. "I love him so much—you don't know how much—it really makes me cry to think of it. Oh this love—if we could only have enough of it. I could be anything or do anything for and by love—but without [it] how desolate and waste and cheerless [life is]."[32]

Shortly after Harriet's visit, when Henry's fortune seemed to be at its highest point, disaster struck the family. On a bleak March day his two-year-old son George Lyman died. He was buried during a snow storm and few friends came to offer their sympathy. Henry choked his grief by immersing himself in his work, but Eunice had a more difficult time recovering. Sick and depressed by the burden of raising her family, she explained her feelings to Harriet, who had been complaining about not having heard from them. "My heart is almost broken by this year's trials," wrote Eunice, "and especially when my kind husband is near me—I hardly know myself—so full of wretchedness and anguish is every thought and feeling. Dear little Georgie! How much pleasure I used to anticipate in showing him to you and father. . . . I have the wildest longings to *look into his grave and see* if he is indeed there, or if this be not a horrible dream from which I may one day wake. . . ." It took Eunice a long time to get over her sorrow and her health never did recover. In the spring of 1846 she was pregnant again for the fifth time, and later in the year she gave birth to a daughter, named Catharine Esther after Henry's oldest sister.[33]

Notwithstanding the family problems that upset and disrupted his affairs during his first years in Indianapolis, Henry found himself more and more concerned about the slavery issue. Several members of the Beecher family had earlier commented publicly on that controversial subject. The most conservative was Catharine, who issued her *Essay on Slavery and Abolition* in 1837. Although she believed that slavery was "pernicious," Catharine opposed abolitionist societies because they fostered "denunciations, recriminations, and angry passions." She felt that women in particular should avoid the slavery issue because God had appointed them to an inferior and "subordinate station" in life. The place of the woman was in the home and not on the lecture platform denouncing slavery. On this issue as on many others, none of the Beecher family agreed with Catharine, and she published her views despite their protests.[34]

More outspoken on the slavery issue than Catharine was Edward Beecher. He had been in Alton, Illinois, in 1837 before the riots in which Elijah P. Lovejoy was murdered. With considerable courage, he had tried to arrange a compromise between the abolitionists and the discontented citizens. Despite his sympathy for Lovejoy, Edward Beecher was not at heart an abolitionist. He had supported Lovejoy's efforts primarily on the grounds of freedom of speech, stressing "the safety of free inquiry and the danger of allowing the progress of discussion to be arrested by force."[35]

More active in the antislavery movement than Edward and Catharine but less outspoken in his views was George Beecher. A graduate of Yale and one of the brightest members of the family, George had been converted to abolitionism by the accounts of the Lane debates. In 1837, he had become a member of Theodore Weld's band of seventy missionaries and had crusaded for the cause in the neighborhood of his church in Putnam, Ohio. At the first meeting of the "New School" Presbyterian General Assembly after the schism in 1838, George Beecher, as the representative of the Synod of Genesee, had raised the question of what attitude the church should take toward slavery. Under his direction, a committee was formed and a resolution presented, subsequently adopted by the General Assembly, to refer all action on this issue to the local presbyteries and synods. The Synod of Indiana quickly had followed this advice and urged its member churches "to take speedy and decisive measures to purify itself from this long continued and enormous evil."[36]

Thus George Beecher directly influenced his brother's stand on slavery because Henry belonged to the Synod of Indiana. When Henry came to Indianapolis, the decision of the synod placed him in a dilemma. For although the surrounding countryside in Indiana had few slaves and was noticeably antislavery in outlook, Indianapolis itself was divided on the issue. As late as 1845, a black man was murdered in the town during a racial scuffle on the Fourth of July. Though Beecher himself was opposed to slavery, he waited until 1846 before speaking out on that subject.[37]

In his opening sermon in May, Beecher frankly stated his reasons for previously avoiding the slavery issue. "I have for myself deliberately concluded," he declared, "and acted in my ministry on the conclusion, that on subjects upon which society had not yet been instructed, on questions involving much doubtful casuistry, in questions so mixed that it is hard to separate principles from policy—in all secondary truths . . . the success of the cause and truth required a fretful minister to withhold, when speaking would only injure; and to speak only when there seemed a favorable state of soil to receive the seed."[38]

Beecher decided to speak out on slavery not only because "an unquestionable modification of public feeling" had taken place on that subject, but also because he now had more confidence in himself. The success of his revivals, the growth and prosperity of his church, and the popularity of his *Lectures to Young Men* had bolstered his self-assurance. No longer was he worried about his finances or unsure of his ability as a preacher.

Beecher's sermon, using an idea that he had developed earlier, began with an analysis of the different public attitudes toward slavery. In the South, he pointed out, there were two views of slavery. Some believed that the institution was necessary and beneficent. Others thought "slavery to be undesirable, but . . . are opposed to all consideration of it." Despite the kindness and personal attachment of some masters to slaves in the South, slavery, by giving one individual control over another, had engendered a love of power and destroyed social purity.[39]

In the North, there were many more shades of opinion. The most vociferous were the abolitionists, who had created a hostile reaction in the South. Their language of rebuke, invective, and irony, declared

Beecher, was the least effective means of getting rid of slavery. "No matter how great the evil, if it has been tolerated, if it has custom on its side, if it has not been fully exposed until honest men are satisfied, then the language of instruction and of duty, simple, explicit, clear, calm, and kind, is the language to be employed. . . ." By speaking in the language of extreme partisanship, the abolitionists only aggravated the problem.

If the abolitionists excited the issue and failed to propose "a mode of effecting the removal of the evil," the colonizationists were equally open to censure for their proposals. Their program had no chance for success because the southerners were unwilling to emancipate their slaves and there were not enough funds to pay for the resettlement of the Negroes.[40]

There was also a third, more numerous group in the North, Beecher argued, whose position lay somewhere between that of the other two organizations. These individuals acknowledged the evils of slavery, its political injustice, economic waste, social wrong and religious sinfulness, and considered emancipation to be a duty, but were unable to find a means to abolish the institution. "It is with this great and growing center section that I desire to be ranked," he declared.

Having perceptively characterized the various public attitudes toward slavery, Beecher then explained his solution. Believing that slavery was a sin and that every man had a duty to exert all his influence against it, he stated that he welcomed any influence arising from commerce, political agitation, or anything else, which tended to abate the evil. Nevertheless, he declared, "I am sanguine of relief chiefly and preeminently from God. It is a subject too mighty for man's handling. . . . I do not believe that religion is to remove the evil, and thereby justify inaction. It is because I see in religion a resource and a remedy that I am impelled to apply it."[41] In effect, Beecher's solution was no solution at all. It was simply an appeal for calm discussion and moderation.

Beecher devoted his second sermon in May of 1846 to an attack on the southern biblical defense of slavery. The Bible, he argued, sanctioned Hebrew slavery, which was inherently different from Roman slavery. Hebrew slavery insisted that a fugitive slave should not be returned to his master. Escape was itself taken as evidence of ill-usage.

After a detailed analysis of four different types of Hebrew slavery, Beecher contrasted it with involuntary servitude in the South, which he pictured as resembling Roman slavery.[42]

The last sermon in the series dealt with slavery in the New Testament. Beecher declared that the whole spirit of this part of the Bible was against slavery. As a final plea, he attacked those individuals who defended their own freedom but did not "seem to dream of such a privilege" for others and he urged Christians to aid southerners by "prayers and fervent exhortations" to rid themselves of their calamity.[43]

These sermons were well received because they provided Beecher's congregation with a convenient way of rationalizing the guilt that was aroused in those who thought that slavery was wrong, but did not want to have free blacks around. They appealed, too, because Beecher had identified himself with the "more numerous group" in the North. In a democratic country where all men were considered to be equal, as Alexis de Tocqueville had pointed out, the correctness of any position was judged in part by the number of individuals who held the same point of view. By identifying himself with the majority, Beecher thus implied that his views were superior to those of the others with whom he disagreed. But his comments appealed most of all because they dramatized a different reform stance—that of the disinterested, nonpartisan social critic.

The popularity of Beecher's sermons on slavery convinced him that his tactic of waiting until the public mood had changed was the correct one. By testing the wind in advance, Beecher was to attack slavery in the South without disrupting the social stability of the North. Because of the success of his first attempt at "moderate reform," Beecher now resolved to take a more active part in the antislavery movement.

As Beecher became more involved with public issues and revivalism, he frequently visited other communities and left his family for several weeks at a time. These absences troubled his wife, who never had fully recovered from the death of their son, and Beecher tried often to bolster her spirits. "How I wish I could say or do anything to comfort you!" he wrote to Eunice Beecher from Madison. "I am hardly away from home an hour's ride before I begin to review our life together; the greatness of your love to me, the degree of self-sacrifice you have endured, your willingness to labor, to suffer, to wear out without complaint, and your unhesitating acquiescence in my remaining when your health seems to be sacrificed."

Mrs. Beecher's ill-health intensified her dislike for the West, which she had nurtured since her arrival there eight years earlier. As a daughter of a prominent New England physician, she thought the West provincial and, in the eyes of one of the congregation, "longed for a broader and more brilliant sphere for her husband."[44] Despite this harsh comment, no one could deny the hardships caused by malaria and frequent pregnancies. Though she was ambitious for her husband, Eunice Beecher also longed to return East to restore her own health and that of her family.

In the winter of 1846, Mrs. Beecher's hopes of returning to the East were aroused when W. T. Cutter, a New York merchant who had recently visited Indianapolis, wrote to inquire whether Beecher would be interested in taking charge of a church in Brooklyn. Cutter was a representative of a new generation of business and professional men who had become successful in New York City during the previous decade and who had moved to the nearby suburb of Brooklyn. Impressed by Beecher's preaching ability and his emphasis on the Victorian virtues of industry and thrift, honesty and piety, Cutter offered to establish a new church if Beecher would agree to become the minister of it.

Beecher had given much thought to the question of moving to the East, but he was nevertheless cautious in his letter of reply. "Now, in this work, the labor of *usefulness*," he wrote to Cutter, "if there be one thing which, above all others, I especially abhor, it is this *cant* talk about 'taking care of one's influence'. . . . A man's *influence* is simply the shadow which *usefulness* casts. . . . This keeping one's ear open to hear if God is not calling, this looking out every little while to see if one is not wished for somewhere else, is rather of the nature of *self-seeking*. A minister, like a maiden, ought not to make the first overtures, nor to be over-eager to have them made to him."

Despite these words of caution, Beecher made it known that he would consider the idea of moving East. "But if ever I come to you or go to any other place," he warned, "although I have no plan as to situations, I have, I hope, an immovable plan in respect to the objects which I shall pursue. So help me God, I do not mean to be a *party* man, nor to head or follow any partisan effort." Beecher's vow identi-

fied the problem that was to plague most nineteenth-century reformers
—the problem of maintaining a strong, critical, nondoctrinaire stand
on the issues without being stereotyped as an extremist and identified
with partisan causes. This ideal of moral nonpartisanship was to lie at
the heart of much of nineteenth-century liberal philosophy: the educated citizen, critical and unbiased, who would make an independent,
fair-minded judgment on the issues. It was a noble ideal, difficult if not
impossible to carry out, that identified Beecher's position as a moderate reformer.

Having stated his ideals, Beecher closed his letter informally with
the comment that Cutter's visit had been of some help to him personally because now his congregation was making greater efforts to pay for
his support. Although eight hundred dollars did not seem to him to be
an extravagant salary, he commented, he would gladly accept six hundred if it would be paid regularly.[45]

Encouraged by the open-mindedness of Beecher's reply, Cutter presented his letter to several other prominent Brooklyn merchants, including Henry C. Bowen, son-in-law of Lewis Tappan, and David
Hale. Hale and Bowen were impressed by Beecher's candor and even
before a church was established, offered him a call at a salary of fifteen
hundred dollars, which they promised to pay punctually.[46]

At the time the letter arrived, Beecher was away from town preaching and his sick wife forwarded a copy to him, together with a short
note from herself. "*Do not*," she urged, "*do not let my health have
any influence in your decision.* I shall never be well any where.
George's death has destroyed all that was left of my constitution. I
despair of ever being of much use to any one. Let me then—my love—
wear away what remains of life—in *any place*, where you can do the
most good. It matters little to me—so that I can be with you while I
live."

Beecher was distressed by his wife's ill-health. Yet he still declined
to accept the offer. The proposed church lacked both a place to worship
and a congregation, and there was little indication that it would be
successful. Moreover, Beecher was still convinced that he could do a
great deal of good in the West, where his father urgently wished him
to remain. The Brooklyn merchants, nevertheless, refused to accept
his refusal, and in March, 1847, Henry C. Bowen invited Beecher to
come to New York and address the May Anniversary meeting of the

American Home Missionary Society. Beecher accepted the offer and arrived in Brooklyn on May 17.[47]

Earlier the same month Henry Bowen, Seth Hunt, John Howard, and David Hale had purchased a church building on Cranberry Street in Brooklyn, recently vacated by the First Presbyterian Church, which had moved to a more favorable location. In May, after Beecher had spoken before the missionary society, he preached to a small gathering in the Brooklyn church. On June 13, 1847, the new church was formally organized and a call was at once sent to Beecher, offering him a salary of fifteen hundred dollars, to be increased to two thousand dollars after three years. Only a few days earlier, Beecher had received an offer from the Park Street Church in Boston to become its joint pastor.[48] But that offer was less appealing since, as an established church, it would have less room for experimentation and innovation.

In spite of these offers and the further inducement of Plymouth Church in Brooklyn to pay his way east, Beecher hesitated to accept. In August, he at last was persuaded that moving to the East would be the only way to restore the health of his wife, and he agreed to go to Brooklyn. Henry C. Bowen, who had worked long and hard to persuade Beecher to come East, was overjoyed at the news and offered to lend him "any sum not exceeding one thousand dollars."[49] It was assumed that the sum would be used to pay off any outstanding debts and that it need not be paid back.

Bowen had reason to be excited about obtaining Beecher's services in the East. Like other churches in this period of rapid urban expansion, Plymouth Church wanted a young minister whose approach was fresh and exciting. In this respect, Beecher was particularly appealing. During his eight years in Indianapolis, he had integrated the four major themes of his earlier career and forged them into a persuasive program. Together they became a central part of the Victorian cultural ethos. These themes—the creation of a moral code based on the internalization of values and peer-group pressure, the establishment of the reform ideal of the disinterested, nonpartisan public critic, the emphasis on a massive appeal to the common man through tracts, newspapers, and lyceum lectures, and the easygoing, highly naturalistic Christian doctrine that made religion a matter of common sense for the average citizen—were all to have an enormous appeal to the expanding populations of urban centers like New York and Brooklyn.

Through hard work and constant experimentation, Beecher had re-shaped traditional social ideals to fit the realities of a mass, democratic society. Using lectures, sermons, and the media, he fashioned a new social ethos with which individuals could identify. It was a middle-class culture that combined strong emphasis on individual action with effective peer-group pressure. Like the group techniques used by psychologists and psychotherapists in the twentieth century, the middle-class social ethos gave the individual a sense of security and belonging. It overcame fears of loneliness and alienation, provided standards of behavior, and gave life a great moral purpose. Beecher was not the only proponent of the new social ethos, but his flamboyant character, outspoken style, and romantic Christian revivalism were to make him a natural leader.

Bowen, an aggressive and effective merchant, recognized Beecher's potential and worked feverishly to keep him from changing his mind once the decision had been made. As Bowen wrote, "The truth's we are *willing* to do more for you than you ever *dreamed* of we are in the condition of . . . any loving wife like yours or mine, willing to do just what, 'you say,' for you have 'stolen our hearts.' . . . We want you; come! you must come!"[50]

Despite his clear potential as a major church leader, Beecher was not without faults, and some members of his church were happy to see him leave. Eunice Beecher, in particular, was unpopular and had few friends. "Full of large tales, and enormous exaggerations," commented Deacon Samuel Merrill, "no one believes a word she says—and I believe the opinion is general that her recent sickness was *for the occasion*." Nor was Henry free from criticism. "Mr. B. is a great man in the pulpit," declared Merrill, "but wofully dificient [*sic*] in every other respect. Often he has failed to attend prayer meeting without any excuse. Never has been in Sabbath School more than thrice in his residence here of seven years. Visits almost none among his people. Makes appointments for meetings of Session, and half the time forgets them." Critical though Samuel Merrill was of Beecher, he remained a close friend and admitted that "we, as a *town*, feel that we are loosing [*sic*] a valuable citizen. . . ."[51]

Merrill's criticism was perceptive. Though Beecher had built up his church and had helped to establish several benevolent and charitable organizations in the city, he did so as much to strengthen his own reputation in the city as to help the needy. At heart, Beecher remained a typical New England conservative, dedicated to preserving the social stability of the community and furthering the cause of Christ. But, in doing so, he was not adverse to promoting his own popularity.

Perhaps Beecher was aware of Merrill's criticism when he decided to move East. Starting afresh, he could correct his deficiencies and from New York, center of the missionary movement, he could continue to influence the cause of revivalism. Even more important, he would have direct access to the publishing houses that were to shape and mold middle-class Victorian thought. He also would have the opportunity to build a major reputation for himself. Self-confident and energetic, he vowed to make his church into an effective force in urban affairs.

NOTES

1. For the abrasive tactics of Lyman and Catharine Beecher, see Kathryn K. Sklar, *Catharine Beecher: A Study in Domesticity* (New Haven, 1973), 107–17.

2. On Victorian morality, see *ibid.*, 78–83, and Daniel W. Howe, "American Victorianism as a Culture," *American Quarterly*, XXVII (Dec., 1975), 507–32; also suggestive about contradictions in American values is Robert Wiebe's *The Segmented Society* (New York, 1975).

3. H. W. Beecher, Journal, May 4, 1839, Yale MSS. He described the roads as "horrible, abominable, outrageous." W. R. Holloway, *Indianapolis, A Historical & Statistical Sketch of the Railroad City* (Indianapolis, 1870), 50–80; Ignatius Brown, *Logan's History of Indianapolis since 1818* (Indianapolis, 1867), 34–56; Mrs. Henry Ward Beecher, *Ladies Home Journal*, Dec., 1891.

4. L. C. Rudolph, *Hoosier Zion: The Presbyterians in Early Indiana* (New Haven, 1963), 13.

5. H. W. Beecher, Journal, Sept. 15, 1839.

6. Samuel Merrill to David Merrill, Nov. 14, 1840, Julia Merrill Papers, Indiana Historical Society.

7. Jane Elsmere, *Henry Ward Beecher: The Indiana Years, 1837–1847* (Indianapolis, 1973), 115, 133; Samuel Merrill to David Merrill, July 9, 1941, Merrill Papers; H. W. Beecher, Journal, n.d.

8. William C. Beecher and Samuel Scoville, *A Biography of Henry Ward Beecher* (New York, 1888), 188; Brown, *Logan's History of Indianapolis*, 42.

9. H. W. Beecher to Lyman Beecher, May 1, 1842, quoted in Beecher and Scoville, *Biography*, 189; *Minutes of the Presbyterian Church* (New York, 1843), 58–59.

10. Rudolph, *Hoosier Zion*, 25; H. W. Beecher, "Record of Times & Places of Preaching," Yale MSS; Elsmere, *Henry Ward Beecher*, 145–50.

11. Charles Beecher to Lyman Beecher, Jan. 4, 1842, Schlesinger Library; Lyman Beecher to H. W. Beecher, Dec. 5, 1842, Yale MSS.

12. H. W. Beecher to Lyman Beecher, March 18, 1843, Schlesinger Library; Ambrose Y. Moore, *History of the Presbytery of Indianapolis* (Indianapolis, 1876), 53. The best account of Henry's work in behalf of Charles is Elsmere, *Henry Ward Beecher*, chap. XIV.

13. H. W. Beecher to Lyman Beecher, Sept. 13, 1844, Schlesinger Library.

14. Lyman Beecher to Charles Beecher with a note from H. W. Beecher, Oct. 25, 1844, quoted in Lyman Beecher, *The Autobiography of Lyman Beecher*, ed. Barbara M. Cross (Cambridge, Mass., 1961), II, 359.

15. H. W. Beecher to Lucy Bullard, Oct. 30, 1844, Yale MSS. There is some question whether this was an accident or whether it was suicide.

16. Lyman Beecher, *Autobiography*, II, 360; H. W. Beecher to Eunice Beecher, Nov. 11, 1844, Yale MSS.

17. Brown, *Logan's History of Indianapolis*, 43.

18. *Indiana Farmer and Gardener*, XXX (Nov. 30, 1895).

19. H. W. Beecher, *Seven Lectures to Young Men on Various Important Subjects* (Boston, 1846), 224. See also Clifford E. Clark, Jr., "The Changing Nature of Protestantism in Mid-Nineteenth Century America: Henry Ward Beecher's *Seven Lectures to Young Men*," *Journal of American History*, LVII (1971), 832–46.

20. H. W. Beecher, *Seven Lectures to Young Men*, 174, 203.

21. *Ibid.*, 116. Actually, the Old School wing of the Presbyterian Church held that original sin was universal because after Adam's fall it was handed down from one generation to another. Beecher modifies this by arguing that sin is hereditary only for some men, though all men have an inclination toward it.

22. *Ibid.*, 54.

23. *Ibid.*, 24, 90, 31, 29, 85.

24. This point is made by John Cawelti in *Apostles of the Self-Made Man* (Chicago, 1965), 52, 211. See also the letter on "The Blessings of Poverty" in Timothy Titcomb, *Titcomb's Letters to Young People* (New York, 1859). Titcomb's book was dedicated to Beecher.

25. H. W. Beecher, *Seven Lectures to Young Men*, 48.

26. *Ibid.*, 61. For a perceptive assessment of Franklin's views see John William Ward, "Who Was Benjamin Franklin?" *American Scholar*, XXXII (Autumn, 1963), 541–53.

27. H. B. Stowe to Eunice Beecher, April 15 (no year), undated correspondence, Yale MSS.

28. H. B. Stowe to Eunice Beecher, June 2 (no year), undated correspondence, Yale MSS.

29. Elizabeth M. Harveson, *Catharine Esther Beecher: Pioneer Educator* (Philadelphia, 1932), 81; Forrest Wilson, *Crusader in Crinoline: The Life of Harriet Beecher Stowe* (Philadelphia, 1941), 201.

30. H. B. Stowe to H. W. Beecher, Feb. 1 (no year), undated correspondence, Yale MSS; Lyman Beecher Stowe, *Saints, Sinners and Beechers* (Indianapolis, 1934), 270; H. W. Beecher to E. O. Hovey, Oct. 22, 1840, Katharine Day Collection, Stowe-Day Foundation.

31. H. B. Stowe to Calvin Stowe, July 16, 1844, Schlesinger Library; Harriet B. Stowe to H. W. Beecher (typed copy, n.d.), Yale MSS.

32. H. B. Stowe to Calvin Stowe, Sept. 3, 1844, Schlesinger Library.

33. Eunice Beecher to H. B. Stowe, Dec. 27, 1846 (typed copy), Yale MSS.

34. Catharine E. Beecher, *An Essay on Slavery and Abolition* (Philadelphia, 1837),

14, 99; James G. Birney to Arthur Tappan, July 29, 1837, Mount Holyoke College MSS. Birney wrote to Tappan that "it is said, and it is probably true, that Dr. B. was much opposed to the publication of Catharine's book."

35. Merton L. Dillon, *Elijah P. Lovejoy, Abolitionist Editor* (Urbana, Ill., 1961), 143.

36. Gilbert H. Barnes and Dwight L. Dumond, *The Letters of Theodore Dwight Weld, Angelina Grimké Weld and Sarah Grimké* (New York, 1934), II, 348n; *Minutes of the Presbyterian Church in the United States of America* (New York, 1839), 4, 20; Rudolph, *Hoosier Zion*, 52.

37. Holloway, *Indianapolis*, 80.

38. H. W. Beecher, Sermons, May 6, 1846, Yale MSS. Lyman Abbott, in his book *Henry Ward Beecher* (Boston, 1903), wrote that he knew of these sermons (p. 63) but never had seen them. Nor did any of the later biographers of Beecher have access to them.

39. H. W. Beecher, Journal, Dec., 1839. Beecher argued at this time that a discussion of the slavery issue should be aimed at the interests of each group in society concerned with the evil. To statesmen he would discuss it as an economic evil, to ordinary citizens he would use an appeal based upon humanitarian grounds.

40. By the 1840s the goal of colonization societies, which sought to return the slaves to Africa and resettle them there, was generally recognized as impractical by many moderate antislavery leaders.

41. H. W. Beecher, Sermon, May 6, 1846, Yale MSS.

42. H. W. Beecher, "Hebrew Slavery," 1846, Yale MSS.

43. The third sermon discussed the "tendency and effect" of revivals.

44. H. W. Beecher to Eunice Beecher, 1847 (typed copy), Yale MSS; Julia Merrill Ketcham, "Reminiscences" (manuscript, Indiana State Library), 79.

45. W. T. Cutter to H. W. Beecher, Dec. 8, 1846, Yale MSS; H. W. Beecher to W. T. Cutter, Dec. 15, 1846, quoted in Beecher and Scoville, *Biography*, 210–12. The original copy of this letter is not in the family papers; however, since all the other material quoted in the family biography has not been altered from the original, I assume that this letter, too, is a faithful copy. For nineteenth-century liberal theory, see Alexis de Tocqueville, *Democracy in America*, and Louis Hartz, *The Liberal Tradition in America* (New York, 1955). Beecher's position is basically similar to that of recent organizations such as Common Cause.

46. H. C. Bowen to H. W. Beecher, Feb. 17, 1847 (copy), included in Eunice Beecher's letter to H. W. Beecher, March 3, 1847, Schlesinger Library.

47. H. C. Bowen to H. W. Beecher, March 26, 1847, Yale MSS.

48. Lyman Abbott, Amory H. Bradford, et al., *The New Puritanism* (New York, 1898), xi; Beecher and Scoville, *Biography*, 214; Silas Aiken to H. W. Beecher, June 10, 1847, Yale MSS.

49. H. C. Bowen to H. W. Beecher, July 14, 1847, Yale MSS.

50. On group psychology see Irvin Yalom, *The Theory and Practice of Group Psychotherapy* (New York, 1970); Daniel H. Calhoun, *Professional Lives in America* (Cambridge, Mass., 1965), 152. In a period when many older and more mature ministers were having an increasingly hard time finding churches, a number of young ones like Beecher secured a permanency of tenure because of their freshness and novelty; on this point, see Henry C. Bowen to H. W. Beecher, July 21, 1847, Yale MSS.

51. Samuel Merrill to Hazen Merrill, Aug. 18, 1847; Samuel Merrill to ?, Sept. 29, 1847, Merrill Papers, Indiana Historical Society.

4

Pastor to an Urban America

In September, 1847, Henry Ward Beecher delivered his farewell sermon, packed his few personal belongings, and boarded the newly completed Indianapolis and Madison railroad for the first stage of his journey to the East.[1] Earlier in the summer his sick wife and their three children had left for her parents' home in Massachusetts.[2] Beecher hoped that the visit in New England would restore his wife's health and improve her spirits. As soon as he found a place to live and was established in his new church, he planned to bring his family to Brooklyn.

When Beecher arrived at his new church in 1847, Brooklyn was just beginning a vast expansion that in less than two decades was to make it the third largest city in the nation.[3] New buildings were going up, new businesses were being established, and vacant land was quickly disappearing. Swollen by foreign immigration and the influx of people from New York, the population of Brooklyn was to grow in only twenty years from 30,000 to 295,000.[4]

This phenomenal growth created a variety of economic and social tensions. Faced with the large foreign immigration, the older and wealthier citizens of the city began to move to Brooklyn Heights and the neighboring area. They were joined there by a new class of business and professional men who had made their fortunes recently and wanted to improve their social position. Disliking the Irish and German immigrants and feeling uneasy about their newly acquired wealth, these Victorian *nouveaux riches* wanted desperately to appear socially respectable. Many of them feared that the new immigrants, with their unusual social customs and Catholic faith, might destroy traditional American ideals and values. Eager to prove that they were socially responsible and had concerns other than the pursuit of wealth, they became addicted to every new scheme for self-improvement and self-culture. Industry and thrift, sobriety and chastity were their ideals; self-reliance and self-control were their goals.[5]

Plymouth Church, where Beecher was to spend the rest of his life, was an early result of the population expansion in Brooklyn. Located near the well-to-do Heights section of the city, the church drew its membership predominantly from the new middle class, though its trustees were some of the wealthiest merchants in the community.[6] Horace B. Claflin's wholesale dry goods establishment did more than seventy thousand dollars worth of business annually, and Henry W. Sage, who joined the church in 1857, was able later to give Cornell University more than a million dollars.[7] Despite these wealthy members, Plymouth Church retained the image of a church that reached all segments of the population. James Parton, writing after the Civil War, contrasted it with the churches on Fifth Avenue in New York that had lost contact with the lower classes.[8]

To increase his effectiveness as the minister to Plymouth Church, Beecher soon after his arrival in Brooklyn began to shape his diverse social views into a more coherent philosophy that would appeal to the interests and ideals of his parishioners. In doing so, he fused attitudes toward religion, the family, success, and social control into a new Victorian middle-class morality. He began by elaborating on the concept of the minister that he had developed in Indianapolis. The duty of the minister, Beecher declared in his first sermon, is to preach Christ "in his personal relations to individual men."[9] To fulfill this obligation, the minister had the "right and duty to introduce into the pulpit *every subject* in wh[ich] his people are concerned; the morals of trade, of commerce, or politics are his property." In particular, Beecher vowed to keep a vigilant eye on the course of business. "It is here," he emphasized, "that the Devil teaches Christians to use the world's selfish maxims; it is here that he persuades them to smother their conscience, to abate its circuit. . . . No minister can preach an unadulterated gospel to a dying world thro' the portals of a worldly—or dishonest, or hypocritical, or commercial church."[10]

Beecher's outspoken and unconventional attitude toward the ministry, together with his careless dress and rough manners, at first startled his congregation and frightened the pastors of the neighboring churches. "Don't ask me what I think of him," wrote the wife of one of the church trustees to her brother, "I can't tell you for the life of me. I only know that I am intensely interested. There is a sort of fascination about the man which I should think was produced in a good measure by his earnestness, his fervor, his seeming naturalness."[11]

Beecher's efforts to produce a revival at first showed little sign of success. Few individuals seemed interested in religion, and the ministers of the nearby Congregational and Presbyterian churches resented Beecher's aggressive attitude toward revivals.[12] It was not long, however, before Beecher began to produce results and the neighboring ministers softened their opposition to his efforts. "Indeed," he wrote to his father in December, "I feel that a work of grace has begun already. There have been several conversions; and there are more than twenty cases of seriousness. . . . Nor are the signs of good confined alone to us. I think that many churches in Brooklyn and several in New York are beginning to be revived in some measure."[13]

Beecher's hopes were soon realized. With sermons like "Counting the Cost" and "Salvation Very Easy and Yet Hard," he sparked a revival that fall in which fifty-six new members were added to his church.[14] Catharine Beecher, who was staying with her brother's family and completing a book on the religious training of children, wrote to her father approvingly, "I never heard any that so fully came up to my idea of 'preaching Christ.' " Such praise from his older sister was significant. Henry was finally recognized by Lyman's other children as the one who would most likely succeed in taking their father's place as a major church leader.[15]

The revival increased Beecher's confidence and convinced him that he had made the right choice in coming to Brooklyn. His church was prosperous and active, and its future looked bright. His salary, more-over, had increased, and he was beginning to pay off some of his debts. And his wife's health, though unimproved, had not become any worse. Most important, he had formed a circle of friends who were better edu-cated and more sympathetic than those he had left in Indianapolis.

This became particularly evident later in December when his one-year-old daughter Catharine died. In an intimate letter to his sister Har-riet, Henry contrasted the death of Catharine to that of his son George who had died in Indianapolis.

> Then, I was in a missionary field—enduring hardship and thinking in myself always how to stand up under any blow, even if it were a thunder stroke—with Paul's heroism at once firing and putting me to shame. Our noble boy suddenly sickened.
>
> Our people did not know *how* to sympathize. Few came while he lived—fewer yet when, on a bleak March day, we bore him through the storm, and standing in the snow, laid his beautiful form to his cold, white grave. Eunice was heartbroken. My house was a fountain of anguish. It was not for me to quail or show shrinking. So I choked my grief and turned outwardly from myself to seek occupation.
>
> But two years found me in a different scene. And when Caty sickened and began her quiet march toward the once-opened Gate, to rejoin her brother (cherub pair) we found our house full of friends. Many of the truest, deepest hearts asked no bidding but with instinctive, heart-thought right, lived with us almost literally. And when her form was to go forth from us, they embosomed her in flowers, winter though it seemed. . . .[16]

These friends not only were sympathetic, they also were well edu-cated and could be constructively critical. As one friend commented in reply to a note from Beecher, "there is one sentence in your letter which I want you to try to look square in the face without a grin. It is this. 'It seems to me that the only thing on earth that truth is good for, is to convert men from evil to holiness.' Do tell," quipped the friend, "is that all?"[17]

Criticism such as this made Beecher aware of the sloppiness and in-consistency of many of his statements, and he began to rethink his theological views. To his sister Harriet he admitted that in the West he had had little chance to develop a systematic theology. "During all that time," he wrote, "my mind was *intensely* unsettled in theology. I had a very different mental philosophy from that of the framers of theology. I had dropped so many technical views, through a preference for those more in accordance with my own philosophy, as to produce the vague impression that in time I should serve the remaining views in the same manner.''[18]

To clarify his religious views, Beecher now studied the most recent developments in theology and slowly began to modify the revivalistic outlook his father had done so much to foster in the 1830s. Revivalism during the Second Great Awakening had rested upon three basic foundations: a view of God as judge and lawgiver, a belief in the moral ability of the sinner to play a part in his own salvation, and a conviction that the strength of the churches in America derived from the "voluntary principle," the ideal that justified the separation of church and state. The conception of God as a stern judge had been handed down to Lyman Beecher's generation by Samuel Hopkins and Nathaniel Emmons, followers of Jonathan Edwards, while the belief in moral ability derived from the theological innovations of Nathaniel W. Taylor of Yale, who held that although men were sinful by nature, they still had the ability to work for their own salvation. The voluntary principle, in a similar fashion, first developed as a rationale to justify the disestablishment of the churches in Connecticut and Massachusetts in 1818 and in 1833.[19]

Basic to the evangelical religion of Lyman Beecher and Charles G. Finney, who were the organizers rather than the theologians of the Second Great Awakening, was the belief in a "stern God of Justice." These men were convinced that the apocalypse was near and that, at the last trumpet, unrepentant sinners would not be shown any mercy.[20] This attitude had been the basis for Lyman Beecher's anguished concern for the souls of his children, and it had given an impetus to the early stages of the temperance and antislavery movements.[21]

While their belief in a stern God of justice gave the revivalists a sense of urgency, their faith in man's ability to participate in his own salvation convinced them that change was possible. In a similar fashion, the voluntary principle provided them with a rationale for organizing their efforts. The voluntary principle, which became the watchword of the revivalists, justified competition between the different denominations as beneficial to religion. Moreover, it was in keeping with the emphasis of Jacksonian America on independence and self-reliance.[22] Voluntary support of the churches proved that they were independent and self-sufficient and could survive and prosper without the support of the state.

The voluntary principle, as it was conceived of by the revivalists, rested upon several important assumptions. The first was that proper social behavior in a democratic society, like religious faith, could not be coerced by laws alone but had to be founded upon trust. People obey laws, the revivalists argued, not simply because they fear apprehension by the police, but because they believe that the laws society has established are necessary and just.[23] Closely associated with this view was a second assumption, which held that people were basically rational and would change their way of life if they could be persuaded that it was in their best interest to do so. Finally, the revivalists believed that, in order to move men, the ministers had to arouse their feelings and touch their emotions. Emotional excitement, carefully cultivated in the context of a mass meeting, was the necessary spur to action and commitment. Building upon these assumptions, Lyman Beecher and the other revivalists argued that it was better to use "moral suasion" than "legal coercion" to reform men's lives and created a vast network of Bible, tract, and missionary societies to spread the gospel and improve society.[24]

By 1850, two of the three foundations of evangelical religion—belief in a stern God of justice and faith in the voluntary system of benevolent societies—were beginning to be modified, while the third—the commitment to arousing the emotions—was becoming further refined and strengthened. Henry Ward Beecher's reexamination of his faith, his gradual rejection of many of his father's views, and his creation of a new romantic Christian liberalism were thus important elements in the sweeping change taking place in the outlook of Protestantism before the Civil War.

Beecher's interest in theology first was aroused by a book written by Horace Bushnell, minister to a church in Hartford, Connecticut. Bushnell had published his *Views of Christian Nurture* in 1846, arguing that the child should grow up as a Christian and never have to undergo a conversion experience.[25] Discontented about revivals that threatened to split his own church, Bushnell developed a new theology around God's love, as defined by Christ's sacrifice, and advocated a symbolic and intuitive attitude toward religious truth.[26] These views, which were embodied in his sermon on the Atonement delivered in Cambridge, Massachusetts, in 1848, stirred up a controversy that came to Beecher's attention later the same year.

In a letter to John Howard Raymond, professor at Madison University (now Colgate), Beecher revealed his first impression of the Hartford minister. "Although I cannot agree with Bushnell," he wrote to Raymond, "I can as little with his respondents; nor do I see any benefit in a controversy. . . . When will ministers learn that putting up fences and disputing about landmarks is not an equivalent for the careful cultivation of the soul."[27]

Beecher's interest in Bushnell was further stimulated later that year by a letter from his younger brother, Thomas Beecher. Thomas, the son of Lyman Beecher's second wife, had gone to Illinois College in 1843 and now was beginning to think about entering the ministry. Thomas was particularly attracted by "Bushnell's scheme of love and that Christian philosophy that springs from the Bible as based upon the heart."[28]

Henry was overjoyed at Thomas's new interest in religion and hurriedly wrote him a letter of encouragement. "I glory and rejoice to know that you are high enough upon the sides of Mt. Zion to begin to see the wide circuit of life—and that you are advanced so far as to know how much deeper *feeling* is than thinking." As for Bushnell, Henry continued, "it seems to me that it is this outward sympathy, springing from an inward sympathy with God, that Bushnell principally lacks. He lives toward God, toward truth, toward the good, the beautiful, the perfect. But that tremendous sweep, which the Pauline, because Christlike, mind takes, when from the crystal mountains it descends . . . he is not ignorant of—but *it is not the* force of his life."[29]

The difference between Bushnell and Beecher, as John Howard Raymond perceptively pointed out, was that Bushnell's approach to religion was intellectual while Beecher's was largely emotional.[30] Although both arrived at a similar point, the stressing of God's love for man, they arrived at it from different directions. Bushnell rejected the excesses of revivalism because he disliked its disrupting influence on the community, whereas Beecher modified his view of God because, like his brothers and sisters, he could not accept the harshness of his father's belief that God was omnipotent and merciless. For different reasons, therefore, both men broke away from a central tenet of New School evangelical theology and established a precedent that was followed by many other clergymen during the 1850s.

Beecher's new conception of God rested on the assumption that love, not fear, should be the motivating force in every Christian's life. "I do not see why," he wrote to a friend, "a man of fine feelings, who receives impress from superior motives rather than from the lower, may not be blessed to his conversion without the use of fear at all." [31] By rejecting his father's conception of God as stern and omnipotent, Beecher took a step that exhibited a considerable degree of maturity and self-confidence. For his attitude toward God was closely related to his attitude toward his own father. Lyman Beecher seemed to his children to embody in his personality the two characteristic attributes of the evangelical conception of God—an intense but unsentimental love of his children and a strong belief in judgment. It was thus difficult for any of the children to modify their view of God without seeming to reject their own father. Nevertheless, members of the family eventually did reject the stern God of retribution that their father preached. [32] The only exception was Catharine, who though rejecting the notion of judgment, still retained an emphasis on self-sacrifice, fear, and guilt. That Henry could take this step despite the continual warnings of his father that "he had no business to tell sinners of the love of God without telling them of the wrath of God" was thus a sign that he at last had achieved a degree of independence from his father's overpowering personality. [33]

Beecher's rejection of his father's theology was symptomatic, as William G. McLoughlin has pointed out, of "the rebellion of a whole generation of Americans against their fathers." [34] It was an indication, on a popular level, of the beginnings of a basic shift in intellectual outlook—the rejection of the Lockean experiential epistemology, which emphasized the importance of sense perception and reason as the source of knowledge, and the adoption of the idealistic philosophy of Coleridge and Kant, which stressed the intuitions, the feelings, and the emotions. Like the English and German romantics, Beecher found inspiration for his beliefs in nature and the higher cultural achievements of society. "Art, natural scenery, literature are buttresses that hold up the tower and spire of [my] theology," he wrote to a friend. "God has written voluminously and not in one department alone. *My theology* requires me to search out truth in ten thousand places besides the Bible. I think that the Bible is but God's finger, pointing the direction where truth is to be found." [35]

The world of nature was to Beecher a living illustration of the beauty and grandeur of God—a place where the soul could experience goodness and find perfection. So wonderful, indeed, was the natural world, that Beecher continually drew upon it to reinforce the basic tenets of his faith. Typical was his statement that

> Love is the river of life in this world. Think not that ye know it who stand at the little tinkling rill—the first small fountain. Not until you have gone through the rocky gorges, and not lost the stream; not until you have stood at the mountain passes of trouble and conflict; not until you have gone through the meadow, and the stream has widened and deepened until fleets could ride on its bosom; not until beyond the meadow you have come to the unfathomable ocean, and poured your treasures into its depths—not until then can you know what love is. [36]

To us today, Beecher's vision of the natural world appears to be so much sentimental gush, but to a generation of Americans who had grown up in the country and moved to the city, it had an enormous appeal.

In addition to replacing his father's stern God of justice with a more beneficent deity and finding inspiration in the world of nature, Beecher shared with Bushnell a concern for the family as an agency of Christianization and social control. Building upon the sentimental conception of the Victorian family that prevailed at mid-century, Beecher argued that the family's duty was not only to introduce the child to the Gospel, but also to instill in the child the proper habits of social behavior. As he argued in 1849 in a sermon entitled "Progress of Society by Educating the Individual," the "family is *the* most important *institution on earth.*"

Beecher's achievement, as the title of his sermon indicated, was to unite for popular consumption two diverse streams of thought—the idealism of Continental Romanticism with the individualistic gospel of evangelical Christianity. The resulting social outlook fell halfway between the individualistic, anti-institutional, perfectionist philosophy of Jacksonian revivalists like Charles G. Finney and the organic, institutional views of Horace Bushnell. In his usual fashion, Beecher took a compromise position that relied upon the institutions of the church and the family to strengthen and reinforce the independence and self-reliance of the individual. As Beecher asserted in his sermon on education, "our age is more and more marked as a period of change. The questions of our day are questions of reorganization—of progress of reforms. The spirit of our people and, I think God may *say the public spirit* of the world, is for amelioration and expansion and growth toward individual and social excellence." [37]

Although both Beecher and Bushnell stressed the importance of the family and shared a belief in the intuitive nature of religion and a faith in a merciful God of love, they differed strongly in other respects. Whereas Bushnell emphasized the family and worked to develop a theological alternative to evangelical religion, Beecher continued to think of himself as a revivalist and reformer. He remained an activist, unconventional in his approach and careless of theological fine points. "In writing or speaking when fairly roused up," he confided in a friend, "I do not seem to think, *I see*. If I speak of images it is because they glow, I see landscapes or cliffs—or forests, or prairies and the *impression* is as minute and vivid as if it were really before my eyes." [38] So diverse and different were Beecher's views in fact, that it would be misleading to speak of him as having a "systematic theology." As Leonard Bacon, pastor of the First Church in New Haven, later commented, "it is well understood that Brother Beecher is erratic. No other person would undertake to be responsible for all his sayings and doings." [39]

Beecher's religious views, though disorganized and unsystematic, did have an activist impulse which gave him a sense of urgency that Bushnell lacked. While Bushnell viewed wealth as an index to virtue, Beecher warned against the perils of riches. And while Bushnell was pessimistic about the chances of reforming society, Beecher had an optimistic outlook that saw civilization as progressing toward higher and more perfect social structures.

Nevertheless, both men, when taken together, represented the new direction in which Protestantism was heading. They not only rejected the harsh, judgmental approach to religion of Lyman Beecher's generation, they redefined and reshaped the three basic tenets on which the new faith would rest: that Christianity was based on God's gift of love, that the natural world was a reflection of God's immutable laws, and that the family was the ideal instrument for fostering true Protestantism. All three tenets rested on the pervasive, unquestioning Victorian belief in the importance of environment. God's love for man was simply a part of the boundless abundance that mid-Victorian Americans took for granted along with the vast forests, extensive farm lands, and rich mineral deposits of the North American continent. It was a gift, to be discovered and exploited at will. Similarly, the natural world was a source of immutable, fixed laws. For the rapidly growing and ethnically plural society of the eastern seaboard, the changing seasons, with their cycles of growth, decay, and rebirth, became a source of truth and inspiration. Progress and advancement were unquestionably possible. Most important, the environment could be reshaped, manipulated, and transformed at will. The Christian family, protected from the violence and aggressiveness of the outside world by elaborate codes of manners and emotionally charged ties of affection, would nurture the true faith that, once mature, could be used to reform and renew the nation. If Bushnell was the theologian for the new romantic Christianity, Beecher was its prophet. The two charted the way for the intellectual and emotional redirection of Protestantism that was taking place in America before the Civil War.[40]

Beecher's espousal of romantic Christianity, with its conception of a merciful God of love and its dedication to reforms that would maintain social stability, was the cement that bound together the different elements of Victorian middle-class morality. It reassured urban Americans that the world was governed by moral laws and that Truth and Virtue did indeed exist. It urged individuals, moreover, to take an active role in social reforms. Beecher not only spoke for this activist position but also set an example by his own behavior. Following the program he had set forth in his first sermon, Beecher soon became involved in a debate over the Mexican War. The war had resulted, Beecher argued at Providence, Rhode Island, from America's love of possession and desire for gain.[41] It was the artful provocation of an expert bully, designed to destroy a poor but peaceful country. He was particularly incensed by the idea of "manifest destiny." "It is the manifest destiny of some men to pilfer; of others to steal; of others to rob; of others to murder," he declared.[42]

Even more specious than the campaign for manifest destiny was the argument that an invasion of Mexico would Christianize her people: "To send fleets to batter and ruin seaports—to pour armies upon a rude and undisciplined mob of half-starved slaves, to ravage provinces, take and hold their cities has been common to all ages; but to do it for the sake of *civilization and religion* is an achievement of the Anglo-Saxon race. . . . I should think that war and injustice were quite enough without *hypocrisy*." Furthermore, Beecher argued, the war should be blamed on the two major parties, who were hypocritical about its outbreak and primarily concerned with maintaining their own power. Their manipulations enabled the slave states to assert their influence during the peace negotiations.[43]

Discontent with recent political developments such as the Mexican War prompted Beecher to associate with a newly formed weekly, *The Independent*. This journal was founded in 1848 by a group of clergymen to further the interests of Congregationalism and to advance the antislavery cause without incurring the recriminations attached to abolitionists of the Garrisonian "immediatist" stamp.[44] Beecher's decision to join this publication was astute; it gave him access to a key channel of communication in the 1850s. Since Victorian Americans were intensely interested in moral education and questions of ethics, the religious press was to achieve a power and influence in the Civil War period equal to that of the secular newspapers.

At the beginning of every issue during the first few months of its existence, the editors reaffirmed Beecher's position of nonpartisanship. *The Independent* was not to be the organ of any ecclesiastical body or political party. Nevertheless, they insisted, the paper would take a stand on all political questions that involved great moral issues. On the question of the extension and perpetuation of slavery, which they considered most significant, the editors backed the Free Soil position and yet were not committed to the Free Soil party.[45] Beecher's association with *The Independent* represented the logical means of furthering his moral crusade and spreading the Gospel. Moreover, having contributed to newspapers in both Cincinnati and Indianapolis, he was aware of the power of the press in an urban environment and vowed to take advantage of it.

In the spring of 1848, Beecher's interest in the antislavery issue was further stimulated by correspondence with his brother Charles, pastor of the Terre Haute church, who had lived in Louisiana for a decade and knew slavery from first-hand experience.[46] Having worried about the problem of slavery for a number of years, Charles now became convinced that the nation would soon suffer divine retribution for its sins. "I for one expect either to die by violence or to live in the fastness and retreats of the forest," he wrote to his sister Harriet. "The plot is laid. The explosion will come."[47]

Although Henry did not share his brother's alarm, he decided in 1848 to make his opposition to slavery known to the public. An opportunity occurred in the fall when Beecher learned that two mulatto sisters, residents of Washington, would be sold back into slavery unless money to buy their freedom could be raised. On December 7 a large meeting was held at the Broadway Tabernacle and Beecher, as one of the speakers, extemporized a mock auction to raise the funds.[48] With ease he imitated the cries of the auctioneer: "And more than that, gentlemen, they say she is one of those praying niggers; who bids? A thousand—fifteen hundred—two thousand—twenty-five hundred? Going! last call! *Gone*."[49] The effect was electric. Some people shouted. Others cried. The hat was passed and money was quickly raised to free the slaves. The crowd's reaction overwhelmed the young preacher and convinced him of the effectiveness of an appeal to outraged middle-class morality. He had touched upon a sensitive issue that had captured the popular imagination. He was pleased, moreover, by the publicity that this event created. Although he was genuinely concerned about the horrors of slavery, he was not averse to using the abolitionist attack to build his reputation.

Further action on the slavery issue was abruptly curtailed on the night of January 13, 1849, when a fire burned over a large area of Brooklyn and destroyed Beecher's church. The fire proved to be a blessing in disguise, for the membership had outgrown the old church building and a new one was needed. But the new structure demanded a great deal of planning and Beecher was left with little time for any other activities. As he wrote to his brother Thomas, "I am now in the very straits of building plans—specifications—sections—effects— styles—sittings—elevations and depressions."[50]

The new church, which cost $36,000 and was completed in January, 1850, was designed by Beecher to focus on his preaching.[51] Instead of a pulpit, the church had a central platform, around which the seats were arranged in a large semicircle. The radically new design not only enabled the congregation of three thousand to hear the sermon easily and the preacher to speak without raising his voice, but also gave the appearance of a closeness between the pastor and the congregation. It was symbolic of Beecher's desire to be more personal and informal in his dealings with his congregation.

The labor demanded by financing and building the new church placed a strain on Beecher's health, and in March, 1849, he became severely ill. For the next two months he was confined to bed, and he did not return to his pulpit until the fall. It was winter before he was able to write for *The Independent* and resume his usual duties.[52] Shortly before Beecher returned to his pulpit, Henry Clay, in January, 1850, introduced in Congress a series of resolutions designed to settle the dispute over what was to be done with the territory that the United States had acquired from Mexico after the war. These resolutions, which became the basis for the Compromise of 1850, marked the recognition of slavery as a central issue in national politics and had a profound effect on the leadership and followers of the antislavery movement.[53] What formerly had been an academic argument over the future of slavery now became a political question of national importance.

The New England clergy were particularly incensed by the Clay resolutions. Since most of them still retained their earlier conviction that the West was to be the seedbed for the future development of the nation, it seemed as if Clay and Congress, by leaving the status of slavery in the territories undecided, were giving the southern states an unfair advantage and jeopardizing the future growth of the country.[54]

The clergy were upset, too, because the appearance of the slavery question in the political arena raised a fundamental question—the question of what "means" should be used to oppose the despised institution.[55] When this question had come up several decades earlier, the revivalists had decided that "moral suasion" was more effective than "legal coercion." They had shared the Jacksonian faith in the common man and had, as Alexis de Tocqueville pointed out, "made it the pride of their profession to abstain from politics."[56]

Since the 1830s, however, the revivalists had run into difficulties in their efforts to reform the nation through moral suasion. The churches had split over doctrinal questions, money had run out during depressions, and the vices of the earlier age had not been wiped out. The pressing question in 1850, therefore, was whether they should continue to oppose slavery by using voluntary persuasion or whether they should turn to political parties and work through them. This question was to lie at the base of the antislavery activities of the New England clergy in the 1850s.

Henry Ward Beecher, like the other New England clergy, had been deeply concerned about the question of "means" in the 1830s and 1840s and had then decided to limit his activity to using moral suasion. Not only was legislation ineffective, he believed, but the political parties were corrupt and would not work for altruistic ends. So opposed to parties was Beecher that he had declared in Indianapolis that "had I a son able to gain a livelihood by toil, I had rather bury him than witness his beggarly supplications for office, sneaking along the path of man's passions to gain his advantage."[57]

When Clay first introduced his compromise resolutions, therefore, Beecher immediately protested, though he was careful not to associate himself with any political party. Moral suasion, he still believed, was the only way to prevent the unjust compromise. Writing in *The Independent*, Beecher attacked Clay's resolutions as a betrayal of American and Christian principles, dictated by crafty politicians and made to serve party tactics.[58] The clash between North and South, which created the crisis, Beecher held, was the inevitable result of the different organization of society in the two sections, a clash between the incompatible and mutually destructive principles of democracy and aristocracy. The North, organized around democratic principles, had gained its strength, virtue, and civilization from the condition of its laborers. Work was considered voluntary and honorable. In the South, by contrast, it was a badge of degradation, fastened on an abject class. Since the condition of work in a society measured the character of the common people and because the common people represented the position of the country on the scale of civilization, the South had become inferior to the North and was seeking to make up for its deficiency through a subtle and clever compromise.[59]

Thus, the real horror of slavery for Beecher was its denial of the most basic Victorian values. By making labor dishonorable, slavery destroyed industry, discipline, and thrift. And what was worse, it denied education and undermined virtue: "It takes liberty from those to whom God gave it as the right of all rights. It forbids all food either for the understanding or the heart. It takes all honesty from conscience. It takes its defense from virtue, and gives all authority into the hands of lustful or pecuniary cupidity. It scorns the family, and invades it whenever desire or want of money prevail. . . .'' Slavery led to prostitution, destroyed the virtue and purity of black women, and denied a common humanity to the black man. "There is a scale in society extending from the rich and cultivated down to the poor and ignorant,'' Beecher argued. "Christ did regard this difference, and he worked at the bottom first. What is the spirit of Christianity? Is it not a spirit of love and mercy to the sinful, the helpless?"[60] Slavery was hideous because it denied education, abused the family, disregarded industrial values, destroyed chastity and virtue, and rejected the most basic tenet of Christianity, the equality of every man in the eyes of Christ.

In his attack on slavery as the destroyer of Victorian values, Beecher unconsciously revealed a tension in the Victorian cultural ethos between an enlightenment commitment to equal rights and the romantic vision of self-improvement, advancement, civilization, and progress. The world was marching forward and moving up on the scale of perfection. The problem was how to build a case for the moral superiority of the middle-class without opening it up to the criticism of being elitist and aristocratic. Beecher's answer, shared by a wide following, was to differentiate good from bad distinctions. Good distinctions included those based on character and cultural achievement. Evil distinctions were those based on race or money alone. Though industriousness was praised and might lead to increased income, riches and the single-minded pursuit of wealth were corrupting.

The difficulty in making such fine distinctions became apparent in January when Beecher attacked Clay's resolutions and drew attention to the role of the business community. The uneasiness and hostility Beecher had displayed toward aggressive businessmen in Indianapolis now reappeared. "Among all the arch-defenders," he emphasized, "there is not one who would think it worthwhile uttering a syllable in defense of slavery in our land if it were not for pecuniary reasons."[61] "With such men" he declared, "a moral principle is an abstraction—a thing for philosophic leisure. . . . Enterprise is the sum of all manhood with them; profits are the great realities of life. . . ."[62]

This stand aroused opposition from the organ of the business community, the *Journal of Commerce*, and it eventually led to a long dispute. The *Journal of Commerce*'s attack came when Henry C. Bowen, publisher of *The Independent* and trustee of Plymouth Church, refused to attend a meeting of merchants at Castle Garden, New York, at which the Fugitive Slave Law was endorsed. In response to the attack by the *Journal*, Bowen published a "card" which had been suggested by Beecher. It read, "We wish it distinctly understood that our goods and not our principles are on the market."[63] This resulted in the cancellation of about one-half of *The Independent*'s three thousand subscriptions and the addition of five thousand new ones, a shift which considerably altered the paper's constituency.[64]

Although Beecher's attack on the business community was extreme, he tried to preserve his belief in moral suasion and was careful not to alienate the southerners. "The very solemnity of the clerical duty in this day," he argued, "makes it imperative to clothe their spirits in the mantle of Love; to give earnest heed that they speak not rashly, that no distempered enthusiasm take the place of earnest truth and calm statement. . . ."[65]

However, as the compromise resolutions were passed one by one, Beecher found it increasingly hard to maintain a sympathetic attitude toward the South. In attempting to preserve his position as a moderate, he was faced with a dilemma. If he did not denounce the proposals for political compromise, there was, he believed, a real danger that the voters would be tricked. Yet by painting the threat in vivid colors, he ran the risk of alienating the southerners. The problem was how to prevent a compromise while preserving at the same time a "moderate, kind, Christian exhibition of the truth . . . to . . . prepare the way for emancipation."[66]

Beecher's dilemma was further complicated by his relationship with the radical abolitionists. Since his first public statements on the slavery problem, Beecher had denounced the radical Garrisonian wing of the antislavery movement. His hostility continued during the 1850s, and he frequently singled out William Lloyd Garrison and Wendell Phillips for censure. "Had he [Garrison] possessed the moderation or urbanity of a Clarkson, or the deep piety of a Wilberforce, he [would] have been the man of our age," he declared on more than one occasion.[67]

Despite Beecher's dislike for the views of Garrison and the other radical antislavery leaders, events in the 1850s conspired to associate him more closely with them. When he learned in May, 1850, that Wendell Phillips had been barred from speaking in New York City, Beecher invited him to deliver his address in Plymouth Church and personally introduced him. But Beecher also made it clear that he was defending Phillip's freedom of speech and not his views. "If he were 10,000 times blacker than he is (I mean his *belief* and not his *skin*)," Beecher declared in his introduction, "I would still stand up for his right to speak his own sentiments. . . ."[68] A year later, having met Garrison while on a lecture trip in Boston, Beecher accepted his invitation to address the Garrisonian American Anti-Slavery Society. Although he insisted in his speech that he shared Garrison's hatred of slavery but not his approach, the audience was not clear about the distinction between principle and tactics.

Beecher's attack on Henry Clay's compromise resolutions was abruptly interrupted in the late spring of 1850 when his health began to fail once again. The church trustees noticed his condition and voted him a three-month vacation in which to rest and recuperate. On July 9, having procured the services of his brother Charles for his congregation, Beecher left for Europe, where he hoped to recover his strength.[69] He spent the next several months visiting England and France. Although he seemed to enjoy his vacation, Beecher frequently was homesick and often had feelings of guilt for having left his wife and family behind. "Sometimes the ingratitude of my life comes up before me with such an overshadowing darkness," he wrote to his wife, "that I almost expect a bolt from it to destroy, but instead I see even more than the bow of promise. I feel my strength is improving and I hope when I return to your arms and to my pastorate, to be able to resume my labors with a degree of efficiency which for many months past has been denied me."[70]

These feelings of guilt and ingratitude are not difficult to explain. If one looks at the periods of "sickness" and "exhaustion" during Beecher's early career, a significant pattern emerges. Beecher became ill, each time for a period of several months, whenever he ran into a situation that questioned his confidence, ability, or integrity. As a child he became "sick" when he was unable to undergo the conversion experience he desperately sought. Similarly, in 1849, he became "ill" when his attempt to create a great revival in Brooklyn appeared to be a failure and his church burned down. And finally, he became "exhausted" when his opposition to the Compromise of 1850 made him the center of controversy. In each case, Beecher's illnesses seemed to coincide exactly with a period of unusual stress or frustration in his life.

It is also significant that Beecher's attitude toward the meaning and cause of sickness changed drastically at mid-century. As a youth, Beecher had viewed sickness as a form of God's retribution, a punishment for sin and wickedness. But in the 1840s his attitude shifted considerably. Once the origins of disease were discovered and knowledge of medicine was enlarged, illness became both understandable and excusable. Sickness now brought pity, not censure, sympathy, not admonishment. The retreat into "illness," so characteristic of mid-Victorian America, thus became both a sign of the pressures on members of the new urban middle class and a means of escape when they could not face reality. When Beecher became "exhausted," he may well have subconsciously been following the pattern set by his peers. Beecher's European trip "for reasons of health" thus became publicly acceptable, and he returned in September rested and eager to begin work.

During Beecher's absence, the Fugitive Slave Law had been passed by Congress. It denied a slave the right to testify in his own behalf and provided special United States Commissioners who could call bystanders to their aid and form a *posse comitatus* to help catch fugitives. The law created a major problem for Beecher. Although he was strongly opposed to it and especially disliked the provision which required a bystander to help capture a fugitive, he hesitated to argue that the law should be disobeyed for fear that he would create a precedent that would undermine civil authority in general. Thus, in his first article in *The Independent* on the subject, Beecher cautiously recommended passive disobedience. "We shall not attempt to rescue," he declared, "nor interrupt the officers if they do not interrupt us."[71]

Harriet Beecher Stowe agreed with her brother's stand on the bill and wrote him of her feelings. "It did my heart good to find somebody in as indignant a state as I am about this miserable wicked fugitive slave business," she declared. "Why I have felt almost choked sometimes with pent up wrath that does no good." Harriet, too, was having trouble retaining her Christian sympathy for the southerners.

"They certainly lay themselves open to the worst suppositions who can want to hush up and salve over such an outrage on common humanity, to say nothing of religion," she commented.[72] Confident of her brother's ability to expose the weakness in the Fugitive Slave Law, Harriet encouraged him to continue his efforts. "Strive, pray, labor, Henry," she wrote. "Be the champion of the oppressed and may God defend and bless you."[73]

Encouraged by his sister's exhortations, Beecher wrote another article on the Fugitive Slave Law in November, giving a fuller exposition of his views. Beecher's opposition to the law rested on two grounds. The law was ineffective, he believed, because morality could not be legislated. And the law was objectionable because it violated men's consciences by requiring them to sin against one another. This latter aspect of the law made it particularly dangerous, for conscience was the basic source of self-restraint and self-control within society. ". . . the nation that regards conscience more than anything else, above all, is like New England with its granite hills, immovable and invincible," he emphasized, "and the nation that does not regard conscience is a mere base of sand, and quicksand, too, at that." Because the Fugitive Slave Law violated a central tenet of Victorian morality—"the higher law, the law of conscience, the law of God, the law upon which obedience to all law is based," the public was obligated to disobey it. "The invincible truth of the Christian's creed," Beecher asserted, was *"obedience to laws even though they sin against me; disobedience to every law that commands me to sin."*[74] Outspoken as this position was, it was typical of the reaction of the northern Congregational clergy.[75] Even a conservative on social issues like Horace Bushnell took the same stand, declaring that the first duty he owed "to civil government is to violate and spurn such a law. . . ."[76]

Harriet Beecher Stowe was heartened by her brother's article. "I wish I had your chance," she wrote to him, "but the next best to that is to have you have it. So fire away. Give them no rest day nor night." She was thinking, she added, about a series of articles she had contracted to write for the *National Era* and she asked Henry for suggestions, "something to make slavery a *picture* instead of a political idea."[77] The articles, which she began to publish in May, eventually became *Uncle Tom's Cabin* and transformed her overnight from an unknown Maine housewife into an international public figure.

Beecher remained concerned with the slavery issue through the winter of 1851, but his church and lecture activities gave him little time to play an active part in the crusade. Not until May did he speak out again. The speech was primarily a reiteration of his earlier statements. Businessmen and politicians were accused of supporting slavery, the Fugitive Slave Bill was attacked, and a moderate and considerate attitude toward the southerner was urged. The new element was his concern for the condition of the free Negro in the North. "What has the North done for its colored population?" asked Beecher. "Here is a class downcast and downtrodden among us—the poor, the despised, the weak. . . . The doors of the schools and colleges are shut against them, and the doors of the trades are shut." The duty of the North, Beecher urged, was as much to educate its own colored population as it was to prevent the extension of slavery.[78]

Having expressed a concern for the rights of the free Negro in the North, Beecher then qualified his support. "I am for Colonization," he reassured his audience. "Do your duty first to the colored people here, educate them, Christianize them, and *then* colonize them." The apparent inconsistency in Beecher's stand, which combined an unusual concern for the rights of free blacks with an acceptance of the neo-colonization movement, was not as hypocritical as it appears. Though Beecher was genuinely committed to a defense of the free blacks' rights, he was skeptical about the ability of any reformer to overcome the prejudice inherent in American society. The only alternative to having blacks face continual hatred and prejudice was to provide them with a middle-class set of values and allow them an opportunity to use their talents elsewhere. Like so much of American Victorian thought, Beecher's compromise combined both idealism and paternalism. Given his extreme concern for social stability, his solution, despite its obvious limitations, seemed to his contemporaries to be a plausible alternative.[79]

Beecher's speech also exhibited a new sophistication in handling audiences. When at one point during his address he was interrupted by hisses, he commented that he had been heard without pause for some time and it was only fair to give his opposition a chance. Later in his speech, when Beecher mentioned that slavery allowed some men to have twenty wives, a voice from the audience answered that some men in New York also had twenty wives. "I am sorry for them," Beecher replied. "I go in for their immediate emancipation."[80]

In the fall of 1852, the American Home Missionary Society met at Albany, New York, to examine the relationship between the Presbyterians and Congregationalists and to decide what stand to take on the slavery issue. Beecher originally did not plan to attend the meeting, but the news that the clergy might take a more radical stand on slavery prompted him to change his mind.[81] At stake was the question of whether both denominations should continue their commitment to moral suasion or whether, following the lead of the Garrisonian wing of the abolitionist movement, they should break all ties with their southern clerical brethren.

When Beecher reached Albany on the fifth of October, he found that most of the six hundred clergymen present were deeply interested in the slavery issue. Several days later when the discussion of the churches' attitude toward missionaries in the South began, the radicals gained a majority and presented a resolution to refuse aid to churches that admitted slaveholders. The executive committee, of which Beecher was a member, headed off this movement by passing a compromise resolution that subsequently was ratified by the convention. Declaring that "the tendency of the Gospel . . . [was] to destroy sin in all its forms," the resolution stated that the missionary society would grant aid to all southern ministers who would preach the gospel in such a way as to bring to pass the speedy abolition of slavery.[82]

This statement, which reaffirmed the traditional faith in moral suasion, was to be the basis for the stand on slavery taken by most Congregational ministers during the 1850s.[83] These ministers remained "independent moderates." They were "moderate" because they backed the nonextension of slavery while assuring southerners that nothing would be done to injure the system in the South. Unlike the Garrisonian radicals, they did not want to break all ties with the South or to withdraw from the Union. They were "independent" because they refused to join with any antislavery or other reform agency.

This moderate stand was accepted and defended by Beecher. For more than two years, he had argued that to abolish slavery in the South, public sentiment in the North had to be changed and then allowed to act upon slavery. "Take from Slavery its right to merchandise, forbid the disruption of families, the sale of slaves from the homestead where they were born, and the system will stink in the nostrils of Southern planters as it now does in our own." The people of the North had only to shut the slave states up and let them alone. And when slavery began to die out, the duty of the North was to deny it the political concessions that the southerners would demand to compensate for their losses.[84]

Nor was Beecher concerned with the length of time it might take slavery to die out. "If it were given to me to choose, whether it be destroyed in fifty years by selfish commercial interests, or standing seventy-five years, be then the spirit and trophy of Christ," he commented, "I had rather let it linger twenty-five years more, that God may be honored and not mammon in the destruction of it."[85]

The weakness of Beecher's arguments against slavery becomes most evident when one speculates about what might have happened if southerners had accepted his advice to give blacks the Bible, to teach them to read, to protect the sanctity of their marriages, and to provide them with certain limited legal rights. If southerners had been willing to modify their system instead of defending it as an absolute good, the result might well have been a society similar to the South Africa of the 1960s, a nation with a dependent lower class held in subjection by highly efficient police and military organizations.

Thus Beecher, in his preoccupation with the prevention of social dislocation of any kind, was unable to offer an alternative that would quickly change the position of blacks in the South. Though he detested slavery, two years after the Omnibus Bill was passed he still reasserted his faith in the efficacy of moral suasion. As the decade wore on, he would find it increasingly difficult to maintain his compromise position. In his efforts to warn the nation of the danger of political concessions on the territorial question, he would become increasingly associated with the radicals, despite all his efforts to the contrary.

NOTES

1. H. W. Beecher to Eunice Beecher, Sept. 12, 1847, Yale MSS.
2. H. W. Beecher to Eunice Beecher, Sept. 5, 1847, Yale MSS.
3. Harold C. Syrett, *The City of Brooklyn, 1865–1898* (New York, 1944), 13.

4. *Ibid.*, 20.

5. See Stephan M. Ostrander, *A History of the City of Brooklyn and Kings County*, ed. Alexander Black (Brooklyn, 1896), 84.

6. Stephen M. Griswold, *Sixty Years with Plymouth Church* (New York, 1907). Griswold argues, somewhat misleadingly, that "it was not a wealthy congregation" (p. 27).

7. *Dictionary of American Biography*, ed. Dumas Malone (New York, 1935), IV; Cornell University, *Memorial Exercises in Honor of Henry Williams Sage* (Ithaca, 1898), 5.

8. James Parton, *Famous Americans of Recent Times* (Boston, 1867), 394.

9. H. W. Beecher, Sermon Notebook, p. 44, Library of Congress.

10. H. W. Beecher, Sermon, Oct. 10, 1847, Yale MSS.

11. John Raymond Howard, *Remembrance of Things Past* (New York, 1925), 48.

12. H. W. Beecher to Lyman Beecher, Dec. 14, 1847, Schlesinger Library.

13. *Ibid.*

14. H. W. Beecher, Sermons, 1848, Yale MSS.

15. Catharine Beecher to Lyman Beecher, Jan. 3, 1848, Schlesinger Library. For similar comments, see Jane Elsmere, *Henry Ward Beecher: The Indiana Years, 1837–1847* (Indianapolis, 1973), 101, 159.

16. H. W. Beecher to H. B. Stowe, n.d., Yale MSS.

17. John H. Raymond to H. W. Beecher, Sept. 11, 1848, Yale MSS.

18. H. W. Beecher to H. B. Stowe, n.d., Yale MSS; Robert Baird, *Religion in America* (New York, 1856), 534.

19. For a discussion of the voluntary principle, which also was known as "voluntaryism" to distinguish it from "voluntarism," which referred to freedom of the will, see Baird, *Religion in America*, Book IV, and Sidney Mead, *The Lively Experiment* (New York, 1963), 124.

20. Henry F. May's introduction to Harriet Beecher Stowe's *Oldtown Folks* (Cambridge, 1966) is the best brief description of the theological background of the Beechers. For a fuller discussion see Sidney Mead, *Nathaniel William Taylor 1786–1858, a Connecticut Liberal* (Chicago, 1942) and Edmund Wilson, *Patriotic Gore* (New York, 1962), chap. I.

21. William G. McLoughlin traces Finney's attitude toward God in *Modern Revivalism* (New York, 1959), 90.

22. See also Perry Miller, *Life of the Mind in America* (New York, 1965), 40–43.

23. Anne C. Loveland, "Evangelicism and Immediate Emancipation in American Antislavery Thought," *Journal of Southern History*, XXXII (May, 1966), 172–88. The influence of "moral suasion" and "political coercion" also is mentioned briefly by James M. McPherson in "Grant or Greeley? The Abolitionist Dilemma in the Election of 1872." *American Historical Review*, LXXI (October, 1965), 61.

24. Although Beecher and the other clergy argued that it was better to use moral suasion than legal coercion to reform the individual, they were not averse to using legal means to supplement their preaching if there was a chance to pass a law. The ideal of moral suasion, which lies at the heart of the voluntary principle, was to trouble second-generation leaders like Beecher, who wanted to remain faithful to the views of his father. For a study of the role that moral suasion played in the antislavery movement see John Demos, "The Anti-Slavery Movement and the Problem of Violent 'Means,' " *New England Quarterly*, XXVII (Dec., 1964), 501–26; Winthrop Hudson, *Religion in America* (New York, 1965), 154.

25. Frank H. Foster, *A Genetic History of New England Theology* (Chicago, 1907), 413; see also H. Shelton Smith, ed., *Horace Bushnell* (New York, 1965), intro.

26. Barbara M. Cross, *Horace Bushnell* (Chicago, 1958), 100, 142.

27. H. W. Beecher to H. J. Raymond, Aug. 30, 1848 (typed copy), Yale MSS.

28. Thomas K. Beecher to H. B. Stowe, Sept. 3, 1848, Schlesinger Library.

29. H. W. Beecher to Thomas K. Beecher, Nov., 1848, Schlesinger Library.

30. J. H. Raymond to H. W. Beecher, Sept. 11, 1848, Yale MSS.

31. H. W. Beecher to Rev. Charles Jones, Oct. 22, 1852 (typed copy), Yale MSS.

32. The best-known case of the rejection of Lyman Beecher's views was Catharine's. Her fiancé drowned on a trip to Europe before he had undergone the conversion experience. Lyman Beecher said that the fiancé must have gone to Hell but Catharine could not accept that assertion. *Autobiography of Lyman Beecher*, I, 370; see also Kathryn K. Sklar's excellent book, *Catharine Beecher: A Study in Domesticity* (New Haven, 1973), 85–89, 118, 127–29, 141.

33. Family Reminiscences, in Beecher Papers, Stowe-Day Foundation.

34. William G. McLoughlin, *The Meaning of Henry Ward Beecher* (New York, 1970), 38.

35. H. W. Beecher to ?, Nov. 29, 1851, Yale MSS.

36. H. W. Beecher, *Sermons by Henry Ward Beecher* (New York, 1869), II, 231.

37. H. W. Beecher, Sermon, Oct., 1849, Yale MSS. On this point, I differ with W. G. McLoughlin's statement that both Bushnell and Beecher "were therefore advocates of Christian nurture, of institutionalized Christianity, of an organic view of society as opposed to the anti-institutionalism, individualism, and perfectionism of Jacksonian revivalists like Charles G. Finney or Jacksonian reformers like Theodore Weld and William Lloyd Garrison." I see Beecher as occupying a middle position between Finney and Bushnell, not the same position as Bushnell and Henry W. Bellows. See McLoughlin, *The Meaning of H. W. Beecher*, 39–40.

38. H. W. Beecher to ?, Nov. 29, 1851, Yale MSS.

39. Leonard Bacon to the *Puritan Recorder*, Sept. 29, 1852, quoted in Theodore Bacon, *Leonard Bacon, A Statesman of the Church* (New Haven, 1931), 356.

40. Cross, *Horace Bushnell*, 40, 48. The best analysis of the tension between the Victorian belief in the family as a retreat and the desire to use it as an instrument of social reform is Kirk Jeffrey's "The Family as Utopian Retreat from the City: The Nineteenth Century Contribution," *Soundings*, IV (Spring, 1972), 21–41.

41. Frederick Merk, *Manifest Destiny and Mission in American History* (New York, 1963), 122.

42. H. W. Beecher, notebook fragment, Feb. 5, 1848, Yale MSS.

43. H. W. Beecher, Sermon, April 27, 1848, Yale MSS.

44. Louis Filler, "Liberalism, Anti-Slavery and the Founders of *The Independent*," *New England Quarterly*, XXVII (Sept., 1954), 294.

45. *The Independent*, Dec. 21, 1848.

46. See the fascinating letters of Charles Beecher to Catharine A. Foote, May 8, May 26, 1839, Schlesinger Library.

47. Charles Beecher to H. B. Stowe, May 1, 1848, Yale MSS.

48. "The Edmonson Sisters," *The Independent*, Dec. 21, 1848.

49. William C. Beecher and Samuel Scoville, *Biography of Henry Ward Beecher* (New York, 1888), 293.

50. H. W. Beecher to Thomas K. Beecher, Jan. 29, 1848, Cornell University Archives.

51. Beecher and Scoville, *Biography*, 223.

52. Lyman Abbott and S. B. Halliday, *Henry Ward Beecher: A Sketch of His Character* (Hartford, 1887), 46.

53. Holman Hamilton in his *Prologue to Conflict* (New York, 1964), 54, points out that Stephen A. Douglas rather than Clay was the chief architect of the Compromise.

54. Stanley Elkins, *Slavery: A Problem of American Institutional and Intellectual Life* (Chicago, 1959), 185–89, discusses the growth of the antislavery movement in the 1850s.

55. See Demos, "The Anti-Slavery Movement and the Problem of Violent 'Means,' " and Michael Fellman, "Theodore Parker and the Abolitionist Role in the 1850's," *Journal of American History*, LXI (Dec., 1974), 666–84.

56. Alexis de Tocqueville, *Democracy in America*, trans. Henry Reeve and ed. Phillips Bradley (New York, 1945), I, 309.

57. H. W. Beecher, *Seven Lectures to Young Men*, 45.

58. H. W. Beecher, "Shall We Compromise?" *The Independent*, Feb. 21, 1850.

59. *Ibid.* For an excellent discussion of the meaning and value attached to the term *labor* by middle-class Americans, see Eric Foner's *Free Soil, Free Labor, Free Men* (New York, 1970).

60. H. W. Beecher, *Patriotic Addresses*, ed. John Howard (New York, 1887), 174, 180.

61. H. W. Beecher, Sermon, Feb., 1850, Beecher Papers, Library of Congress.

62. H. W. Beecher, "Mr. Webster—Mr. Seward—Recapturing Slaves," *The Independent*, March 21, 1850.

63. Frank L. Mott, *A History of American Magazines* (Cambridge, Mass., 1839), II, 370.

64. Bacon, *Leonard Bacon*, 343.

65. H. W. Beecher, "Politics and the Pulpit," *The Independent*, May 23, 1850.

66. H. W. Beecher, Sermon, May 6, 1846, Yale MSS.

67. H. W. Beecher, "Cause and Cure of Agitation," *The Independent*, Nov. 14, 1850.

68. H. W. Beecher to Eunice Beecher, Jan. 8, 1851, Yale MSS; unidentified newspaper clipping, *Scrapbook*, May 10, 1853, Beecher Papers, Library of Congress.

69. Beecher and Scovill, *Biography*, 339.

70. H. W. Beecher to Eunice Beecher, Aug. 16, 1850, Yale MSS.

71. H. W. Beecher, "Fugitive Slave Bill at Its Work," *The Independent*, Oct. 3, 1850.

72. H. B. Stowe to H. W. Beecher, n.d., Yale MSS.

73. H. B. Stowe to H. W. Beecher, n.d., Yale MSS.

74. H. W. Beecher, "Law and Conscience," *The Independent*, Nov. 7, 1850.

75. Robert Senior, "New England Congregationalists and the Anti-Slavery Movement, 1830–1860," Ph.D. thesis, Yale University, 1954, 283.

76. Horace Bushnell to Dr. Bartol, May 6, 1851, quoted in Mary A. Cheney, *Life and Letters of Horace Bushnell* (New York, 1880), 247–48.

77. H. B. Stowe to H. W. Beecher, Feb. 1, 1851, Yale MSS.

78. H. W. Beecher, "American Slavery," *The Independent*, May 13, 1851.

79. *Ibid.*; William Stanton, *Leopard's Spots: Scientific Attitudes towards Race in America, 1815–1859* (Chicago, 1960). The extent of northern prejudice is clearly set forth in Leon Litwack's *North of Slavery, the Negro in the Free States, 1790–1860*

(Chicago, 1961); the best commentaries on northern racial attitudes are George Fredrickson's *The Black Image in the White Mind: The Debate on Afro-American Character and Destiny, 1817–1914* (New York, 1971) and Daniel W. Howe's "American Victorianism as a Culture," *American Quarterly*, XXVII (Dec., 1975), 507–32.

80. H. W. Beecher, "American Slavery," *The Independent*, May 13, 1851.

81. H. W. Beecher to Eunice Beecher, Oct. 5, 1852, Yale MSS.

82. *Proceedings of the Albany Convention*, quoted in Senior, "New England Congregationalists and the Anti-Slavery Movement," 292; see also Clifford S. Griffin, *Their Brothers' Keepers: Moral Stewardship in the United States, 1800–1865* (New Brunswick, N.J., 1960), 182–89.

83. Senior, in "New England Congregationalists and the Anti-Slavery Movement," has traced the stand on slavery of the Congregational ministers, but he does not relate it to their faith in moral suasion.

84. H. W. Beecher, "Cause and Cure of Agitation," *The Independent*, Nov. 14, 1850, and "American Slavery," *ibid.*, May 13, 1851.

85. H. W. Beecher, "A Word with the *Tribune*," *The Independent*, June 2, 1853.

5

The Pleasures of Being a Public Man

Beecher's frequent and outspoken attacks on the Compromise of 1850 increased his stature in the community and made him a much sought after public speaker. But prominence as a public figure was not an unmixed blessing; it limited his privacy, exacerbated his difficulties with his wife, and led to bitter public controversies. Though Beecher loved the limelight and found it difficult to turn down speaking invitations that would add to his reputation, he soon found that being a public man was not as pleasant as he had dreamed it would be. He was pestered by requests for charity, mobbed by public admirers, and hounded by reformers who wanted him to speak in behalf of their causes.

Prosperity did have its benefits. In addition to improving his financial situation, Beecher's numerous lectures and newspaper articles provided a forum in which he was able to develop more systematically his views about society, the increasing chaos of urban life, and man's relationship to the natural world. By reshaping earlier attitudes toward individual freedom and institutional involvement, by seeing the simple, everyday events of childhood and youth as symbols of the security and opportunity of the American economic system, and by expanding on the public's conception of nature and man's relationship to it, Beecher further enhanced his reputation as a spokesman for Victorian morality. This reputation in turn dramatically increased his role in the antislavery movement and forced him to come to terms with the question of tactics. Although he remained preoccupied with the ideals of moderation, nonpartisanship, and reform through moral suasion rather than legal coercion, he was forced, as the decade wore on, to take a tougher stand against the expansion of slavery. He thereby unintentionally helped to polarize the debate over slavery, increasing the emotionally charged atmosphere that preceded the outbreak of war.

Beecher was involved in a variety of reform movements and took a stand on many social issues during the 1850s. Among his favorite campaigns was the temperance crusade, which, like moderate abolitionism, was implicitly dedicated to the maintenance of Victorian morality. Participation in the temperance crusade implied a concern for poverty and disease, a desire to clean up politics, and, as the word itself suggested, a belief in moderation and self-control.[1] Because of his concern about the evils of alcoholism, Beecher, in February, 1852, was invited to speak at a temperance banquet in New York in honor of Neal Dow, the mayor of Portland, Maine, who recently had persuaded his state legislature to pass an act prohibiting the sale of liquor.[2] Beecher made a brief, impassioned speech about the physical harm produced by alcoholic spirits, but carefully refrained from discussing the Maine law. On this question, as on the slavery issue, he remained committed to the use of moral suasion.[3]

Because Beecher had spoken on behalf of the temperance crusade, Thomas W. Higginson, a Boston reformer, wrote him a year later to ask if he would be willing to join a World's Temperance Association and to inquire about his views on the women's rights issue. Beecher replied that he would not join the temperance organization because he wished to preserve his right to take an independent stand. "As to the women's question," he continued evasively, "my ground is simply this. I do not *prefer* that women should become public teachers or speakers, etc., but if they have the desire, and *will*, then they must have *fair play*, and a chance to do just what they have the ability to do." He closed his remarks and signed himself, "truly yours without

regard to gender," adding, "don't ask me to be solemn about the
women question. I can't do it." [4] Although Beecher took a more liberal
view of the women's rights question than his sister Catharine, clearly
he recognized that the subject was not popular with the public and
wanted to stay away from it for the time being.

Another major issue to concern Henry Ward Beecher in the early
1850s was that of education. Although he had long known about Catharine's interest in educational reforms, Henry had been too committed
to other crusades to follow her example. Even Harriet Beecher Stowe
at first had doubted the usefulness of Catharine's educational schemes.
As she later admitted to Henry, "I considered her [Catharine] strange,
nervous, visionary, and to a certain extent unstable. I see now that she
has been busy for eight years about *one thing*—a thing first conceived
upon a sick bed when she was so sick and frail that most women would
have felt that all they could hope for was to lie still and be nursed. . . .
Then she conceived this plan of educating our country by means of its
women and this she has steadily pursued in weariness and painful-
ness. . . ." [5] At the urging of his sister Harriet, Henry began to take a
more serious interest in the crusade for public education. A short time
later, after his concern for education had become known, Henry was
invited to speak before the annual meeting of the Society for the Promotion of Collegiate and Theological Education in the West. Taking
advantage of the offer, he delivered a major speech on the subject
"Man and his Institutions." [6]

In the speech, Beecher first set forth his ideas about the social function of institutions and then applied these views to the debate over
education. Man was by nature an individualistic and unique being, he
asserted, yet man also had to live within society. Man therefore combined "in himself harmoniously two apparently incompatible elements, perfect independence and perfect cohesion with others. He is at
the same time sharply individual, and thoroughly composite. He is at
once solitary and social; a perfect being, and yet organized as an element into a community of beings."

Since the individuality of man was the source of his power, it was
the duty of society through its institutions, to enhance the strong points
of each man's character. "While the first of all civic truths is the *liberty, power*, and individuality of man," he asserted, "the second truth
must be, the necessity of *the civil state, of laws, of wise institutions*."

Although some men saw a conflict between the development of man's individuality and the protection of the community, Beecher saw the two as complementary. The laws and institutions of the community checked man's passions and thereby enabled the other parts of his nature to develop more fully. Thus they contributed to his true freedom. "Man is the elementary power, and the supreme value," Beecher asserted. "But for his own greatest good he requires institutions; they are the means by which man acts, and without which he never could develop himself, or make use of his power were it developed."

The danger occurred only when institutions became ends in themselves, suppressing man's creative energies and limiting his freedom. In the America of the 1850s, the threat of tyrannous institutions appeared to Beecher to be particularly grave. "Our people seek to organize every thing," he reminded his audience. "We organize for inquiry. We organize to answer. We organize to give advice. We organize for pleasure. We distribute tracts by system. We institute our charity, until we are in danger of seeking to do nothing with the generous glow of personality, and everything in corporate character." There was, therefore, a desperate need for Americans to create the kind of institutions that would express the creative powers of individual citizens.

Beecher made a plea for the creation of protective institutions because he feared that the self-reliant individual of the Jacksonian era was becoming lost in the increasingly complex and interdependent society of the 1850s. Like many Americans, Beecher believed that the haphazard growth of business and industry was depriving people of their rights and freedoms. What he wanted to achieve, as spokesman for Victorian Americans, was a new individualism that would be strengthened by institutions. Beecher's notions of personal autonomy, self-control, and self-advancement were particularly appealing to the middle-class clerks, teachers, lawyers, and managers of small industry who wanted to retain the older sense of individualism in a society of growing institutional complexity.

To illustrate his argument for freedom and power through institutions, Beecher went on to describe his views about the ideal school and college. Educational institutions, he believed, should serve two major functions. First, they should act as centers of research and learning that would provide material benefits for society. This had been true in the past, he asserted. Because of the nation's educational institutions, men had created "better roads, lighter wheelbarrows, finer kerchiefs, lighter fingers to make them, neater carpenters and snugger homes, fewer needs and more supplies; in short, civilization among the masses." Second, schools and colleges should be philanthropic institutions designed to help the less intelligent and the less fortunate. "If colleges give *learning* to the few, they give *intelligence* to the many," he commented. ". . . if they stand upon a higher plane, it is as stationary engines, to draw society up the long inclinations." Colleges, in Beecher's view, should act as the leaven of society, diffusing knowledge to the poorer and less able members of the social structure.

Because educational institutions served socially beneficent purposes, men of wealth had a duty to support them, Beecher asserted. Money given to them would have a usefulness that would outlive the benefactor. ". . . who can measure," he asked, "the scope and breadth of that working which he shall perpetuate who trusts his spirit, not upon the birdwing of song, or in the crystal vase of a book, but who incarnates himself in an institution suited to the universal want, common to all times, and whose nature it is to be parent power, prolific of subsidiary powers, sending forth whatever influences and agencies are required by society in all its depths?" The answer was that only those men who were sensitive to the needs of the age would know how effective a donation to a school or college might be.

By pleading for better financial support for education, Beecher touched upon an old, commonplace theme. What was new in his argument was not his plea for financial support, but rather his attempt to redefine the relationship between individualism and institutions. Although Beecher previously had defended the need for primary and secondary schools on the grounds that they brought both social control and refinement to the general public, he now stressed the use of institutions to preserve individualism. In doing so, he helped to modify the earlier Emersonian conception of the self-reliant individual. People no longer could be totally self-controlled and self-reliant. They now had to use institutions to develop their native powers to the fullest extent. While Emerson saw men as attaining freedom *outside* of institutions and later Progressive reformers like Herbert Croly saw man as asserting his individuality within institutions, Beecher took a middle position, asserting that institutions could be used as stepping-stones to the formation of a fuller, more powerful individuality. It was a novel argument that redefined the traditional conception of individualism in a way that brought it more into focus with the social realities of the 1850s and eased the adjustments of many Americans to the strains and tensions produced by industrialization.

In addition to his activities in behalf of educational reform, Beecher also spent a good deal of time on the lyceum lecture circuit. The lyceum system, which had been created in the 1820s to provide practical knowledge for the working class, by 1850 reached even the smallest towns. With its large membership, the lyceum system hired some of the best speakers of the day—Edward Everett, Rufus Choate, Horace Mann, Bayard Taylor, Josiah Quincy, and Ralph Waldo Emerson.[7] These men provided entertainment as well as instruction. In an era when few public theaters or other amusements existed, they made the lyceum an important source of recreation.

Oliver Wendell Holmes, Sr., a good friend of the Beechers, once humorously described the typical audience: "Front seats; a few old folks—shiny-headed—slant up best ear towards the speaker—drop off to sleep after a while. . . . Bright women's faces, young and middle-aged, a little behind these but towards the front. [In the back] an indefinite number of pairs of young people—happy but not always very attentive."[8]

Beecher joined the ranks of the lyceum lecturers in the 1850s partially from the need for money and partially for altruistic reasons. In his youth Beecher had had difficulty living within his means. Now, living near New York City, he found increased temptations to spend. He developed the habit of visiting New York's jewelry and department stores to look at their new wares. Semiprecious stones interested him and he began to collect them, sometimes carrying the uncut stones around in his pocket. "Several establishments knowing my weakness," he wrote to a friend, "send me word whenever they have anything curious and their *workmen* seem much pleased that one should go down into their dark cellars, or corners in attics, to see them at work."[9] Though Beecher was interested in jewelry and uncut stones, his real passion was books. He frequently visited dealers in new and secondhand books and always returned home with a new purchase. During the 1850s he spent more than five hundred dollars a year on books.[10]

To compensate for these expenditures, Beecher turned to lecturing. This was a logical choice, for in a number of ways, the lyceum system was a natural adjunct to the evangelical religion of the period.[11] Both depended on the oratorical abilities of the speaker, and the chances were that if a preacher could arouse his congregation, he would also be able to appeal to the lyceum audience. If the lyceum proved to be a source of entertainment, so too did many clergymen. Moreover, both evangelical Protestantism and the lyceum placed an emphasis on personal improvement. Where the clergyman urged the sinner to work for his salvation and dedicate himself to God, the lyceum lecturer exhorted the workingman to become a success through self-help.

Beecher looked upon his revival sermons and lyceum lectures in the same light—both helped to improve the character of the common people. Yet, he was not entirely open about his own motives, and there was a certain naïveté in his comment to his wife that "when I see men absorbed in politics, or mere material wealth, I cannot help feeling that my activities are not selfish, but for the public good."[12]

Beecher usually delivered his lectures during the middle of the week, traveling through New England and speaking on successive nights. During the summer he extended the length of his trips, sometimes reaching Chicago. Before each lecture, despite the degree of preparation, Beecher was always nervous. Writing to his wife on one trip, he commented with relief, "so, the long agony is over, and I am safely through another dreaded job. But then, I shall dread the next just as much. . . . Success never inspires the hope or certainty of succeeding, so . . . that each time I feel the same burden beforehand, and the same anxiety."[13]

Beecher would usually choose a general theme, like character, perfect a lecture on the subject, and deliver it for a year or so. His lecture on patriotism was delivered more than thirty times in 1854 and 1855.[14] Beecher was not an imposing or elegant speaker. His movements were abrupt rather than graceful, and his quick jumps of thought, flashing from one illustration to another, frequently went astray. But the lectures had a kind of spontaneity and charm that captured the audience. His energetic statements and rough style of speaking gave Beecher a boyish quality—one which *Harper's Weekly* described as "his fresh feeling, his exuberant and rollicking humor, [and] his genuine love of men. . . ."[15] These traits never failed to impress the audience. As

Charles Eliot Norton, a severe critic, commented after hearing one of Beecher's lectures, "it was not great oratory, but it was a fine, large, broad, sensible, human sympathetic performance."[16]

Beecher's other main interest in the 1850s was the preparation of weekly articles for his column in *The Independent*. Beecher used these "Star Articles," so called because they were signed by an asterisk, to speak out on the slavery and temperance questions, and to refine his conception of the gospel of success. Following the format that he first developed in his *Lectures to Young Men*, he discussed topics such as "Health and Education," "Character and Reputation," and "Genius and Industry," using illustrations drawn from his own experience. The theme running through all the articles was the necessity of the self-repressive virtues of industry, frugality, perseverance, and discipline for the development of a truly Christian character.[17]

Beecher's articles on politics and the gospel of success were well received, but they were not as popular as the columns dealing with subjects that, at first glance, seemed more frivolous—"Haying," "Summer Rain," "Strawberries and Cream," "Apple-pie," "Snow Power," and "Winter Beauty."[18] What was remarkable about these articles was Beecher's ability to find in common, everyday experiences a reaffirmation of Victorian religious and social views. Take, for example, a short piece that he wrote in the early 1850s entitled "A Discourse on Flowers." In Beecher's eyes, flowers were more than just colorful ornaments, grown to one's fancy. They were a revelation of God's grandeur and beauty. "It is the end of art to inoculate men with the love of nature," he explained. "But those who have a passion for nature in the natural way, need no pictures nor galleries. Spring is their designer, the whole year is their artist." There was, moreover, a democratic aspect to flowers. "A very common flower adds generosity to beauty," he commented. "It gives joy to the poor, the rude, and to the multitudes who could have no flowers were nature to charge a price for her blossoms." Even dandelions, in Beecher's view, had a message for Victorian Americans. "Their passing away is more spiritual than their bloom," he remarked. "Nothing can be more airy and beautiful than the transparent seed-globe, a fairy dome of splendid architecture."

Flowers not only revealed the beauty and generosity of God, but they also provided solace and relief to people who were tired of living in the dirty, cluttered cities of the eastern seaboard. "How one exhales, and feels his childhood coming back to him," exclaimed Beecher, "when, emerging from the hard and hateful city, he sees orchards and gardens in sheeted bloom—plum, cherry, pear, peach, and apple, waves and billows of blossoms, rolling over the hillsides, and down through the levels! My heart runs riot. This is the kingdom of glory." To thousands of Americans who had been born in the country and had moved to the city, such words brought back memories of the simpler, more easygoing existence of their youth.

Although flowers were to Beecher symbolic of the virtues of rural life, their most important message was to proclaim the meaning of Christ's death and resurrection. To illustrate this idea, Beecher described his advice to a poor family that had just lost a child. "If you cannot give a stone to mark his burial place," he consoled, "a rose may stand there; and from it you may, every spring, pluck a bud for your bosom, as the child was broken off from you. And if it brings tears for the past, you will not see the flowers fade and come again, and fade and come again, and fade and come again, year by year, and not learn a lesson of the resurrection—when that which perished here shall revive again, never more to droop or die."[19] Given the recent deaths of his own children, this comment revealed Beecher's own attempt to come to terms with personal misfortune.

Thus, in a single newspaper article on the meaning of flowers, Beecher touched on three themes that were central to the middle-class, Victorian ethos: the belief in a democratic society where both beauty and opportunity were open to all men, the faith in a God that was immanent in the world of nature and in a life that was ordered by all-encompassing natural laws, and the memory of a simpler, rural existence whose values contrasted starkly with the noise and ugliness of city life.

In subsequent articles, Beecher went on to present more fully his conception of nature and man's relationship to it. The trouble with modern religion, he asserted in an article entitled "Nature a Minister of Happiness," was that the clergy described God as a collection of attributes rather than as a real being. Where the Hebrew found God in nature, the American found him in the catechism. "We can never come to a sense of *a living and present God*," Beecher asserted, "until we also include in our methods the old Hebrew way of beholding

God in living activity, moving in the heavens and along the earth.
. . ."[20] Only in the natural world, then, could man, relieved of the
repression and inhibition made necessary by society, finally relax and
allow his imagination and feelings to have full play. Alone in the
woods, man could unwind and be totally free. Beecher grew lyric as
he described the pleasure of a man on a fishing trip deep in the mountains. Since his comments summarize his conception of true Christianity, they bear quotation in full:

> Here indeed is good companionship—here is space for deep and strange
> joy. If the thought of the city intrudes it seems like a dream; it can hardly
> be real that there can be stacked houses, burning streets, reeking gutters,
> everlasting din of wheels, and outcry of voices, or that you were ever
> hustled along the uproarious streets! In this cool twilight, without a
> voice except of wind and waters, where all is primeval, solitary, and
> rudely beautiful, you seem to come out of yourself. Your life lifts it-
> self up from its interior recesses, and comes forth. Your own nature—
> your longings—your hopes and love, your faith and trust, seem to lie
> with quiet and unshrinking life; neither ruffled nor driven back, nor over-
> laid by all the contracts and burdens of multitudinous life in the city. Oh!
> Why may not one carry hence that freshness which he feels—that sim-
> plicity, that truthfulness to what is real, and that repugnance to all that
> is sham? Why may not one always find the way to heaven and to spiritual
> converse, as short and as facile as it is in these lovely mountains?
>
> It was in such places that Christ loved to stray. It was in such places
> that he spent nights in prayer. . . . Christ's love of nature, his constant
> allusions to flowers, his evident familiarity with solitudes, as if he was
> never so little alone as when separated from all men, mark any degree
> of the same relish in us as a true and divine taste.[21]

Beecher's romantic conception of Christianity, as seen in this passage, provided an outlet for Victorian inhibitions and repressed feelings. Women, in particular, stifled by the conventions of domesticity
that chained them to the home and dictated their actions, found an
emotional release in religion and joined the churches in increasing
numbers. In addition to providing an outlet for pent-up emotions,
romantic Christianity also furnished appropriate charitable and benevolent enterprises into which suppressed energies might be redirected.
As espoused by Beecher, Protestantism served as a psychological
safety valve, a channel for the frustrations and aggressions of the

middle class that had arisen from the repression of sex and the constant burdens of self-discipline and self-control.

Since many of the charitable and missionary enterprises of the mid-Victorian period served to relieve feelings of guilt and frustration, it is not surprising that the attitudes of the middle class toward the poor were often tinged with overtones of elitism and superiority. Beecher unconsciously reflected this outlook in another one of his Star Articles, written in his study as he watched the fog move in over Brooklyn harbor:

> How restful is all this! Irritableness and impatience are gone. The woes and frets of life are then not hard to be borne. To live for the things which occupy God; to lift up our fellow-men, through all the round of human infirmities; to build the substantial foundations of life, to enrich the conditions of society, to inspire better thoughts, to fashion a noble character, to stand with Gospel trumpet and banner, and see flocking toward it troops of regenerated men, who, ere long, shall throng about our Lord, the Christ of God; these seem, then, neither unsubstantial ambitions nor impractical works.[22]

Beecher's paternalistic and elitist outlook became more pronounced during the 1850s as he became more closely identified with his well-to-do parishioners. Soon, he was rationalizing their habits of conspicuous consumption and feelings of elitism. "In an age when men more and more feel the duty of employing their strength and their wealth for the education of their fellows," he wrote in *The Independent*, "it becomes a question of supreme moment, to what extent a Christian man may surround himself with the embellishments and luxuries of beauty." Beecher went on to reassure the public that the collection of works of art, the construction of elaborate brownstone houses, the purchase of antiques and fine furniture, and the indulgence in luxuries were all acceptable if they contributed to the education of one's fellow man. It was a weak rationalization, but middle-class Americans nevertheless adopted it enthusiastically and put it to use.

To support his defense of beauty and art, Beecher argued in yet another Star Article that men in society were ranged in a hierarchy according to their intelligence and ability. "Natural aristocracy is the eminence of men over their fellows, in mind and soul," he argued. Men of quality could spend their money as they pleased. "The question is not what proportion of his wealth a Christian man may divert from benevolent channels for personal enjoyment through the elements of the beautiful. For, if rightly viewed, and rightly used, his very elegancies and luxuries will be a contribution to the public good." [23] Such a theory, as William G. McLoughlin has pointed out, "made luxury and extravagance not only respectable but pious." [24]

Nevertheless, if Beecher rationalized the pursuit of wealth and conspicuous consumption, he also continued to warn against riches and extravagance. As he noted in another Star Article, "no man can tell whether he is rich or poor by turning to his ledger. He is rich or poor according to what he *is*, not according to what he *has*." [25] As is evident from this comment, there was a glaring contradiction between the two sides of Beecher's social philosophy—his defense of frugality, discipline, and character, and his rationalization of leisure, wealth, and luxury. It was a contradiction that was inherent in middle-class morality itself. For the first set of ethical imperatives, which were originally designed to help men make money, were now used by middle-class parents to instill in their children the virtues of obedience and self-control, while the second set, which formerly were warnings about riches, now became a rationalization for wealth and luxury.

Beecher's achievement, as indicated in his Star Articles, was to extoll the different elements of the middle-class social ethos without letting the contradictions come to the surface. To do this, he balanced warnings about the perils of riches with suggestions about benevolence and good works. And above the warnings and advice was the reassuring canopy of romantic Christianity, absorbing the frustrations produced by the restrictive social ethos and allaying the guilt produced by the possession of luxuries in urban areas where poverty was always evident. It was an outlook that had an enormous appeal for Victorian Americans who wanted desperately to prove that they could be both refined and socially responsible.

Beecher's newspaper articles and lyceum lectures, when added to his antislavery and temperance activities, increased his income and made him a nationally recognized clergyman. But they also had a major drawback—they contributed to the increasingly bitter discontent of his wife. Eunice Beecher's health, which had been poor in Indianapolis, was further weakened by frequent pregnancies. In December,

1850, she gave birth to twin boys, and for several months they added a new brightness to her life. But they died within half a year and she again became depressed. In June, 1854, she gave birth to her ninth and last child. Worn out by the long years of childbearing, she never recovered her health. By the middle of the decade her hair had turned grey and her face had begun to take on the hard, stern look that characterized most of her later pictures.[26]

Sickness and ill-health contributed to Eunice Beecher's unhappiness and made her dependent on her husband at a time when public life was drawing him away from home with increasing frequency. The speeches and journalistic commitments, when added to his regular church duties, left Beecher little time to spend at home. Gradually, Eunice Beecher began to resent her husband's frequent absences.

Eunice saw her husband most often during the summer months, when the church gave him a two-month vacation. As Henry declared to a friend, "my family are jealous of my vacation. The children think that July and August are the only months in which they have a father."[27] In 1854 Beecher purchased a farm in Lenox, Massachusetts, where the family spent several summers. When Lenox proved to be too far away, Beecher bought another farm in Matteawan, near Fishkill on the Hudson River.[28]

The combination of ill-health, insecurity, and annoyance with her husband made Eunice Beecher irritable. Of Henry's brothers and sisters, only Harriet was on good terms with her. Catharine, who could be blunt at times, mentioned Eunice's discontentment when she wrote, "now I fancy I hear some of your modest speeches about not caring to hear from you—not loving you—liking you only because you are Henry's wife and all that trumpery that has not a word of truth in it. . . . We all have deficiencies and we all have got to be shipped all the way thro' life before we shall be fixed anyhow decently so as to be ready for heaven."[29] Such advice was not easy to take and Eunice grew to dislike Catharine, who would visit for months at a time on the pretext that it was impolite for a maiden lady to stay alone in a hotel.

Beecher's prominence as a public figure thus proved to be a mixed blessing. Although it enhanced his reputation and increased his appeal as a lyceum lecturer, it also involved him in controversies, created enemies, and fostered discontent within his family. As Beecher became more involved with the slavery issue during the remainder of the decade, he became enmeshed in an increasing number of controversies and found his family life more and more overshadowed by his activities as a reformer.

Although Beecher's interest in education, temperance, lyceum lectures, and Star Articles occupied a good deal of time during the early 1850s, the slavery issue and matters related to it continued to absorb most of his attention. The first controversy began in the spring of 1852 when Beecher became involved in an argument that resulted from the publication of *Uncle Tom's Cabin*. The dispute concerned Harriet Beecher Stowe and the Reverend Joel Parker. Since Parker lived in New York and communication by mail was slow, Harriet appointed her brother as her representative, and he, too, soon became a party to the dispute.

The controversy arose over a footnote on page 191 of Harriet's book in which she quoted Parker as having said that "there are no evils in slavery but such as are inseparable from any other relations in civil and social life." Parker had held a pastorate in New Orleans and was strongly opposed to the antislavery movement. Harriet had intended to remove the footnote, cited as an example of the proslavery bias of some clergymen, to avoid angering Parker, but in the rush and excitement of the first days of publication she forgot about the matter.

On May 8, Joel Parker wrote to Calvin Stowe, enclosing a note to Harriet in which he demanded a "full and public retraction" of the footnote.[30] Harriet had just left to visit Henry in Brooklyn, so Calvin forwarded the letter to her there and sent Parker an apology for his wife's actions. Harriet's visit to New York was spectacular. Only two months after its publication, *Uncle Tom's Cabin* had sold over fifty thousand copies, and Harriet had become a celebrity. New Yorkers lionized her, following her travels throughout the city and greeting her with acclaim. Convinced that she was now a spokesman for a great cause and positive that she had read the quotation somewhere, Harriet refused to retract her statement and ignored Parker's letter.

Parker waited for more than a week and then wrote another letter, this time threatening a libel suit. Harriet's reply, dated May 25, was delayed in the mails, and by the time Parker received it, he had engaged the services of a prominent lawyer, Benjamin Butler, for his defense. In her letter Harriet explained that she had not meant to attack Parker personally but merely thought that his views were typical of the proslavery argument. Any further communications, she added, should "be addressed to my brother H. W. Beecher, who is in full possession of the subject."

Upon Benjamin Butler's recommendation, a conference was arranged between Hiram Barney, Butler's former law partner and a member of Beecher's church, and Beecher. Barney, who had read Parker's original statements, argued that Mrs. Stowe had misinterpreted them; he felt that all that was necessary to satisfy Parker was a simple retraction in the newspapers. Beecher however, was not convinced and resolved to wait until the documents he had sent for arrived.

The documents were delivered shortly after Barney left Beecher's house. Upon reading them, Henry concluded that his sister had not only misquoted Parker, but also had taken the words out of context. Parker had been arguing with another clergyman that evils such as the separation of families and the restriction of education were not limited solely to slavery but could be found wherever human nature was depraved. When Harriet was shown the documents, she agreed with her brother and immediately wrote to Parker, asking for a private interview with him.[31]

The interview took place on the following Monday, but no agreement was reached. Parker wanted a simple retraction. Harriet argued that she had to explain to the public that she only used the quotation because she wanted an example of clerical support for slavery. Although no agreement was reached, Harriet, who had to leave for New Haven the following day, promised to send Parker a letter with the retraction in a more acceptable form.[32]

At this point, the controversy became more complicated. Harriet reread Parker's original statement in New Haven and was no longer convinced that it was she who had made the mistake. The statement read, "What then are the evils inseparable from slavery? There is not one that is not equally inseparable from depraved human nature in other lawful relations." With this statement as a basis, Harriet wrote a rough draft of a letter of retraction, conceding only that "the language of the quotation in the book is not the precise language of Mr. Parker and the reader may fairly judge of this when the two quotations are placed side by side."[33]

If considered out of context, there was indeed little difference in the meaning of both quotations. Both seemed to be justifying the evils of slavery by saying that they were no worse than the evils found in everyday life. It was the context that made the difference. Parker had in fact made proslavery statements. In her hasty search for an example, Harriet simply had taken the wrong quotation. Perhaps because Parker had justified slavery or perhaps because there was little difference between Harriet's quotation and Parker's, if taken out of context, Harriet refused to give in.

Harriet's draft of the letter of retraction together with a note giving Henry "*carte blanche* to act in the matter," were mailed to her brother in Brooklyn. Henry did not like the draft. It seemed a "grudging acknowledgement." "When any apology is made before the public," he wrote Harriet in reply, "it ought to be so explicit, as at once, to gain for the maker the credit of honesty, frankness, and honor. . . ."[34] Nevertheless, he took it to Parker and the two struggled over it for several hours. After trying to revise Harriet's version for some time, Henry became impatient and, with Parker's agreement, drew up two hypothetical letters to take the place of Harriet's draft.

This decision on Beecher's part was characteristic of his outlook. Quick, impulsive, and careless of detail, Beecher refused to revise his own writings and disliked reviewing those of others. Working with Parker over Harriet's draft made him impatient, and he resolved to end the controversy quickly and easily by composing a new version on the spot. Parker, not thinking the letters anything but a rough draft, agreed that they "might lead to settlement" and asked Beecher to show them to his counsel, Mr. Butler.[35]

That night Beecher hurried over to see Butler. The lawyer read the correspondence, commenting that it seemed all right to him if it was agreeable to Parker. Both Parker and Butler assumed that the matter would be further discussed before any action was taken. But Beecher concluded that an agreement had been reached. He was eager to see the controversy settled, for on Monday he was leaving for Indiana to begin a lecture tour. So without further thought, he handed the letters of retraction to a friend who saw to it that they were published in the *Tribune*, the *Era*, and *The Independent*.

Parker was shocked when he saw the letters in the press and immediately wrote an indignant letter to the Stowes stating that he neither had written nor signed the correspondence. But the Stowes would not listen to his argument.[36] Henry Ward Beecher, they insisted, had made the decision, and Parker would have to consult with him if he wanted an explanation. Seeing that he would have little chance in a lawsuit with Harriet, Parker, in a gesture of defiance, resolved to attack Henry and gave all the material on the controversy to his friend the Reverend S. Irenaeus Prime, the editor of the religious weekly, *The Observer*.

Irenaeus Prime, an Old-School Presbyterian, had reason to dislike Beecher. His paper was the arch-rival of *The Independent*, and Beecher had opposed its conservative views in many of his Star Articles. Prime had tried to discredit Beecher's activity at the Albany Conference of the American Home Missionary Society by declaring that Beecher was a radical abolitionist.[37] Now that he had new material, he resolved to publish it in full, giving it the worst possible interpretation. In this manner he hoped to discredit not only Beecher's social views, but also his religious position.

On July 31, *The Observer* printed the correspondence of the Parker-Stowe dispute and accused Henry Ward Beecher of forgery and venality. "We have been . . . particular in reciting the facts in this case. . . ," wrote Prime. "The whole story shows the *morality* of modern ultraism in general and *Uncle Tom's Cabin* in particular."[38] Beecher was quick to reply in a dramatic twelve-column article in *The Independent*. It was bad enough that he had been unjustly attacked, but the insult to his sister was even worse:

> It was my prayer to God when I began this narrative that my brain might not reel nor be left to error; and it was my promise, if He would give me grace and wisdom to strike a true blow for a sister that should set her free from the accursed enchantment in which her reputation stood spellbound before the public, that I would hardly ask a thing for myself. But God has given me all and more, and the work is done, and eternity will not untwine the cords with which this monstrous iniquity is bound for the sacrifice.[39]

The controversy ended by justifying Harriet's stand. The public sympathy that her novel aroused would have made it very difficult for Prime to be convincing even if he had a stronger case. Moreover, many individuals agreed with Henry that Prime's attack had been part of a conspiracy to undermine the influence both of the novel and of Beecher in the antislavery movement. Although the New York *Tribune* declared that Beecher was guilty "of great, and perhaps criminal imprudence," most people agreed with *The Independent*'s comment that he had not deliberately tried to misrepresent Parker.[40]

Nevertheless, the incident reflected poorly on both Harriet and Henry. Henry's exaggerated and maudlin stand revealed a hypersensitivity to criticism that had lingered from childhood. Harriet, too, displayed these traits and was slow to forgive her critics. Even after the controversy had run on for some time, she refused to let up in her attack on Prime. Eventually, she brought even her brother Edward into the dispute. Writing to Henry, she stated that "Edward, who in his way is no fool particularly in exhuming all sorts of inconvenient declarations and arranging them in most uncomfortable proximities, is already up to his chin in documents which he reads and makes notes of with that grave, thoughtful smile peculiar to him."[41]

By the end of the year the Parker-Stowe controversy had died down and the public interest in the Compromise of 1850 had all but disappeared. As Beecher wrote in *The Independent*, "we are satisfied that agitation is all out of the question. . . . Peace in New York [is] so deep, so broad, and so abundant, that we cannot get away from it."[42]

Between 1852 and 1854, Beecher spoke out little on the slavery issue. Despite his fear that the Compromise of 1850 had set a bad precedent and would pave the way for future political concessions to the South, he avoided committing himself to a political party and relied instead on moral suasion to warn the North of its danger. But the passage of the Kansas and Nebraska Act in May, 1854, and the subsequent violence in Kansas where a proslavery legislature was elected through fraud and violence forced him to change his point of view. Convinced that these new developments were part of a larger conspiracy, Beecher began to disregard his commitment to moral suasion. Like many of the other moderates among the northern clergy, he began to see in political agitation the only means of blocking the southern desire to extend the boundary of the slavery empire.[43]

Beecher began his campaign against the Kansas and Nebraska Act by reasserting his earlier position that the struggle before the nation was one based upon two incompatible principles—liberty and slavery. He then appealed to the voters of the North as trustees of the property in the territories. "Place slavery on that soil and you light the fires which shall desolate it," he declared in a speech at the New York Tabernacle. It was the duty of the northerners to preserve the territory for northern settlers and to keep it open to the gospel.[44]

To prevent future political compromise, Beecher had a specific plan. He would reform and unite public opinion in the North by holding meetings, by sending petitions to Congress, and by circulating the speeches of Chase, Sumner, and Seward. As part of this campaign, Beecher undertook a large number of speaking engagements during the spring and summer of 1854. In these speeches and lectures he developed most fully his conspiracy theory about the South.[45]

Southern politicians, Beecher declared in March, could not be trusted, because they defended an institution that epitomized every evil and crime that could be committed.[46] They had proved themselves earlier to be devoid of moral principles. Now, once again, they were thinking of extending their detested institution. They were scheming for new empires to be bought by war and debased by slavery.[47] This scheme contained within itself the germ of a new doctrine, argued by Calhoun, that free and slave institutions should be accounted as equal. Slavery by its very nature, emphasized Beecher, perpetually impoverishes the state and degrades its citizens. The horror of Calhoun's claim, Beecher insisted, was that the southerners were trying to compensate for their natural deficiencies by obtaining political power. "For a man that is broken, but won't fall, propped up by extortionate laws, is like a weary traveler whom a vampire cools waving his slumberous wings, while he sucks the life blood out. This is the real nature of the demand for sympathy of the slave institutions under government. It is a bankrupt demand for a system of national aggrandisement: a division of power."[48]

The civil war in Kansas between pro- and antislavery forces that broke out in the spring of 1856 fitted logically into Beecher's conspiracy theory. The South, which in an earlier breach of trust had violated the Missouri Compromise, now was seeking to gain the free territory by force. "That gigantic conspiracy," declared Beecher, "was developed of which Kansas is but a single finger, but whose whole hand is yet to grip the throat of the Nation."[49] The conflict in the territories now had reached a crucial stage. Peace in Kansas would be peace everywhere. War there would lead to war all over the land.[50] The South once had seduced the North from its trusteeship of the territories.

If the balance of power changed again, he warned, it would soon control and channel public opinion. The North was marching straight for disunion, for the advantage given the South would soon drive the North to take drastic actions.

The violence of Beecher's opposition to the Kansas and Nebraska Act contradicted his earlier plea for moderation. Nevertheless, unaware of the inconsistency of his position, he continued to maintain his earlier view that the northerners should have sympathy for the plight of their brethren in the South. He still hoped to persuade the southerners to revise some of their laws pertaining to slavery.

Beecher himself did not realize that his angry and fiercely antagonistic attitude toward the political extension of slavery in Kansas in effect canceled his moderate and conciliatory attitude toward the slaveholders in the South and made his position closer to that of the radicals. Some men who recognized this inconsistency, however, looked down on Beecher for it. In 1855 a group of prominent intellectuals that included Henry Whitney Bellows, Henry James, Sr., George Ripley, Horace Bushnell, and Frederick Law Olmsted happened to discuss Beecher's influence in the antislavery movement at a social gathering. These men, who considered themselves, in Olmsted's words, to be part of an "aristocratic class" in New York, were highly critical of the Brooklyn minister.[51] Writing to a friend, Bellows described their comments about Beecher:

> James had just heard his Anti-Slavery lecture and was bitterly disappointed. He pronounced him shallow and vulgar. Ripley thought his coarseness the chief source of his success and defended it as a well chosen weapon. Bushnell, who hated his style, attributed his influence to his heart which he said was as big as that of an ox. I maintained that it was the length of his range, his extra octaves which gave him his charm . . . a very high sentiment and a very low manner—the union of moral philosopher and comedian; his passion and his desire to do good united.[52]

In their assessment of Beecher, James and the other intellectuals were of course correct. He was, indeed, often shallow, coarse, and vulgar. What Beecher did was to modify the "elevated style" of oratory that was popular in the 1850s so that it would be more comprehensible to the general public. Beecher used the balanced sentences, rhetorical questions, parallel constructions, extended metaphors, and biblical references that were the hallmarks of the "elevated style," but he combined them with homely, commonsense arguments. For example, he frequently discussed the "sublime theme" of liberty, both as a grand principle and as the reaction of a man whose house was broken into and whose watch was stolen. James and the other intellectuals found such arguments abominable and in bad taste. Crude and oversimplified as Beecher's statements were, they nevertheless struck a responsive note among the northern public. James and Bellows might think him vulgar, but thousands of Americans believed what he said and followed his every word from the lecture platform and the newspapers.

Beecher's protests against the Kansas atrocities were part of a general reaction among the New England clergy to the events that were taking place in the territories. In the spring of 1854, when Eli Thayer founded the Massachusetts Emigrant Aid Society, many ministers used their churches as recruiting stations for the Kansas emigrants. Committees were set up to circularize the clergy in New England in an effort to enlist them in the society as life members.[53]

After border incidents in the new territory broke out, various meetings were held to raise funds to buy Sharp's rifles for the emigrants. Beecher had at first given his support to this effort by calling the rifles a "truly moral agency" with more power than a hundred Bibles. Since the conscience of the southerner was destroyed by slavery, the Bible was of little use and only force could make him uphold the laws.[54] This stand brought an immediate attack from Garrison's *Liberator* and Beecher's old foe, the *Observer*. The use of force, they held, contradicted a truly Christian state of mind based upon love. Beecher nevertheless maintained that defending lives "calmly, deliberately, and with Christian firmness" was a truly Christian attitude.[55]

Backing up his words with action, Beecher attended a well-publicized meeting in New Haven and, with Professor Benjamin Silliman, Sr., pledged money for twenty-five rifles to be sent to the New Haven Colony in Kansas. He followed this with a campaign in his own church and in the next month sent to the colony twenty-five additional rifles together with twenty-five Bibles. The rifles were to provide for the defense of the state, the Bibles for its foundation on principle.[56] The Sharp's rifles soon became known in the North as "Beecher's Bibles" and his church, the "Church of the Holy Rifles."

The most interesting aspect of this incident was that, though large numbers of clergymen in the North backed the settlers in Kansas and helped to raise funds for rifles, Beecher, as a popularizer of the movement, gained the undeserved reputation of being one of its leaders. His opponents, by misrepresenting his position in order to discredit him, helped to identify him more closely with the radicals in the North.[57]

In addition to his efforts to aid the Kansas emigrants, Beecher repeated a method he had used earlier to dramatize the slavery issue. He held a mock slave auction. On Sunday morning, June 1, 1856, Beecher stepped up to the platform after the closing hymn and announced that he was about to do something unusual. A slave trader in Richmond had bought a girl from her master, pitied her fate, and decided to set her free. He had paid $100 toward her original price and raised funds from others until only $500 remained to be paid.

At this point Beecher motioned to the side of the church and said, "Come here, Sarah, and let us see you. What shall you do now?" he asked his hushed and stunned congregation. "May she read her liberty in your eyes? Shall she go free? Christ stretched forth his hands, and the sick were restored to health; will you stretch forth your hands and give her that without which life is of little worth?" The plates were passed and Lewis Tappan, who had joined the church that same year, pledged amid the tears and sobs of the congregation to make up the difference. All told, not including jewelry, $738 was raised and Tappan's offer was unnecessary.[58] This incident, coming shortly after the caning of Charles Sumner in the Senate, added to the emotional tension in the North.

The approach of the election of 1856 stirred Beecher to his most active participation in the antislavery campaign during the decade. He became convinced of the importance of the nonextension program of the newly formed Republican party. Obtaining a leave of absence from his church, he threw his energies into the campaign for the election of John C. Frémont.[59] He at last had given up his stand on moral suasion. Though he still believed that moral suasion was useful, he now felt that it had to be supplemented with political involvement.

Beecher justified his changed attitude in an article in *The Independent*. He now was convinced, he stated, that the South was inevitably forced by the nature of slavery to expand its boundaries. Without expansion, slavery would no longer produce a profit and would dwindle and die. "When it is believed that these events in the South came from a law stronger than volition, from a law that underlies society and compels its movements," said Beecher, "the question of political choice assumes a very different shape."[60]

During the campaign of 1856, Beecher continually waved the torch of "bleeding Kansas." To labor for the righting of the desecration of Kansas, he declared, "was the truest, noblest, and most Godlike work of religion." The only question was whether the nation would ratify the wickedness there. Buchanan, Beecher asserted, was the anointed successor of Pierce, a man beloved of the South. Every vote for him was an open and undisguised endorsement of the Kansas outrages. Every vote for Fillmore was simply a disguised vote for the same. "There is but one question," Beecher emphasized, "Freedom or Slavery—for or against."[61]

Despite Beecher's participation in the political campaign and his outspoken language, he still considered himself a moderate. He still believed that the first step in abolishing slavery should be the reformation of public opinion in the North in such a way as to make it act on the South. As part of this program, Beecher began in 1856 to agitate for better treatment of the Negro in the North. Beecher's efforts had a note of urgency about them, for he was convinced that emancipation of the Negro would take place in the near future. Assuming that emancipation was only a matter of time, Beecher emphasized that "no duty is more urgent, more apparent to far-sighted Christian wisdom than that of preparing for this future exigency."[62]

Carrying out his campaign to educate the Negro, Beecher became a trustee and financial secretary of a free Negro school in the District of Columbia. This school was known as "The Washington Association for the Education of Colored Youths" and had been founded by H. W. Bellows, Leonard Gale, Francis P. Blair, and Gamaliel Bailey. Designed for the free black children in Virginia and Maryland, and for the "children of such slaveholders as will emancipate," its stated purpose was to educate the Negroes to be teachers and missionaries.[63]

To raise funds for this association, Beecher delivered two sermons in 1856 and 1857 entitled "Education, the Colored Man's Moses" and "Africa among Us." The treatment of the free Negro in the North, he emphasized, was a repudiation of the Christian spirit and a negation of Christian duty. Despite the antipathy of the North toward the Negro and "even if science should demonstrate their inferiority," Christianity treated all men as equal. Since colonization in Africa or in the western countries was unfeasible, education of the Negro in the North was the only solution for the bitter questions of social position and race relations. In repudiating his earlier commitment to colonization and shifting away from a total reliance on moral suasion, Beecher broke away from the major wing of the abolitionist movement. Where most northern abolitionists romanticized blacks as having a highly religious and feminine nature but denied that they could ever play a full role in society, Beecher took a more radical stand and demanded that they be treated equally. It was a strong stand that angered some members of his congregation and further added to his notoriety.[64]

The shift in Beecher's reform philosophy could also be seen in his changed stand toward intemperance. The shift became apparent in March, 1855, when Beecher wrote an article for *The Independent* on the Maine Law, a subject then being widely debated in New York. The controversial law, passed under the leadership of Neal Dow in Maine, prohibited the sale of liquor and provided law enforcement officials with a "search and seizure" clause to aid them in carrying out their orders.[65] Beecher defended the Maine Law, declaring that it was fresh and pure, "sprung directly from the masses, unadulterated by passing through the corrupt channels of party politics."[66] Such a bill, he commented, would be a blessing for New York State because it would prohibit intoxicating drinks, the source of much poverty, vice, and crime. The search-and-seizure clause of the bill, moreover, was not, as many claimed, a violation of their personal rights. "All the outcry against the vindication of the citizen's rights, the invasion of the sacredness of the household, the imperiling of personal liberty by dangerous and tyrannical processes," he declared, "is the outcry made up by designing men, and echoed by ignorant ones."

This and subsequent statements reflected a dramatic shift in Beecher's earlier stand on the temperance issue. Just as he had changed in the antislavery movement from arguing for "moral suasion" to a position of political commitment, so too in the temperance crusade he changed from fighting alcoholism through voluntary societies to a stand favoring legislation. In each case, Beecher justified his stand by referring to the Republican party, a new organization based on principles. While Beecher still argued for moral suasion, he now urged that it be supplemented with political involvement.

Beecher's new attitude toward political coercion marked an important turning point in his career as a reformer and had a strong impact on his revivalist activities. For in the debate over the extension of slavery into the territories, he had come to reject the dream of the preceding generation of clerical leaders of reforming the world through voluntary societies and moral exhortations. Beecher's decision to enter the ranks of the Republican party was significant, too, because he now had an enormous public following. As a minister, lyceum lecturer, newspaper correspondent, and reformer, he reached a national audience numbering in the millions. And this national following brought with it considerable power. No longer the poor, backwoods minister he had been in Indianapolis, Beecher now began to play a role in public affairs that few clergymen, either before or since, have been able to match. Sensitive to the public mood and eager to improve his own reputation, he resolved to keep his name before the public as much as possible. By doing so he could help maintain the legal and institutional heritage of liberty in the North while adding to his own stature.

NOTES

1. New York *Times*, Feb. 19, 1852.

2. Joseph R. Gusfield, *Symbolic Crusade: Status Politics and the American Temperance Movement* (Urbana, Ill., 1963), 61; H. W. Beecher, *Patriotic Addresses*, ed. John Howard (New York, 1887), 313.

3. New York *Times*, March 11, 1852.

4. H. W. Beecher to Thomas W. Higginson, May 28, 1853, Higginson Papers, Houghton Library, Harvard University.

5. H. B. Stowe to H. W. Beecher, n.d., Schlesinger Library.

6. H. W. Beecher, "Man and His Institutions," speech, New York, 1856, reprinted in *Permanent Documents of the Society for the Promotion of Collegiate and Theological Education at the West* (New York, 1860). For an excellent discussion of the changing meaning of individualism, see John William Ward, *Red, White and Blue: Men, Books, and Ideas in American Culture* (New York, 1969).

7. Carl Bode, *The American Lyceum* (New York, 1956), 135.

8. Oscar Sherwin, *Prophet of Liberty: The Life and Times of Wendell Phillips* (New York, 1958), 132.

9. H. W. Beecher to Mrs. Emily Drury, n.d., Schlesinger Library.

10. H. W. Beecher, Personal Papers, box 78, Yale MSS.

11. Carl Bode makes this point in the *The American Lyceum*, 32.

12. H. W. Beecher to Eunice Beecher, Painesville, Ohio, June 30, 1854, Yale MSS.

13. H. W. Beecher to Eunice Beecher, Providence R.I., Sept. 5, 1854, Yale MSS.

14. H. W. Beecher, lecture fragment, Yale MSS.

15. *Harper's Weekly*, July 17, 1858.

16. Quoted in Lionel Crocker, *Henry Ward Beecher's Art of Preaching* (Chicago, 1934), 42. For other descriptions of Beecher's style of speaking see James Parton, *Famous Americans of Recent Times* (New York, 1867), 358, and Adam Badeau, *The Vagabond* (New York, 1859), 279ff.

17. H. W. Beecher, *Eyes and Ears* (Boston, 1862).

18. *Ibid*.

19. H. W. Beecher, *Star Papers, or Experiences of Art and Nature* (New York, 1855), 94, 95, 99, 105.

20. *Ibid.*, 312.

21. *Ibid.*, 169.

22. *Ibid.*, 209.

23. *Ibid.*, 293, 297.

24. William G. McLoughlin, *The Meaning of Henry Ward Beecher* (New York, 1970), 112; see also McLoughlin's chap. V, "The Protestant Ethic and the Spirit of Capitalism," and chap. VI, "Art for the People, Culture for the Masses."

25. H. W. Beecher, *Eyes and Ears*, 246.

26. William C. Beecher and Samuel Scoville, *A Biography of Henry Ward Beecher* (New York, 1888), 352; see also the pictures among the family papers in the Yale University library.

27. H. W. Beecher to Mrs. Emily Drury, July 7, 1858, Yale MSS.

28. H. W. Beecher, Personal Papers, Box 76, Yale MSS.

29. Catharine Beecher to Eunice Beecher, Jan. 5, 1851, Yale MSS.

30. Forrest Wilson, *Crusader in Crinoline: The Life of Harriet Beecher Stowe* (Philadelphia, 1941), 261; Joel Parker to Harriet B. Stowe, May 8, 1852, Yale MSS. Wilson devotes chap. 1, part IV, to this controversy. My material comes primarily from the Beecher Family Papers at Yale.

31. H. B. Stowe to Joel Parker, May 25, 1852; unsigned draft in the hand of H. B. Stowe, May 25, 1852, Yale MSS; Wilson, *Crusader in Crinoline*, 314.

32. Wilson, *Crusader in Crinoline*, 315.

33. Unsigned statement in the hand of H. B. Stowe, May 25, 1852, Yale MSS.

34. H. W. Beecher to H. B. Stowe, June 11, 1852, Yale MSS.

35. Wilson, *Crusader in Crinoline*, 317.

36. H. B. Stowe to Joel Parker, July 2, 1852, Yale MSS. She wrote "you will perceive at once that the case lies between you and my brother Henry, who judging from the letter to me, considered himself to be acting with all kindness and good faith, as he *always does act*. . . ."

37. Editorial, "Perseverance in Wrong," *The Independent*, Nov. 4, 1852.

38. Extract from *The Observer*, Sept. 1852, quoted in *The Independent*, Oct. 7, 1852.

39. Wilson, *Crusader in Crinoline*, 312–22.

40. New York *Times*, Oct. 30, 1852; *The Independent*, Nov. 25, 1852.

41. H. B. Stowe to H. W. Beecher, Nov. 1, 1852, Yale MSS.

42. H. W. Beecher, "Death of Agitation," *The Independent*, Jan. 23, 1853.

43. One petition to Congress opposing the Kansas and Nebraska Act contained the

signatures of more than three thousand clergymen from New England alone. Robert Senior, "New England Congregationalists and the Anti-Slavery Movement," Ph.D. thesis, Yale University, 1954, 378.

44. "Mass Meeting at the New York Tabernacle on the Nebraska Question," New York *Times*, Feb. 20, 1854.

45. H. B. Stowe to H. W. Beecher, Jan. 13, 1854, Yale MSS; this conspiracy theory had been used earlier by Beecher during the mob outbreaks when he associated the use of violence with a current of discontent that had been deliberately fostered by the "Owens, Wrights, and Kneelands." See *Journal and Western Luminary*, July 21, 1836, Presbyterian Historical Society.

46. H. W. Beecher, "Slavery in Nebraska," New York *Times*, March 20, 1854.

47. H. W. Beecher, "The Peaceful Method of Dealing with Slavery," *The Independent*, Oct. 12, 1854.

48. H. W. Beecher, "Slavery in Nebraska." The quotation is from the original sermon in the Yale MSS.

49. H. W. Beecher, "Silence Must be Nationalized," *The Independent*, June 12, 1856.

50. "Meeting at the North Church in New Haven," New York *Times*, March 22, 1856.

51. Frederick Law Olmsted to Wolcott Gibbs, Nov. 5, 1862, quoted in Henry W. Bellows, *Historical Sketch of the Union League Club of New York* (New York, 1879), 12–13.

52. H. W. Bellows to C. A. Bartol, Jan. 20, 1855, Bellows Papers, Massachusetts Historical Society.

53. Senior, "New England Congregationalists," 385.

54. H. W. Beecher, "The New York *Observer*'s Ideas of Artillery," *The Independent*, Feb. 7, 1856.

55. H. W. Beecher, "The *Observer* and the *Liberator*," *ibid.*, March 6, 1856.

56. New York *Tribune*, April 4, 1856; New York *Times*, March 6, 1856.

57. H. W. Beecher, "The *Observer* and the *Liberator*," *The Independent*, March 6, 1856.

58. "A Slave Made Free in Plymouth Church," *ibid.*, June 1, 1856; Beecher and Scoville, *Biography*, 299.

59. Lyman Abbott and S. B. Halliday, *Henry Ward Beecher: A Sketch of His Character* (Hartford, 1887), 46.

60. H. W. Beecher, "On Which Side is Peace?" *The Independent*, June 26, 1856.

61. H. W. Beecher to C. O. S. Shurtleff, Sept. 3, 1856, Yale MSS; Sermon Book, Sept. 16, 1856, Yale MSS; H. W. Beecher, "The Only Question," *The Independent*, Sept. 11, 1856.

62. H. W. Beecher, "For Colored Schools," sermon, December, 1856, Yale MSS.

63. Undated document, Yale MSS.

64. H. W. Beecher in the New York *Times*, Dec. 15, 1856; see also the manuscript versions of the two sermons in the Yale MSS; on northern abolitionist attitudes toward blacks, see George Fredrickson, *The Black Image in the White Mind: The Debate on Afro-American Character and Destiny, 1817–1914* (New York, 1971).

65. H. W. Beecher, "A Public Outrage by Public Men," *The Independent*, March 15, 1855.

66. H. W. Beecher, "The Search and Seizure Clause," *ibid.*, March 29, 1855.

6

Harvesting the Seed

By associating with the Republican party in 1856 and entering the debate over antislavery tactics, Beecher unknowingly became involved in the creation of a new reform philosophy that went far beyond a simple attack on slavery. In their opposition to the westward expansion of the plantation system, Salmon P. Chase, Carl Schurz, George Julian, Abraham Lincoln, and other advocates of the new ideology developed a broad-based attack on the whole southern way of life. Central to their argument was the middle-class notion that free labor, as the source of social mobility and economic independence, was absolutely necessary for a functioning democracy. Without it, as in the South, dependency corrupted all. For these Republicans, a belief in free labor and its extension, free soil for the farmer to work, came to represent a set of cultural assumptions and a way of life.

Beecher not only shared the major assumptions of the Republican ideology—the stress on self-improvement and self-control, the belief that all classes would reap the benefits of economic progress, the suspicion of wealth gained through inheritance or manipulation, and the conviction that the problems of the poor could be solved through industrialization and hard work—he reinforced these beliefs by merging them with ideals of romantic Christianity. The process of fusion was not intended. It was the fortuitous result of Beecher's participation in both the revival of 1858 and the expansion of the abolitionist crusade after John Brown's Raid. Since Beecher moved from one movement to the other and played a major role in each, he helped implant the secularized ideals of romantic Christianity within the ideology of the Republican party.[1]

The process began after the Kansas-Nebraska controversy had died down. Having spent a good deal of money and effort canvassing New York State on behalf of John C. Frémont, he finished the year by resolving to rebuild his finances and to redirect his attention to ministerial duties that had been relatively neglected. One of his immediate concerns was to get out of debt. Despite a salary of more than four thousand dollars and the income from his articles in *The Independent*, he was unable to make ends meet. In addition to the mortgage on his farm in Matteawan, Beecher owed money to a number of book dealers and jewelers in New York City. The purchase of a new brownstone house in Brooklyn and the provision for the education of his eldest daughter further added to the burden. To recoup his finances and pay some of his outstanding bills, Beecher contracted to give an extensive tour of lyceum lectures during the spring.

The stock market collapse in October, 1857, further added to Beecher's financial difficulties. The silk firm of Henry C. Bowen, the owner of *The Independent*, failed, and the newspaper fell behind in its payments to Beecher for his articles. As a consequence, he wrote to his wife from Buffalo, where he was lecturing, and advised her to sell all their stock, even if they had to take a loss on the sale. "We shall need *money* this winter more than stock," he reasoned.[2]

Beecher used the depression as an occasion to renew his attack on the business community and to reiterate his version of the gospel of self-help. A year earlier he had warned that "our prosperity is so great, and our resources so ample, that we are in danger of running into temptation." During the first weeks of the depression, he again repeated this view. In an article in *The Independent* entitled "Lessons from the Times," Beecher argued against "the fatal belief that property may be made by legerdemain." While rivalry and competition in limited quantities served a definite purpose, he commented, when severe and continued they harmed the community by tempting men to cheat. "If only all men were honest, truthful, intelligent, and generous," he continued, "how easy would commercial life become."[3]

By November, things were beginning to look up and Beecher began to change his attitude toward the depression. In a sermon to his congregation, he argued that the financial crisis was not a form of divine chastisement but rather a means of testing. Trials and tribulations were a blessing because they fostered patience and humility. Encouraged by the apparent strength of the economy, Beecher now saw little need to worry about the commercial crisis. "Credit grows in the country as parsley in a garden," he commented. "It can't help growing." The lesson of the struggle was that individuals should be concerned less about business and more about community.[4]

In the early months of 1858, the shock of the depression and the continuing strain of the antislavery crisis produced widespread anxiety and insecurity that helped fuel a new wave of revivals. Prayer meetings were held daily, attended by businessmen and clerks during their lunch hour, and the new converts were publicized in the press. Thousands joined the churches and benevolent activities were greatly increased.

The revival of 1858 differed in a number of respects from those that had preceded it. Unlike the organized awakenings of the 1830s, the revival of 1858 was a spontaneous outbreak, led by the laity rather than the clergy and confined primarily to the cities. Businessmen in particular, long suspect by evangelicals for their devotion to trade and commerce, were among the most prominent converts.[5]

The first signs of the new revival were received with interest by Beecher, who had long worried about the future of evangelical religion. A decade earlier he had purchased a notebook in which he planned to record his views and observations on revivals.[6] But the pressure of events and his involvement in the antislavery crusade had left him with little time for reflection and he had never completed more than a couple of pages. With the possibility at hand of carrying the awakening to Brooklyn, he now resolved to postpone his other activities and devote full time to spreading the new revival.

Beginning with the last Sunday in February, Beecher held daily prayer meetings and met individually with those in doubt. He also spoke to numerous audiences in other churches and contributed a series of articles on revivalism to *The Independent*. Beecher's incessant activity worried his wife and she complained that "if you could only feel that you might trust the harvesting of the seed you have so faithfully sowed to your church a little more it seems that they would be far more effective Christians and your health and usefulness be prolonged."[7] Despite the wish of his wife, Beecher continued his relentless activity.

The revival bore its first fruit later in the spring when 190 new members were added to the church rolls. In June another 160 persons joined the church.[8] In his sermon of thanksgiving, Beecher declared that he viewed the new additions to the church as a testimony to his conception of the ministry. He had taken it for granted, he stated, that his duty was "to preach a *living* Gospel to *living* men, about *living* questions. . . ."[9]

The new converts considerably improved the financial position of Plymouth Church. In January, 1858, before the revival began, the church raised $16,300 in pew rents at the annual auction of seats. In the following year this sum jumped to $26,052, an increase of about 60 percent.[10] Such an increase was a mixed blessing, however, for it aroused unfavorable comments from other churches and forced Beecher to defend the high pew rents paid by his own congregation. Plymouth Church had always contributed generously to charities, Beecher stated in reply to his critics. Therefore there was no need for members of the congregation to give up their seats as well.[11] Although many parts of the city were still suffering from the depression, Beecher saw little need to increase the efforts of the church on behalf of the poor and needy.[12]

Despite the criticism that Beecher received for the high pew rents, the general effect of the revival was to improve his reputation. Henry W. Bellows, the leading Unitarian minister in the city, who previously had had little esteem for Beecher, happened to meet him on a train and came away with a new impression. "He [Beecher] is unpretending, simple, and genuine in his manners," wrote Bellows to his wife. "His conversation boils with earnestness and bubbles with playfulness. He says many striking and memorable things; but above all (and this surprised me) is marked by common sense. . . . You may be sure that Beecher is a very *prudent* man—and that it is *prudence* winged by *genius* that carries him so far ahead. He has moreover great sweetness and makes you love him."[13]

Still another clergyman who disliked Beecher's style of preaching yet could not help admiring him was Horace Bushnell. Writing to his wife after a visit to Beecher's church during the revival, Bushnell admitted that "Beecher preached the most dramatic and, in one sense, most effective sermon I have ever heard from him, but in all the philosophy of it unspeakably crude and naturalistic; and yet I was greatly moved notwithstanding, and, I trust, profited."[14] Professor Edwards A. Park of Andover Theological School was so impressed by Beecher's ability that he wrote a letter to the president of Harvard, recommending Beecher for a Doctor of Divinity degree. Beecher "agrees in opinion with no one," stated Professor Park, "but is, 'for substance of doctrine,' orthodox. He has an immense power over the *people*," continued Park, and "he is *read* by the learned."[15] The Harvard authorities, however, distrusted his identification with the Republican party and refused to grant him a degree.

Beecher's activities during the revival clearly revealed the extent to which he had modified his evangelical faith. Unlike the earlier revivalists, he no longer threatened his congregation with eternal damnation. The love of God, rather than the fear of retribution, was the chief reason for joining the church. As he wrote to a young man at the outset of the revival, the love of God was the only remedy for man's sin. "If this remedy fails I know of no other," he stated. "If love will not save you, fear will be of no avail."[16] A letter from his brother Charles, who was preparing Lyman Beecher's autobiography, made him even more aware of the extent to which his views had changed. "Is eternal punishment a reality?" wrote Charles despairingly. "Father thought so. He never doubted. Strike that idea out of his mind, and his whole career would be changed, his whole influence on us modified."[17]

Then, too, Henry Ward Beecher no longer demanded that a person conduct a long and agonizing self-scrutiny before conversion. Discussing the difference between his attitude and that of Charles G. Finney, Beecher declared that "I very soon saw that in conducting a revival my business was to bring to bear upon men the influence of the gospel . . . and then to let every one repent, become converted and come into the church according to his temperament. If when he has got in, he says, 'I love God and hate sin,' that is enough to begin with."[18]

Beecher, in other words, now conceived of conversion as the gradual development of character rather than as the instantaneous experience of divine grace. As he explained in an introduction to a book about the 1858 revival, "my own observation has led me to the conclusion that more persons become true, spiritual Christians without the sudden joy, and without the consciousness, *at the time* of transition, of a great change, than with it." [19] By redefining the nature of the conversion experience in this fashion and equating it with the development of character, Beecher watered down the principle of disinterested benevolence that the earlier generation of revivalists had used to argue that a true conversion would be followed by socially beneficent action. He thus undermined one of the dynamic principles that had sparked the crusade to spread the gospel and reform the nation in the 1830s.

Besides redefining the conversion experience and watering down the principle of disinterested benevolence, Beecher no longer retained the earlier generation's faith in the effectiveness of revivalism as an instrument for national reform. Participation in the antislavery movement and his experience during the church schism of 1837 convinced him that the conversion experience usually did not bring with it a change in men's social views. Furthermore, rational argument, or moral suasion as it was called, appeared to be hopelessly inadequate for uprooting deep-seated prejudices. Revivals, Beecher believed, ought therefore to be considered simply as useful devices for reaffirming men's belief in God. Because he now looked upon revivals not as an instrument for national reform but rather as an expression of faith, Beecher refused to view the 1858 awakening as anything more than a local phenomenon. In working to spread the revival in Brooklyn, he was simply taking advantage of an existing situation.

Thus the revival of 1858 was not the culmination of the efforts of the earlier generation of revivalists. It was rather the last gasp of a passing system. In the years between 1830 and 1858, various factors had gradually undermined the revivalist tradition. The increase of non-Protestant immigrants, the divisions within the Protestant denominations, the passing of the earlier evangelical leaders, and the professionalization of the movement all contributed to its decline. [20] But the major blow came from the theological innovations that modified the old conception of a stern God of justice, redefined the nature of the conversion experience, and rejected the use of revivalism as an instrument for national social reform. Beecher's new attitude toward revivals, therefore, was indicative of a general change that was taking place within the Protestant churches at mid-century. Revivalism, of course, continued to live on in the hands of the professional revivalists, and it was given a new lease on life in the 1860s by Dwight L. Moody, but it no longer dominated the main stream of Protestant religion as it had done in the 1830s.

The force that romantic Christianity did exert came not so much from the churches themselves as from the secularization of religious ideals and their incorporation into popular morality. As Beecher's experience clearly indicated, the transformation of Protestantism in the 1850s was accelerated by the participation of many northern clergymen in the antislavery crusade. By speaking out against the extension of slavery, these ministers gradually became involved in politics, much to the dismay of the more conservative members of their congregations. As Adam Badeau pointed out in reference to Beecher, "I do not think the pulpit his sphere; he seems to me a stump speaker who has mistaken his way and stumbled into a church. . . . It is notorious that he preaches politics, temperance, abolitionism . . . more than religion.
. . . The influence of religion itself is injured, its sacredness lessened, its effect curtailed by such a course."[21] But Beecher was faced by a dilemma—the dilemma of relevance. He had the choice of adapting the faith to the conditions of the times so that it would have a greater appeal or of defending the old dogmas and seeing the church attendance decline. Beecher took the first alternative and thus helped to pave the way for the Social Gospel.

The process of transformation was also clearly influenced by the attempts of benevolent societies and denominations to define their stand on slavery. One such struggle took place in 1859 at the annual meeting of the Tract Society, to which Beecher had been invited. For several years the society had been torn by a battle between those who wanted to denounce slavery and those who wanted to maintain an apolitical stance. Beecher favored the more liberal clergymen and resolved when invited to address the society to use the opportunity to argue for a modification of the conservative position.[22] Speaking before the association in May, Beecher began by discrediting the rumor that an attack on slavery would lead to disunion. "Indeed," he declared, "I fear that this people is too selfish ever to break asunder. Our danger is not disunion. The devil has too large investments in this land to admit of disunion." Beecher then went on to argue that a refusal to permit discussion of the slavery issue in the literature published by the Tract Society was a violation of the principle of freedom of speech. If, suggested Beecher, the society would take a stand on slavery, he would personally oversee the distribution of its tracts and pamphlets.

When his offer failed to elicit a favorable response, Beecher tried a different tack. "These men [the publishing committee of the society] have mistaken the temper of the times, and the spirit of the common people," he warned. "There is a public sentiment that will drown this society."[23]

Although Beecher's speech had little effect on the Tract Society, it was important because it clearly represented a modification of the earlier generation of revivalists' belief that the society should avoid questions around which a difference of opinion existed. As the members of the Tract Society had declared in 1825, the organization was "founded on the broad principle of uniting in its support Christians of all evangelical denominations of Protestants, so far as they may be disposed to co-operate in its objects; . . . and its publications themselves convey those great truths and doctrines in which all of these communions can agree."[24] By joining with those clergy who urged the Tract Society to take a stand on slavery, Beecher rejected one of the key principles on which the benevolent societies of the 1830s and 1840s had rested. His involvement with the antislavery crusade thus accelerated the transformation of revivalism that was already well underway in the 1850s.

Four months after Beecher's speech, the slavery issue was again suddenly thrust into public notice by the daring raid of John Brown and his followers on the federal arsenal at Harpers Ferry. The raid, which was supported by funds from Theodore Parker, Gerrit Smith, and other abolitionists, shocked the North and raised the antislavery debate to a new intensity. By supporting John Brown's raid, the more radical abolitionists seemed to have rejected pacifism and embraced violence as the means for overthrowing the detested institution.[25]

During the long trial that followed Brown's arrest, the northern public, which first viewed him as a madman, began to look upon him as a hero and martyr. Pictures of Brown sold in New York for a dollar apiece and the abolitionists extolled his virtues. Speaking in Plymouth Church, Wendell Phillips praised Brown's bravery, while George B. Cheever, a New York minister and radical abolitionist, warned the nation from the pages of *The Independent* that "God himself is about to uncap the volcano, if an insensate, hardened people persist in the violation of his law.''[26]

While Phillips and Cheever were praising Brown for his noble deed, Beecher took a more cautious stand. Speaking before his congregation, he expressed his sympathy for Brown's misfortunes, but was careful to condemn his ''mad and feeble schemes.'' He then went on to assert that although slavery was a threat to middle-class standards, ''a pest to good morals, a consumption of industrial virtues, a burden upon society in its commercial and economic arrangements, a political anomaly, and a cause of inevitable degradation in religious ideas, feelings, and institutions,'' that did not mean men could attack it in a manner that would gratify their fancies or passions. The southerners, Beecher argued, should not have to fear that any northerner would try to free the slaves.[27]

''The right of a race or nation to seize their freedom is not to be disputed,'' he continued. ''It belongs to all men on the face of the globe, without regard to complexion. . . . But, according to God's word, so long as a man remains a servant, he must obey his master. The right of the slave to throw off the control of his master is not abrogated. . . .'' Nevertheless, the use of this right had to conform to reason; any attempt at rebellion would be foolish because it could only lead to disaster. Preoccupied with the maintenance of public order and social control, Beecher was unwilling to encourage slave rebellions.[28]

To explain the apparent inconsistency between his advocacy of the right of rebellion and his qualification of that right, Beecher set forth his conception of liberty. His definition of that concept was similar to his definition of the right of revolution. Using an argument that would appeal to his middle-class parishioners, Beecher declared that ''a regulated liberty, a liberty possessed with the consent of their [the slaves'] masters, a liberty under the laws and institutions of this country, a liberty which should make them common beneficiaries of those institutions and principles which make us wise and happy—such a liberty would be a great blessing to them.'' But freedom without restraint and obedience to laws would result not in liberty but in anarchy. In arguing for a qualified, limited conception of liberty, Beecher reflected the middle class's inconsistent attempt to combine freedom and social control. Like the Republican party, whose ideology remained torn between an emphasis on equality of opportunity and a dislike of extremes of wealth, Beecher sought a moderate, balanced conception of liberty, combining reciprocal privileges and duties.[29]

Beecher's belief in the rights of liberty, rebellion, and economic opportunity rested on two fundamental assumptions that were also shared by romantic Christian theology. The first was the conviction that material and social progress were inevitable if people would work for them. Slowly but surely the laborer would achieve middle-class financial independence and the slave would win his freedom by demonstrating his capacity to exercise self-restraint and judgment. But these victories could be won only through patient hard work and moderation. Extreme attempts at immediate freedom or wealth would destroy the only social and political system in the world that was capable of guaranteeing liberty and financial success. Like the romantic Christian theology that stressed character development, dedication, and self-control, Beecher's espousal of freedom for the slave was carefully qualified in order to avoid any extremes that might upset the status quo.

It is easy, in our revulsion at the inconsistent nature of Beecher's definition of the rights of black people, to label his comments as a malignant form of covert racism. But such a view would misconstrue the assumptions on which his position rested. Though Beecher was inconsistent, he was indeed opposed to slavery, and the solution that he proposed for its destruction merits examination. When Beecher declared that "bad slaves will never breed respect, sympathy, and emancipation," and that "truth, honor, fidelity, manhood—these things in the slave will prepare him for freedom," he was not trying to provide a new rationale for slavery, though that might well have been the effect of his remarks.[30] What Beecher was trying to do, by arguing that slaves should be Christian gentlemen, was to make the violation of liberty so offensive to southerners they would voluntarily free their slaves. If this proposal seems to be a hopelessly naïve and simpleminded tactic to us today, we should remember that his sister's novel, *Uncle Tom's Cabin*, had as its central character the Christ-like Uncle Tom, whose sufferings brought a feeling of outrage and revulsion to millions of Americans and swept them into the antislavery camp.

Beecher's moderate abolitionist stand thus rested squarely on his faith in romantic Christianity. The emphasis on character development, the rejection of swift or radical changes, the belief in a universal ethical system based on peer-group pressure and social ostracism, and the faith that love could be the universal healer of all wounds were taken from his religious faith and fused into his attack on slavery. Moreover, because of his extensive lecturing on behalf of the Republican party, Beecher helped incorporate these basic assumptions into the party's ideology. Consequently, when Beecher responded to John Brown's raid, he spoke for thousands of Republicans and represented a major wing of the antislavery crusade.

In 1859, therefore, Beecher's goal remained that of creating "a public sentiment based upon the truths of Christian manhood," which would act on the consciences of southerners. He hoped, as his father had, to use public opinion as an instrument of social control. To his credit, it must also be noted that Beecher now waged an active battle to restore the rights of free Negroes in the North. As he argued:

> If we would benefit the African at the South, we must *begin at the North.*
> . . . No one can fail to see the inconsistency between our treatment of those amongst us who are in the lower walks of life and our professions of sympathy for the Southern slaves. . . . Can the black man engage in the common industries of life? There is scarcely one from which he is not excluded. He is crowded down, down, down, through the most menial callings, to the bottom of society. We tax them, and then refuse to allow their children to go to our public schools. . . . We do not own them, so we do not love them at all. The prejudice of the whites against color is so strong that they cannot endure to ride or sit with a black man, so long as they do not own him.[31]

Beecher's position in 1859, then, was a contradictory mixture of religious convictions, middle-class morality, moral suasion, and the defense of legal and procedural rights. Beecher considered his position to be a moderate one, but the public at large, depending upon which aspect of his program they emphasized, viewed him either as a conservative or as a radical.

The real difference between Beecher and radicals like Cheever and Phillips became somewhat clearer during a dispute that took place at the annual meeting of Plymouth Church in January, 1860. The controversy centered on whether the church should financially support the American Board, a part of the American Home Missionary Society. Opposition to the American Board was led by Theodore Tilton, who had become a member of Plymouth Church in the early 1850s while he

Henry Ward Beecher, ca. 1835

The Beecher family, ca. 1859, photographed by Mathew Brady. Standing, from left, Thomas, William, Edward, Charles, Henry; seated, from left, Isabella Beecher Hooker, Catharine, Lyman, Mary Beecher Perkins, Harriet Beecher Stowe.

Henry Ward Beecher, ca. 1880

The Peekskill house, built in 1878

was working for the New York *Observer*. Attracted by Beecher's views on temperance and slavery, Tilton joined *The Independent* and eventually became Beecher's right-hand man. When Beecher was unable to find time to write his weekly article, Tilton would make it up from parts of Beecher's most recent sermons. While Beecher remained a moderate in his antislavery views, Tilton gradually became a radical, arguing with William Lloyd Garrison that all ties with slaveholders should be severed.[32]

The question at stake in Plymouth Church was whether the American Board deserved the church's support if part of the board's activity was to maintain mission churches among the slaveholding Cherokee Indians.[33] On the opening day of debate, Beecher asked the church to support the board, arguing that it was gradually drawing the bands tighter around slavery and that it aided the Cherokee mission only because the Indians had promised to change their stand. His argument, Beecher maintained, was the same it had always been. "If in any single case a man can prove that, though he holds the legal relation of slaveholder, it is against his wish and without his moral consent; that he is doing all that the laws of the peculiar circumstances of trust in which he is placed will allow, to give his slaves their rights; and that he is preparing them for liberty and training them as free; —then we hold that this man, in so far as slaveholding is concerned, is worthy of confidence, and religious fellowship."[34]

This argument was immediately attacked by Theodore Tilton, who stood up in the congregation and began to explain his views. Although he apologized for speaking out and declared his love for Beecher, Tilton was caustic in his comments, arguing that "he did not think the venerable age of the American Board was urged seriously in its defense by Mr. Beecher."[35] Tilton then attacked the past record of the missionary society, comparing it with the temperance society. If the temperance society excluded all tipplers, why shouldn't the missionary society refuse aid to all slaveholders? At the end of his speech, Tilton brought out a Sharp's rifle that had been sent to Kansas by the church in 1856 and urged the congregation to return to its original stand on principle.

Beecher interrupted Tilton to explain that he supported the present position of the American Board, not its past, and at the end of Tilton's remarks, he made a fuller explanation. "He would stay in the Church, and in the Union, and in the American Board, to get them in the right path and keep them there."[36] A vote was then taken and the church overwhelmingly supported Beecher. Disturbed by the decision, Tilton published his speech as a protest.

Reflecting on the debate several days later, Beecher commented that "it seems very queer to me to be on the side of *holdback*." But then, he added, "I always knew that I was largely conservative when the time should come."[37] To his brother Charles he explained that since the board had in the last few years yielded more and more to the antislavery feeling of the age, it would be a poor policy "to reward it at length, with kicks and cuffs." "In fact," he continued, "the American Board must hereafter rely upon the Northern antislavery public sentiment and *we* ought to stand by so powerful an organization for good."[38]

After Beecher's stand on the American Board was publicized, many people began to feel that he was changing his position on slavery. To quell the criticism of his opponents, Beecher resorted to the theatric gesture that he had used so successfully in 1856 and ransomed a nine-year-old black girl from the pulpit. The effect on the church was magnetic. Sympathy for the child was intense and many were moved to tears. "The scene is likely never to be forgotten by those who witnessed it," wrote the correspondent for *The Independent*.[39]

In September, Beecher turned his attention to the issues of the coming presidential election. Speaking on religion and politics to a packed crowd in Plymouth Church, Beecher urged them to fulfill their responsibilities to vote and to maintain the principles on which the nation was founded.[40] After the election, Beecher was quick to see Lincoln's victory as a confirmation of his earlier views. The southern conspiracy to gain new lands for slavery had at last been thwarted. But he cautioned the northern people to "be tender to those who do not see as you see."

On the eve of the Civil War, therefore, Beecher continued to emphasize the main tenets of the moderate antislavery position. He condemned extremists who used strong language, and he argued that moral suasion rather than force or violence should be the only means used to oppose slavery. As he had declared in February, 1860, he was "willing to do anything to make the thing [slavery] tolerable while they are preparing for emancipation."[41] Unlike Wendell Phillips and the more extreme radicals, he looked upon John Brown's raid as an error and condemned violence of any kind.

Yet, despite these points of difference, the general public identified Beecher with the radical antislavery leaders in 1860. The question thus remains: if Beecher thought of himself as a moderate, how did he gain a reputation as a radical? One scholar suggests that "it was the Northern need for a simple emotional concept of antislavery which gave Beecher so strategic a place in its thought and feeling."[42] Undoubtedly this is part of the answer. Beecher had a flair for the dramatic and a sensitivity to the public mood that enabled him to influence public opinion. The purchase of Sharp's rifles to send to Kansas and the mock slave auctions made the evils of slavery seem more real to thousands of people.

Still another reason many thought of Beecher as a radical was the vitriolic language he used in his lectures and *Independent* articles. Likening the South to a vampire and the Compromise of 1850 to a ball of frozen rattlesnakes brought into the house to thaw, or referring to the North as trying to vomit the slave out of its presence by colonization, Beecher placed himself in the Garrisonian school of bitter invective. By trying to arouse the North to take a firm stand against any further political compromises, Beecher committed the very mistake he accused the radicals of making. His extreme statements unconsciously annulled his plea for moderation and moved him closer to the camp of the radicals.

Some of Beecher's reputation as a radical was also undoubtedly due to the attempts of conservatives to discredit him. In several cases, especially those which involved Irenaeus Prime and Joel Parker, theological differences led to a savage attack. Thus Parker and Prime tried to paint Beecher as a radical abolitionist in order to discredit his views on slavery and to undermine his ecclesiastical position.

Moreover, Beecher's association during the 1850s with the radicals, including Garrison, Phillips, and others, led many to believe that he was one of their number. He did, in fact, share certain beliefs with them. Like Garrison and Phillips, Beecher had been a strong advocate of temperance and had frequently denounced the evils of drinking. In 1850 and 1859, he had even offered his church to Wendell Phillips when Phillips was unable to obtain a hall in which to speak. Although

Beecher had made it clear that he was acting in the interest of free speech rather than radical abolitionism, people did not always remember the distinction.

Finally, there was a basic ambiguity in Beecher's own views. By taking a radical stand for free blacks in the North and sometimes qualifying it, by defending the principles of liberty and freedom and then redefining them to fit the middle-class preoccupation with law and order, and by portraying a southern conspiracy to take over the federal government and then admitting that he did not fear disunion, Beecher became associated in the minds of many northerners with the radicals even though he was at heart a moderate who believed that Negroes as a race deserved freedom but could only acquire it slowly.

Beecher's mistake and the mistakes of the other moderates is that they did not realize that their position had shifted during the decade and that they, too, were contributing to the explosive atmosphere of 1860. Although they were dedicated to maintaining a moderate and Christian attitude toward the South, they unconsciously undermined this position by using inflammatory language to oppose further political concessions. Without realizing it, they helped to create the atmosphere of hostility in 1860 that made compromise in any form practically impossible. They unwittingly fostered the very situation of hate and mistrust that they most wanted to prevent.

The very fact that Beecher was labeled a radical, in the final analysis, provides an insight into one of the causes of the Civil War. If the success of a radical campaign in history can be measured by the way in which it affects the moderates, then it can be said that the radicals in the North were successful in drawing many of the moderates into their camp before the Civil War. For Beecher was a prominent representative of a great number of preachers who began as moderates and ended by being associated with the radicals. Aroused by the Compromise of 1850 and convinced that there was a general conspiracy on the part of the South to destroy the free institutions of the North, Beecher and others entered into a political crusade that, in effect, nullified their more conservative views. If many northerners thought of Beecher as a radical, to the extent that he unintentionally had entered the Garrisonian camp in his adamant attitude toward compromise, their beliefs were justified. If compromise immediately before the Civil War was almost impossible, it was partially because the radicals had succeeded in associating the moderates of Beecher's stamp with their position.

NOTES

1. Eric Foner, in his excellent study of Republican ideology entitled *Free Soil, Free Labor, Free Men* (New York, 1970), recognizes that an important part of this ideology was strongly influenced by the Protestant ethic. My argument, an extension of his, is that the particular forms of romantic Christianity as preached by Beecher supplemented and reinforced Republican ideology in several important ways.

2. H. W. Beecher, Personal Papers, Yale MSS; Henry Fowler, *The American Pulpit* (New York, 1856), 203; New York *Times*, April 5, 1875; H. W. Beecher to Eunice Beecher, Oct. 23, 1857, Yale MSS. Beecher was not the best-paid minister in Brooklyn; Richard S. Storrs was earning $8,000 in 1851.

3. New York *Times*, March 22, 1856.

4. H. W. Beecher, "Lessons from the Times," *The Independent*, Oct. 8, 1857, and in "The Battle of Business," sermon, 1857, Library of Congress.

5. Timothy L. Smith, *Revivalism and Social Reform in Mid-Nineteenth Century America* (New York, 1957), 64, 143; see also Bernard Weisberger, *They Gathered at the River* (Boston, 1958), 135ff. William G. McLoughlin, in *Modern Revivalism* (New York, 1959), mentions only briefly the revival of 1858 and the causes for the decline of revivalism (see p. 120). McLoughlin's concern is with the professional revivalists rather than with the spontaneous movements.

6. H. W. Beecher, Notebook, Yale MSS.

7. Eunice Beecher to H. W. Beecher, May 6, 1858, Yale MSS.

8. New York *Times*, May 8, June 7, 1858.

9. *Ibid.*

10. Brooklyn *Daily Eagle*, Jan. 8, 1868.

11. William C. Beecher and Samuel Scoville, *A Biography of Rev. Henry Ward Beecher* (New York, 1888), 379.

12. This attitude contrasts with that of the Unitarian minister Henry W. Bellows, who lectured on the "Treatment of Social Diseases" in New York and surveyed the charities in the city. New York *Times*, Feb. 3, 1858; see also Henry Whitney Bellows Papers, Massachusetts Historical Society.

13. H. W. Bellows to Eliza T. Bellows, Oct. 10, 1855. Bellows Papers.

14. Horace Bushnell to Mary A. Bushnell, May 11, 1858, quoted in Mary A. Cheney, *Life and Letters of Horace Bushnell* (New York, 1880), 413.

15. E. A. Park to Dr. Amasa Walker, May 29, 1857, Harvard Archives.

16. Beecher and Scoville, *Biography*, 375.

17. Charles Beecher to H. W. Beecher, April 12, 1857, Yale MSS.

18. H. W. Beecher, "Lecture Room Talk" (typed copy), Nov. 13, 1860, Yale MSS.

19. This view of conversion as a gradual process represents a major change from Beecher's earlier position. In 1849, for example, in an article for *The Independent* entitled "Is Conversion Instantaneous?" (Dec. 27, 1849) he had argued that belief in a

gradual conversion experience was part of a procrastinating nature. See also Beecher's introduction to William C. Conant's *Narratives of Remarkable Conversions and Revival Incidents* (New York, 1858), xix.

20. McLoughlin, *Modern Revivalism*, 120; Charles C. Cole, Jr., *The Social Ideas of the Northern Evangelists* (New York, 1954), 223; Winthrop Hudson, *The Great Tradition of the Protestant Churches* (New York, 1953), 123.

21. Adam Badeau, *The Vagabond* (New York, 1859), 280–81.

22. Clifford S. Griffin, *Their Brothers' Keepers: Moral Stewardship in the United States, 1800–1865* (New Brunswick, N.J., 1960), 193–96.

23. H. W. Beecher, "Speech at the American Tract Society," *The Independent*, May 19, 1859.

24. Robert Baird, *Religion in America* (New York, 1856), 336.

25. C. Vann Woodward, *The Burden of Southern History* (Baton Rouge, 1960), 57.

26. *The Independent*, Nov. 10, 1859; Irving H. Bartlett, *Wendell Phillips, Brahmin Radical* (Boston, 1961), 212.

27. H. W. Beecher, "The Nation's Duty to Slavery," Oct. 30, 1859, in *Patriotic Addresses*, ed. John Howard, 203–23.

28. *Ibid.*

29. *Ibid.*

30. *Ibid.*

31. *Ibid.*

32. T. Tilton to H. W. Longfellow, Dec. 27, 1855, Longfellow Papers, Houghton Library, Harvard University; T. Tilton to H. C. Bowen, May 3, 1861, Beecher Papers, Library of Congress; T. Tilton, *The American Board and American Slavery*, pamphlet (n.p., n.d.), Harvard Divinity School library.

33. Griffin, *Their Brothers' Keepers*, 190.

34. *The Independent*, Feb. 2, 1860.

35. New York *Times*, Jan. 26, 1860.

36. Tilton, *The American Board and American Slavery*, 16.

37. H. W. Beecher to Mrs. Emily Drury, n.d., Schlesinger Library.

38. H. W. Beecher to Charles Beecher, Feb. 2, 1860, Yale MSS.

39. "Ransom of a Slave-girl at Plymouth Church," *The Independent*, Feb. 9, 1860.

40. New York *Times*, Nov. 5, 1860.

41. *The Independent*, Feb. 9, 1860.

42. Louis Filler, "Liberalism, Anti-Slavery and the Founders of *The Independent*," *New England Quarterly*, XXVII (Sept., 1954), 302.

7

War at Last

The election of Abraham Lincoln to the presidency in November, 1860, and the subsequent secession of several southern states made many moderates in the North fear that new concessions might be granted to southerners to keep them in the Union. As rumors of new compromises circulated throughout the nation in the fall of 1860, Beecher became worried. It seemed to him that the moral fiber of the nation was breaking down. "The growth of corrupt passions in connection with the increase of commercial prosperity, luxury, extravagance, ostentation, and corruption of morals in social life," he warned his congregation, "have given alarming evidence of a premature old age in a young country." Thus, when war did break out in April, 1861, Beecher was elated. Though he had consistently opposed violence and bloodshed during the previous decade, he viewed this conflict in a different light. "Bad as war is," he wrote to a friend, "in this land it will be a very Gospel. . . . Look at the self-denial which it will require in a people grown luxurious by prosperity; at the expression which it will give to Northern feeling long held back by prudential reason; at the transfer of public thought for *stocks, money,* [and] bargains to patriotic considerations. . . . War is bad. But there are bloodless wars which stab the soul, which besiege and starve out manhood. These are *worse*. Death is not so bad as living worthlessly." [1]

Beecher looked upon the war as a blessing because he believed it would improve the moral sentiment of the North, imbue the land with a sense of patriotism, and preserve the American heritage of liberty. "Give me war redder than blood, and fiercer than fire," he declared to his congregation, "if this terrible affliction is necessary that I may maintain my faith in human liberty. . . ." [2] By protecting the right of every man to liberty, the war would demonstrate to the world the success of democracy in America.

Beecher's view that the war would vindicate a democratic way of life was shared by other northern clergymen and represented a new shift in their outlook. Until the conflict began, the Protestant clergy had identified the mission of the churches with that of the nation and had worked toward establishing a distinctive sense of national identity. Beecher himself, during his labors in the West, had been convinced that he was planting the seeds that would determine the future growth of the nation. The outbreak of the Civil War, by threatening institutions already established, changed the vision of the clergy from one that emphasized future growth to one that stressed past achievements. [3] As Beecher declared in a sermon, "one side or the other must prevail. Let it be that side that carries forward to the future the precious legacies of the past." [4] The primary duty of the nation was to restore the union and to defend the principles of liberty.

To view the war as a crusade for liberty was to imply that it was a war for the emancipation of blacks, yet Beecher hesitated to describe the conflict in those terms. Unsure about whether the Constitution gave the president the power to free the slaves and whether the northern public would tolerate such an action, he urged his congregation to devote their energies to restoring the union. "This is not a plea against immediate emancipation," he wrote in *The Independent*, "it is but a solemn caution, lest, smarting from wrong, we seize the opportunity inconsiderately to destroy one evil by a process that shall leave us at the mercy of all others that time may bring." [5] This attitude, which the radical abolitionists regarded as one of "shuffling expediency," was supported by other clergymen in the North. Both Philip Schaff and Horace Bushnell agreed with Beecher's views and thought of the conflict as "actualizing the nation."[6] It was a tragedy suffered by both North and South as an atonement for their sins.

Beecher viewed the war not only as a punishment for northern sinfulness, but also as an opportunity to reaffirm values and ideals that had long been taken for granted by the middle class. One of the most important of these values was the belief in the "common people." Although Beecher in the past had sometimes mentioned the importance of the average man, or the "common people," as he called them, he now pictured these individuals as the backbone of the war effort. The common people, he argued, were the source of national patriotism, the root of the nation's material prosperity, and the most alert defenders of liberty and freedom. ". . . when you measure men on their spiritual side, and on their affectional relations to God and the eternal world," he added, "the lowest man is so immeasurable in value that you cannot make any practical difference between one man and another."[7] Since the South lacked an energetic lower class, Beecher was confident that the existence of such a class in the North would be the crucial factor in the success of the northern war effort.

Beecher's stress on the common people, with its equalitarian overtones, seemed at first to contradict the hierarchical and elitist conception of society that he had expressed in his Star Articles during the 1850s. But, on closer examination, the apparent contradiction was resolved by the way he defined the term "common people." "In America," he explained to his congregation, "there is not one single element of civilization that is not made to depend, in the end, upon public opinion. Art, law, administration, policy, reformations of morals, religious teaching, all derive, in our form of society, the most potent influence from the common people. For although the common people are educated in preconceived notions of religion, the great intuitions and instincts of the heart of man rise up afterwards, and in their turn influence back." The average citizen, the common man, was more important in Beecher's eyes than either the rich or the poor because he was the basic source of public opinion.

By stressing the importance of public opinion as the buttress of social order and public morality, Beecher was simply restating a position set forth first by his father and later by the Republican party. Like the Republicans, Beecher believed in a society where class antagonisms were minimal. Hence the middle class was important because it had to lead and set the example for the lower class. But he also believed that the average citizen, the common man, should be the ultimate judge of truth and morality in a democratic society. Educate the man on the street and that man could be trusted to act in the best interests of the nation. As Beecher boasted to his congregation, ". . . not among any other people on earth, is there such order, such self-restraint, such dignity, and such sublime nobility, as there is among the educated common people of America."[8]

Beecher therefore viewed the outbreak of war as a blessing in disguise, for he believed that the conflict between the sections would strengthen and consolidate public opinion so that it could now function as an invincible force in the campaign to restore the principles of liberty and democracy. Thanks to the virtue and dedication of the common people in the North, public opinion once again could be used as a subtle and effective instrument of social control.

To take advantage of the opportunities for social reform provided by the outbreak of war, Beecher undertook a strenuous campaign in the summer of 1861 to fire up the patriotic spirit of the North. In sermon after sermon he stressed the importance of George Washington and the flag as the key symbols of American nationalism. The flag stood for the principles of freedom and authority. "Every color means liberty," Beecher proclaimed from the lecture platform, "every thread means liberty; every form of star and beam or stripe means liberty; not lawlessness, not license; but organized, institutional liberty—liberty through law, and laws for liberty!"[9] Beecher wanted a rational, disciplined middle-class liberty that could be preserved only by the patriotic spirit of the North. Anyone who objected to this view was a misfit. "God hates lukewarm patriotism, as much as lukewarm religion," he wrote in *The Independent*, "and we hate it too. We do not believe in hermaphrodite patriots."[10]

By continually asserting the need for loyalty and patriotism, Beecher helped to create a new, strident nationalism in the North. Whereas his father and the earlier generation of revivalists had equated piety with the maintenance of public virtue, Beecher now equated the destiny of the church with that of the state. He wanted an ordered, disciplined, controlled nationalism that would preserve the country's honor and dignity. The cause of the nation was the cause of Christ. "You are bound, as part of your fealty to Christ," he warned the North, "to think of national character, of national morals, and of national welfare."[11] God had come to a judgment and He would purify and save His people. The war against the South was a holy war in defense of the principles of republican government, the highest stage in the evolution of civilization. "Self-government by the whole people is the teleologic ideal," Beecher asserted. "It is to be the final government of the world."[12] The preservation of liberty, the maintenance of morality, the justification of republican government, and the advance of civilization were thus all equated by Beecher with the northern war effort. A comprehensive and reassuring argument, fusing romantic Christianity and nationalism, it lifted spirits in the North and added a new determination to the campaign against the South.

Beecher's plea for a new, vociferous nationalism foreshadowed the position later taken at the turn of the century by Henry Cabot Lodge, Theodore Roosevelt, and other imperialists.[13] The same fervent patriotism, the same equation of the advance of civilization with the destiny of the nation, and the same belief in the evolution of the human species to higher, more civilized stages of existence that Beecher used in the 1860s were exhibited by the later prophets of American expansionism. The difference was that Beecher emphasized patriotic nationalism in order to strengthen the bonds that held the northern states together at home, while Lodge, Roosevelt, and the other expansionists used the same arguments to defend the acquisition of possessions abroad. Thus, while Beecher opposed such expansionist schemes because they appeared to be part of a slave-power conspiracy, the imperialists at the turn of the century took the opposite approach as they began to plot for an empire of their own.

In addition to trying to build a stronger sense of nationalism in the North in the spring of 1861, Beecher also helped in the actual preparations for war. Together with the leading members of his congregation, he began to recruit troops for a local regiment, "the Brooklyn Phalanx." Beecher devoted a great deal of his own time and money to seeing that the troops were properly trained and equipped. As his daughter proudly wrote to her fiancé, "*almost all* the work for the entire regiment is falling upon our church. . . ."[14]

During the early weeks of spring, while the Brooklyn Phalanx was being readied for action, northern hopes for a quick victory were suddenly dispelled. Union forces were decisively defeated at the first Battle of Bull Run in July, and by August, when the Brooklyn regiments left for Washington, the outlook was growing dimmer. "If the times are fearful," wrote Beecher to a friend, "they are a witness of God to our sins. National oppression will bring punishment both upon those who practice and those who wink at it. We have nourished a wild beast. It is no longer a pretty cub, but ferocious and vengeful. We must slay or be slain." [15]

In September, Beecher's eldest son, Henry, wrote from Washington asking his father to use his influence to get him a position in which he would see more action. "What I really want," wrote his son, "is that you should exert your influence with General Frémont to obtain some staff appointment for me in his department. I care not if it is a rank lower than the one I now hold," he declared. [16] The object was later obtained, wrote Beecher to a friend, when "Theodore Tilton went to Washington for it, and dug it out of Cameron." [17] Mrs. Beecher, who did not want to see her son injured, never forgave Tilton for his help.

During the fall, Beecher's concern with the course of the war was momentarily eclipsed by his troubles with *The Independent*. The paper had been in financial difficulty since the depression of 1857, and Henry C. Bowen, its publisher, was having trouble making ends meet. When war was declared, Beecher borrowed money from his account with the paper to equip his son's regiment. In May, Bowen wrote Beecher an urgent letter, declaring that his account was overdrawn for more than five thousand dollars and asking for immediate repayment. [18] Beecher, who was careless about financial matters, thought that Bowen exaggerated his indebtedness and contemplated withdrawing from the paper. [19] Nor was he the only one connected with the newspaper who was dissatisfied.

Since 1857, Bowen's precarious financial position had forced him to expand the advertising columns in the paper, much to the dismay of the editors, Joseph P. Thompson, Richard S. Storrs, and Leonard Bacon, who looked upon *The Independent* as a nonprofit enterprise for the support of Congregationalism. They were further upset by the vitriolic attacks on the South by George B. Cheever, a local minister and radical antislavery leader. Thus, in September, 1861, when Bowen assigned the paper to his father-in-law, Lewis Tappan, the editors became convinced that Bowen wanted the paper to take on a more radical character and they resigned. Meanwhile, Bowen had reached an agreement with Beecher and offered him the position of editor-in-chief. Since Beecher was in need of funds, he accepted and appointed Theodore Tilton as managing editor. Ownership was then transferred from Tappan back to Bowen.[20]

In his opening editorial, Beecher declared that the paper would continue to promote vital godliness rather than sectarian interests. It would also "assume the liberty of meddling with every question which agitates the civil or Christian community. . . ."[21] For the first few months *The Independent* followed the lines laid down by its previous editors and supported the administration's efforts in the war. Beecher contributed not only editorials but also weekly sermons, while his sister Harriet serialized her latest novel, *Pearl of Orr's Island.*

Beecher's interests were broad, and he frequently requested public figures to give their opinions on selected subjects. To Francis Lieber he wrote asking him if he would supply a piece on "the nature and scope of Martial Law—its relation to our times and the work; and its possible effect upon the government which exercises it."[22] Another correspondent was President Woolsey of Yale, whom Beecher asked to comment on "the Puseyite *tendency* [within the Episcopal church] away from reason and to authority."[23]

Despite the contact with prominent public figures which the editorship gave him, Beecher, like the former editors, gradually became discouraged by the extensive advertising that the paper carried which he considered unfitting for a religious periodical and by the amount of time required by his editorial duties.[24] As he commented to a member of his family, "my paper hangs heavily on my hands. I hope to make other arrangements about it, and shall either be free from responsibility every week, or shall give it up entirely."[25] When Beecher tried to resign, however, Bowen met his objections and he consented to stay on.[26]

Beecher supported the president in his editorials during the winter of 1862, but he became increasingly upset by the administration's refusal to declare the war a crusade for the abolition of slavery. During the past year, his association with radicals like Tilton had convinced him that the purpose of the war should include freeing blacks. "The gist of the war is slavery," Beecher now wrote in an editorial. "This is the pivot on which the whole history turns. . . ."[27] When Lincoln refused to change his stand, Beecher became more vehement. "We have a sacred cause, a noble army, good officers, and a heroic common people," he wrote. "But we are like to be ruined by an administration that will not tell the truth."[28] Throughout the summer, in sermons and editorials, Beecher continued to harass the administration and to call for universal emancipation.

In August, 1862, angered by recent defeats and by a letter from his son, who after fifteen months in the army still had not seen battle, Beecher unloosed his fiercest attack on the administration. It is, he declared, the "extraordinary want of executive administrative talent at the head of the government that is bringing us to humiliation."[29] This bitter criticism of the president provoked strong dissent from Beecher's own family. "I think you in error, and doing great harm by a most noble overestimate of men and public sentiment," wrote Henry's half brother, Thomas K. Beecher. "I am satisfied," he continued, "that the day you succeed in writing your magnificent principles on our national banner; you will have only a flag and a sentiment; the army, the men with one consent will say, 'We ain't going to fight for the niggers.' . . . I can answer for rural New York. The more emancipation you talk, the less recruits you can enlist."[30]

The problem that Beecher faced was how to deal with the strong racial prejudice that existed in the North and West.[31] Although many Union supporters agreed that slavery was an evil, they were unwilling to accept the presence of free blacks. The states of Illinois and Indiana felt so strongly on this matter that they passed laws prohibiting freed slaves from entering their territory and the Republican party at large was forced to adopt voluntary Negro colonization as its official policy.[32] Despite such extensive racial hostility, Beecher nevertheless resolved to disregard public opinion and to continue to try to change northern attitudes.

Beecher's experience with the intense racial hostility produced by the talk about emancipation was frustrating, but the Union defeat at the second battle of Bull Run and the indecisive victory at Antietam in September were even more discouraging. "I am full of apprehension for the country," he wrote to his wife. "I hope that God sees plainer than I do, how things may be settled favorably. I trust that, as often before in our history, unexpected and unforseen deliverances may come.

But I confess to more fear than I have ever had, and, fear is not apt to be my state of mind."[33]

It is interesting to compare Beecher's reaction to the early reverses of the war to that of Henry Whitney Bellows, the leading Unitarian minister in New York City and the president of the United States Sanitary Commission. Bellows, who also was troubled by the early setbacks, wrote to Professor Charles Eliot Norton at Harvard that a dozen or more officers should be shot "to save the country from oozing out at their insubordination," and then added that "two or three hundred men of standing, moral weight, and courage, [should be invited] to form some sort of volunteer Congress . . . to shape a policy for the government."[34] Bellows thus favored a take-over of the government by an upper-class oligarchy. Beecher, in contrast, even during his most pessimistic moments, retained his faith in a democratic form of government. Although he was troubled by what appeared to be a failure of national leadership, he refused to advocate a take-over by an elite.

Nevertheless, though Beecher's criticism of President Lincoln in the editorial columns of *The Independent* was less despairing than that of Bellows, it was quickly attacked by both his half-brother Thomas and his sister Harriet. "The general tone of your articles," wrote Harriet to Henry in 1862, "is deeply discouraging to that very class whose demoralization and division would be most hopeless defeat for us." Go to Washington, she urged, talk with the administration, and see if "you can't throw out a few lines of encouragement."[35] Following his sister's advice, Beecher in November reviewed the course of the war and for the first time urged the nation to take a "hopeful view."[36]

Lincoln's Emancipation Proclamation, issued January 1, 1863, raised Beecher's hopes to a new level. "The proclamation may not immediately free a single slave," he argued, "but it gives liberty a moral recognition." It was now time, Beecher commented, to start thinking of the future of those who would be released from bondage.[37] Speaking at the National Freedman's Relief Association, Beecher declared that the Negro was entitled to a fair opportunity to test the abilities that God had given him.[38]

After the Emancipation Proclamation was issued, the need to change the attitude of the nation toward the war suddenly seemed less imperative and Beecher turned his attention to other matters. In

January he settled his dispute with Bowen over the money he owed by paying Bowen a thousand dollars. But the disagreement was opened again several months later when Beecher asked for payment for the sermons that had been published in *The Independent*. The issue was referred to two referees who concluded, "in view of Beecher's habitual inaccuracy of business, to give him the benefit of the doubt; and they accordingly decide[d] that *some compensation* is reasonably due." Bowen therefore paid Beecher three hundred dollars.[39]

Beecher's editorial duties during the first two years of the war left him tired and worn out. When in May, 1863, his church offered to send him to Europe for a rest, he accepted without argument. Together with John Howard Raymond, head of the Brooklyn Polytechnic Institute, he set out in June for a six-month tour of England and the Continent.

Even before he landed in England, Beecher had been requested by a number of Englishmen to speak for the northern cause. These he refused, declaring that he would not speak until he "had time to form some judgment of things."[40] Upon arrival, this refusal was supported by his "American friends in Liverpool," who feared that any speeches might upset Anglo-American relations already strained by the British seizure of the raider *Alabama*, which was being privately built for the Confederates.[41] Beecher was, moreover, personally unconcerned about British public opinion. "We have nothing to hope from it," he wrote to his wife in June, "and we shall not, bye and bye, care a pin whether they think ill or well."[42]

Having visited a good part of the British Isles, Beecher left in July for the Continent. His friends now put a great deal of pressure on him for a series of lectures to be given when he returned to England in the autumn. Beecher nevertheless remained uncommitted. Skeptical of the utility of such speeches, he pointed out that what the British really feared was "the shadow which the future of our nation already casts. Is there any explanation," he questioned, "that will make England ready to stand second?"[43]

During this period, Theodore Tilton, Beecher's assistant on *The Independent*, kept him informed of events at home. The paper was going well, Tilton commented, but he missed Beecher around the office. Referring to Bowen, whose wife had just died, Tilton wrote "I have just received from him a letter in which he writes like a conquered man, whose sorrows have crushed him into the dust. He says that the world—life—fortune—ambition—all are almost nothing to him, and he has never before felt so willing to die. . . . I hope and this letter helps my hope—that when you come home you will find the former things passed away, and all things become new."[44]

During the summer, Tilton commented on current events, interviewing for the newspaper the governor of Massachusetts, the secretary of the treasury, and the president. He also described the New York draft riots led by Irish workers and the Union victory at Vicksburg in July.[45] By August, Tilton could write that in New York, the result of the summer victories "has been a wonderful change of sentiment (more than I can describe) in favor of the *Negroes*, and against the Irish." Most of the nation, he reported, now looked upon the war as a crusade for universal emancipation. Tilton, afraid that lectures by Beecher might upset the delicate diplomatic relations between England and America, also complimented him on not speaking in public. "Your silence in England was golden," he wrote. "It satisfies all your friends at home. Everybody, without exception, thinks you have managed sensibly and wisely."[46]

As the time for his return to England came closer, the pressure of invitations to speak increased, though Beecher still hoped to avoid them. "How glad I would be," he wrote to a close friend, "if, when in London, I find that I need not speak. In truth, I have no heart for it. England is selfish and cannot be made to recognize it. Her opinion of us has very little value." If beseeched by friends, however, he admitted, "I do not see how I could refuse to listen and comply."[47] And complying was what eventually happened.

Upon his return to England in September, Beecher visited the American ambassador, Charles Francis Adams, and broached the subject of a speaking tour. Adams replied that "the public mind was in a better state now," and that "one or two more judicious addresses would most likely do good."[48] Thus encouraged, Beecher set out on a tour of England and Scotland, hoping, as he expressed it to his wife, to "remove misconceptions and promote *peace* between the two nations in the future."[49]

It took considerable courage to speak to the hostile English audiences, and when Beecher's speeches were reprinted verbatim, including jeers and applause, in the New York *Times* and *The Independent*, he appeared to the American public to be a lone warrior fighting for the northern cause. Thus, when he returned to New York in November, he was greeted as a public hero. Mass meetings were held and the papers were lavish with praise. "It is no exaggeration," said the New York *Times*, "to affirm that the five speeches he has delivered . . . have done more for our cause in England and Scotland than all that has been before said or written."[50] Oliver Wendell Holmes, writing in the *Atlantic Monthly*, added enthusiastically that Beecher's trip was "a more remarkable embassy than any envoy who has represented us in Europe since Franklin pleaded the cause of the young Republic at the Court of Versailles."[51]

Beecher himself contributed to these encomia. At a reception in Brooklyn in November, he asserted that "Parliament would very soon have done what it was afraid to do but wanted to do all the time—declare for the Southern Confederacy. The committee said, 'If you can lecture for us, you will head off this whole movement.' "[52] Thus Beecher gave himself credit for having changed British public opinion from favoring the South to favoring the North. In reality, he had deliberately waited until the English attitude toward the war had shifted before speaking out. He may have removed some misconceptions in the British Isles about northern war aims, but he did little to change English attitudes toward the conflict. The Union military victories in the summer, rather than Beecher's speeches, were responsible for the change in British public opinion.

This tour, perhaps better than any other event, reflects the combination of opportunism and humanitarianism that colored so many of Beecher's reform activities. Begun with the altruistic desire of improving Anglo-American relations, Beecher's speaking tour was later consciously used to enhance his own popularity. The result was that he gained a notoriety far in excess of that which he actually deserved.

Beecher's speeches in England increased his popularity at home, and when he returned to his church he was offered a five thousand dollar bonus to his salary of seventy-five hundred dollars, an addition which he politely turned down.[53] Beecher's new popularity also affected his position within the Republican party. In December he visited Washington at the request of his sister Harriet to obtain a leave of absence for her son, who had been wounded in action. And in January, 1864, worried about the Union attitude toward Mexico, he wrote Secretary of State Seward to ask what his "real position" on that subject was.[54]

Later that same spring Beecher was called to use his influence to help the son of yet another friend. On the night of May 18, 1864, Joseph Howard, son of one of the most prominent members of Beecher's church and editor of the Brooklyn *Daily Eagle*, forged an Associated Press dispatch in the form of a presidential proclamation calling for four hundred thousand fresh troops and appointing a day of fasting and prayer.[55] Bribed by a group of brokers who desired to influence the stock market, Howard circulated the news release to the papers shortly before they went to press. When the forgery was later discovered after two papers had mistakenly printed it, Howard was captured, tried, and imprisoned.

Two months later Beecher wrote to John D. Defrees, superintendent of public printing, requesting that Joseph Howard be pardoned. Since the boy was young and his father was Beecher's close personal friend, Beecher hoped that this mistake might be overlooked. This request Defrees forwarded to Lincoln, adding that "the President has no truer friend than Beecher—and I do trust he may be gratified in a matter which he takes so much to heart."[56]

On August 22, the president informed Edwin M. Stanton that he "very much wish[ed] to oblige Beecher by relieving Howard."[57] Stanton had no objections and Howard was released on the following day. With the reelection campaign approaching, Lincoln was careful to retain the support of Beecher, who had been a caustic critic of the administration the year before.

With the exception of his trip to Washington to get the pardon for young Howard, Beecher limited his activities during the summer months so that he would be rested for the presidential campaign in the fall. In June, together with Horace Greeley, he spoke at a Union Square rally in New York and recommended that the working day be limited to ten hours.[58] Later the same month he gave a speech at a meeting for the benefit of the sick and wounded.[59]

As the end of the war became more predictable, the fall election, in which Lincoln faced General George B. McClellan, took on a new significance. The four coming years were to be the formative years of the new nation. The administration elected in November would be responsible not only for the reunification of the country but also for the reconstruction of the South. As Beecher declared in his first campaign speech, "I regard the destiny of this nation as pivoting on the election in November." [60] It was important to begin thinking about the reconstruction of the South. "The pending election," he stated, "even more than that of 1860, depends on principles. . . . If we sneak back into peace, with all the former evils unredressed, and the same evil men in authority, we shall be worthy only of the world's contempt and scorn." [61]

Between election speeches and work in his church, Beecher occasionally managed to get away to his farm, where he could enjoy the fall foliage. As he wrote to a close friend:

> The air seems to burn now, with glowing leaves! The sun, this afternoon, shook out such a wealth of golden haze, just as he was departing, that one would almost think it but the approach of angels, along the golden way! In one half hour—all was gone. The hills lay cold and blue against the sky, and the river darker yet, rolled clearly beneath them, while clouds began to fill the air, showing that the cold was condensing vapor, as soon as the sun departed. *I am rested*. I feel more like myself this fall, than I have for two years past, Indeed, I have been clearly overworked. But now, I have slipped the *Independent* from my shoulders, and have retrenched lecturing, and this summer, have lain fallow. I am, however, just now busy in the Canvass. I am hopeful and almost jubilant. I forsee a national glory just ahead, that a Christian man may well rejoice in! [62]

In his last article before the election, Beecher set down what he considered the basic conditions for peace. "It must," he argued, "assert and demonstrate the sacredness of the vote; it must make revolution or civil war a crime to be dreaded; it must maintain the doctrine of national unity and discountenance the heresy of absolute state sovereignty; and it must make liberty the law of the republic and slavery the curse." Lincoln, Beecher asserted, was his choice because he was bound by the Republican party platform to uphold the principles for which the war had been waged. [63]

On the day of the election excitement ran high. Beecher was up at daybreak so that he could be one of the first at the polls. For most of the rest of the day he traveled around Brooklyn, calling upon friends and checking on the election returns. By dinner Lincoln's reelection seemed certain and Beecher was jubilant. With his sister Harriet, who was visiting Brooklyn, and the Howards, who lived nearby, Beecher spent the evening discussing the implications of the victory.[64]

The year thus ended on an optimistic note. Lincoln was reelected, the war seemed on the verge of ending, and Beecher had never been more popular. In January, Beecher again visited Washington to see if he could gather some information on the president's reconstruction plans and obtain a better army position for his son Henry. Secretary of War Stanton secured a promotion for young Beecher and the president consented to give him a personal interview. Beecher was strongly impressed by the president's candor and tact. As he wrote to a friend, "let me tell you S[eward] is not one whit shrewder than Lincoln, and not half so honest."[65]

Convinced that the president was not going to give up the principles for which the war had been fought, Beecher returned home in high spirits. The experience of the past four years had helped to reconfirm his faith in patriotism and democracy. Like millions of other middle-class Americans, Beecher had viewed the Civil War not only as a struggle for the restoration of the union, but also as a defense of the democratic way of life. Now, with the North moving ever closer to victory, the ideals that he most valued appeared to be enshrined in the public consciousness.

Beecher was elated, too, because his own personal reputation had been enhanced by his outspoken efforts on behalf of the northern campaign. Although some men criticized him for his blatant attempts to increase his own popularity, Beecher was scarcely troubled by their comments. As he jubilantly remarked to a friend, summing up his feelings about the war, "Is this not a day of great glory? To have been born in these times is a distinct blessing—provided that one has been worthy of the cause of liberty and refused to betray it. As for me, I leave all the struggles of the past days, as the morning leaves the night behind it, and hastens on, to new achievements. The future is full of promise. I mean, in my day, and to the end of it, to labor earnestly to inspire habits, sentiments and character wh[ich] sh[ould] become such a Christian people as ours. . . . The religious papers are criticizing my sermons a great deal. Only let the common people read and believe, and, in the next generation, I shall be orthodox enough."[66]

NOTES

1. H. W. Beecher, "Our Blameworthiness," *The Independent*, Jan. 4, 1861; H. W. Beecher to Emily Drury, April, 1861, Schlesinger Library.

2. H. W. Beecher, "The Battle Set in Array," in *Patriotic Addresses*, ed. John Howard (New York, 1887) 283.

3. This interpretation was suggested to me by George Fredrickson.

4. H. W. Beecher, "The Success of American Democracy," in *Patriotic Addresses*, 356.

5. H. W. Beecher, "Modes and Duties of Emancipation," *ibid.*, 335; see also James M. McPherson, *The Struggle for Equality* (Princeton, 1964), 58.

6. R. D. Webb to A. W. Weston, July 16, 1861, Weston Papers, Boston Public Library; William A. Clebsch, "Christian Interpretations of the Civil War," *Church History*, XXX (July, 1961), 217.

7. Beecher, "The Success of American Democracy," 344–45.

8. *Ibid.*, 346, 352; Eric Foner, *Free Soil, Free Labor, Free Men* (New York, 1970), 18–39.

9. H. W. Beecher, "The National Flag," in Howard, ed., *Patriotic Addresses*, 292.

10. *Ibid.*, 297.

11. H. W. Beecher, "National Injustice and Penalty," *ibid.*, 364.

12. H. W. Beecher, "The Ground and Forms of Government," *ibid.*, 389.

13. William G. McLoughlin makes this point in *The Meaning of Henry Ward Beecher* (New York, 1970), chap. 10, but I think that he exaggerates Beecher's adherence to Anglo-Saxon and British institutions. Although Beecher admired the British, he was also highly critical of them during the Civil War.

14. Harriet E. Beecher to Samuel Scoville, May 31, 1861, Yale MSS.

15. H. W. Beecher to Mrs. Emily Drury, Aug. 15, 1861, Schlesinger Library.

16. Henry B. Beecher to H. W. Beecher, Sept. 24, 1861, Yale MSS.

17. H. W. Beecher to Samuel Scoville, Dec. 8, 1861, Yale MSS.

18. H. C. Bowen to H. W. Beecher, May 3, 1861, Beecher Papers, Library of Congress.

19. H. W. Beecher to Mrs. Emily Drury, May 17, 1861, Schlesinger Library.

20. Theodore Bacon, *Leonard Bacon: A Statesman of the Church* (New Haven, 1931), 467–71; Frank L. Mott, *A History of American Magazines* (Cambridge, 1939), II, 369–71.

21. *The Independent*, Dec. 19, 1861.

22. H. W. Beecher to Francis Lieber, May 20, 1862, Huntington Library.

23. H. W. Beecher to T. D. Woolsey, March 27, 1862, Yale MSS.

24. H. W. Beecher to Mr. Dickinson and William Edwards, May 15, 1862, Beecher Papers, Library of Congress.

25. H. W. Beecher to Samuel Scoville, June 27, 1862, Yale MSS.

26. H. C. Bowen to H. W. Beecher, May 16, 1862, Beecher Papers, Library of Congress.

27. H. W. Beecher, "The Country's Need," *The Independent*, July 10, 1862.

28. *Ibid.*

29. H. W. Beecher, "The Contrast," *ibid.*, Sept. 11, 1862.

30. Thomas K. Beecher to H. W. Beecher, Aug. 10, 1862, Yale MSS.

31. Leon F. Litwack, *North of Slavery: The Negro in the Free States, 1790–1860* (Chicago, 1961), chap. VIII.

32. V. Jacque Voegeli, *Free But Not Equal: The Midwest and the Negro during the Civil War* (Chicago, 1967), 17, 22.

33. H. W. Beecher to Eunice Beecher, Oct., 1862, Yale MSS.

34. H. W. Beecher to Charles Eliot Norton, Aug. 21, 1861, Charles Eliot Norton Papers, Houghton Library, Harvard University.

35. H. W. Stowe to H. W. Beecher, Nov. 2, 1862, Yale MSS.

36. H. W. Beecher, "The Ground and Forms of Government," in *Patriotic Addresses*, 379–98.

37. New York *Times*, Jan. 6, 1863.

38. *Ibid.*, Feb. 20, 1863.

39. Statement of Theodore Tilton and Joseph H. Richards, April 18, 1863, Beecher Papers, Library of Congress.

40. H. W. Beecher to Eunice Beecher, June 11, 1863, Yale MSS.

41. The raider *Alabama* was being privately built for the Confederates and was seized by the British government on April 5.

42. H. W. Beecher to Eunice Beecher, June 11, 1863, Yale MSS.

43. H. W. Beecher to H. B. Stowe, June 17, 1863, Yale MSS.

44. T. Tilton to H. W. Beecher, June 17, 1863, Yale MSS.

45. *Ibid.*

46. T. Tilton to H. W. Beecher, Aug. 7, 1863, Yale MSS.

47. H. W. Beecher to Susan Howard, Sept. 9, 1863 (typed copy), Yale MSS.

48. Benjamin Moran, *Journal of Benjamin Moran*, ed. Sarah A. Wallace (Chicago, 1949), Sept. 24, 1863. II, 1211.

49. H. W. Beecher to Eunice Beecher, Sept. 24, 1863, Yale MSS.

50. New York *Times*, Nov. 4, 1863.

51. Oliver Wendell Holmes, "Our Minister Plenipotentiary," *Atlantic Monthly* (Jan., 1863), quoted in *Patriotic Addresses*, 422.

52. New York *Times*, Nov. 20, 1863.

53. H. W. Beecher to the Trustees of Plymouth Church, Dec. 23, 1864, Yale MSS. Only six years later his salary was increased to $20,000.

54. H. B. Stowe to H. W. Beecher, Dec. 3, 1863, Schlesinger Library; H. W. Beecher to William H. Seward, Jan. 24, 1864, Houghton Library, Harvard University.

55. J. G. Randall and Richard N. Current, *Lincoln, The President* (New York, 1955), 151.

56. J. D. Defrees to John Hay, Aug. 3, 1864, Robert Todd Lincoln Papers, Library of Congress.

57. Randall and Current, *Lincoln*, 155.

58. New York *Times*, June 17, 1864.

59. *Ibid.*, June 24, 1864.

60. *The Independent*, Oct. 13, 1864.

61. New York *Times*, Oct. 23, 1864.

62. H. W. Beecher to Mrs. Emily Drury, Oct. 25, 1864, Schlesinger Library.

63. *The Independent*, Nov. 3, 1864.

64. H. B. Stowe to her daughters, Nov. 8, 1864, Schlesinger Library.

65. H. W. Beecher to Robert Bonner, Feb. 8, 1864 (copy), Yale MSS. This interview clearly revealed Lincoln's skill at reconciliation, since his attitude toward the

Negro, with its emphasis on racial inequality and the prospect of colonization, was somewhat different from views held by Beecher; see Kenneth M. Stampp, *The Era of Reconstruction, 1865–1877* (New York, 1965), chap. II.

66. H. W. Beecher to Mrs. Emily Drury, n.p., n.d., Schlesinger Library.

8

The Great Laws
of Free Labor

On April 14, 1865, several thousand people from all over the North assembled at Fort Sumter in the harbor of Charleston, South Carolina, for what *The Independent* called "the most significant celebration of the century."[1] The purpose of the gathering, which had been planned months in advance, was to commemorate the restoration of the Stars and Stripes over the ruins of the old fort. The chief address was to be given by Henry Ward Beecher. The choice of Beecher as speaker for this occasion—"the ceremony by which the nation and the world were to be assured symbolically and in fact that the Rebellion was for ever crushed"—was significant, for the war, which began in 1861 as an attempt to prevent disunion, had gradually, after the issuance of the Emancipation Proclamation, become a crusade for freedom and equal rights. As a popular reformer and dedicated abolitionist, Beecher was an ideal choice for speaker. The prolonged cheers that greeted his appearance on the platform, wrote the correspondent of the New York *Times*, were "a fitting welcome to the great champion of the rights of man."[2]

Beecher's Sumter speech, which reviewed the causes of the war and discussed the possible terms of peace, raised the difficult and perplexing question of how the free blacks should be incorporated into the life of the nation when the conflict had ended. Beecher was most concerned about questions of tactics. What could be done, he wondered, to maintain in the North a moderate and Christian attitude toward the South during the last days of fighting? And should the North try to make the southerners change their attitude toward the Negro by moral suasion or by legislative enactment?[3]

Beecher's questions were raised against a backdrop of growing northern pessimism about the possibility of amicable race relations. Even the most advanced and liberal northern white opinion during the war had been highly nationalistic, opposed to racial intermarriage, and skeptical about the black man's chances of survival when put into competition with white capitalistic society. President Lincoln and other leading Republicans actively supported a scheme to colonize blacks in Latin America, while other leading humanitarians such as Gamaliel Bailey, editor of the *National Era*, and Charles Elliot, a prominent Methodist clergyman, foresaw a gradual whitening of America from a mutually agreeable and voluntary process of emigration. Dr. Samuel Gridley Howe, the famous physician and reformer, and Theodore Parker, the radical abolitionist, went even further and argued that the Negro race was doomed to disappear because of inherent biological weaknesses.[4]

Although he recognized the Liberals' pessimism about the possibility of harmonious race relations and worried about the general animosity toward blacks in the North, Beecher nevertheless tried for the next two years to mold and shape a national policy for the reconstruction of the South. He had been encouraged to do this by his popularity as a moderate abolitionist in the 1850s and by the enormous acclaim that greeted his speeches in England during the war. In characteristic Beecher fashion, he sought to fuse opposing points of view into a new position that would satisfy all sides.

Beecher's own ideas about Reconstruction had vacillated during wartime. On the question of how the southern leaders should be treated, he had first declared that all the North would ask of the southern leaders was unswerving loyalty and universal liberty.[5] Speaking at Fort Sumter, however, he displayed a different view. The South, declared

Beecher, had been divided during the conflict between conspiratorial aristocrats and the common people. "I charge the whole guilt of this war," said Beecher, "upon the ambitious, educated, plotting, political leaders of the South." The course to take during reconstruction was thus evident. Punish the leaders but let not a trace of animosity remain for the multitude.[6] "I hold," he demanded several days later after learning of Lincoln's assassination, "that the educated, original ruling classes in the rebellion should be made to smart and tingle to the uttermost with condign punishment, whose elements should be; first, trial and condemnation if need be, with remission of sentence of death; secondly, disfranchisement; thirdly, confiscation."[7]

Beecher's attitude toward blacks, like his attitude toward the punishment of the white leaders, underwent a process of modification as the war drew to a close. While the war was in progress, he had argued that blacks deserved all the rights of suffrage and citizenship. "I demand that the broad and radical democratic doctrine of the natural rights of men shall be applied to all men, without regard to race, or color, or condition," he had declared. In addition, he had argued that the blacks deserved "land in fee simple, with ample protection in the shape of a wise self-protecting economy" and "all those means of improvement which we so solicitously secure for our white population —schools, churches, books, and papers."[8]

During his trip to Fort Sumter, however, Beecher elaborated on these earlier views in a letter to Secretary of War Stanton about the proposed Freedmen's Bureau:

> I am anxious to have the bureau in operation. We are in danger of *too much* northern managing for the Negro. The black man is just like the white in this—that he should be left, and obliged, to take *care* of himself and suffer and enjoy, according as he creates the means of either. He needs to be extricated from slavery, to be guarded from imposition, to have the means of Education, and to have, in the case of plantation slaves, a small *start*, in tools, seed etc. Beyond this, I think nursing will only pauperize him. I see in the movements about here a tendency to dandle the black man, or at least, to recite his suffering so as to gain sympathy and money from the public. All this will be checked by your *bureau*.[9]

Beecher feared that beyond giving the Negro the vote and some land, too much federal meddling with the problems of the South would undermine the independence of the blacks and alienate white southerners. To prevent this from happening, he recommended to Stanton that a friend of his, General Oliver Otis Howard, be appointed to the new Freedmen's Bureau, a suggestion that the secretary of war accepted.

Although Beecher's position appeared inconsistent in 1865, it rested on the same major assumptions that had underlain his earlier espousal of romantic Christianity and Victorian morality. The cornerstone on which both systems of thought rested was the notion of balance and moderation. All people had a right to liberty and freedom, but these rights had to be weighed against the general needs of society. Likewise, social advancement for all races was possible, but it could only come slowly, through hard work and self-discipline. The laws of free labor would guarantee progress only if they were allowed to function without restriction. Christianization, education, and peer-group pressure were the great instruments of social advancement, but real progress was never achieved overnight. Social interaction had to rest on love and mutual respect. In all cases of opposing points of view the only solution was to present a moderate, balanced, stable process of growth and improvement, a laissez-faire system in which each group in society could independently achieve its fullest potential.

In October, 1865, Beecher elaborated further on his ideas about race relations. "Declaring the colored man's right to citizenship in this country does not make him your equal socially," he told his congregation. Although black men deserved full legal rights, whites did not have to treat them as their equals. Certain qualifications on the Negroes' right to vote, moreover, now seemed to be necessary. "We ought," he admitted, "to demand universal suffrage, which is the foundation element of our American doctrine; yet I demand many things in theory which I do not expect to see realized in practice. I do not expect to see universal suffrage in the South; but if the Southern people will not agree to universal suffrage, let it be understood that there shall be a property and educational qualification." [10]

By arguing that blacks were not to be considered the social equals of whites and that property qualifications and literacy tests might be attached to the blacks' voting rights, Beecher aligned himself with a growing body of northerners whose advocacy of equality before the law did not rule out vast differences in wealth, power, and social status. This conditioned commitment to Negro equality was widely shared, even by those whites who were most sympathetic to the cause of black rights. The qualifications, though easily translated into de facto inequality in a stratified social system, were not thought of by Beecher as a barrier to social advancement. Unlike many northerners, he assumed that social advancement for the Negro race would only be a matter of time. It was a compromise position which, in typical Beecher fashion, sought to fuse two opposing and contradictory positions: the older enlightenment notions of equal rights before the law and the newer middle-class belief in civilization acquired through self-discipline, social control, and the acquisition of culture.

Beecher's letter to Stanton and his speech at Fort Sumter established the basic outlines of his position on reconstruction during the summer and fall of 1865. His point of view was what he called "a practical rather than a theoretical approach. . . . As new difficulties come up, God will prepare us for a solution of them." Southern society, by following the principles of free labor, would be reconstructed by the vital forces within it. But the change would be slow. "Do not be disappointed," he cautioned, "if the Virginia elections should go spitefully against the administration." The Negro would have to go through suffering and hardship before he would become free and independent.[11]

Many of Beecher's friends were pleased by his Sumter speech but none more so than Robert Bonner, editor of the New York *Ledger* and one of the city's most successful publishers. Bonner had built up his paper in the 1850s by paying large fees to have well-known authors like Fanny Fern and Edward Everett write for him. By the 1860s the *Ledger* had a circulation of more than 275,000 copies per week.[12] In January, 1865, Bonner contracted to have Beecher write a novel for the *Ledger*, seventy-five columns in length, with a "good moral purpose and effect."[13] Though Beecher had never tried his hand at fiction, the spectacular offer of $24,400, the same amount that Bonner had paid Everett, was too attractive to pass up and so he accepted.

Bonner was an astute and perceptive man, blessed with a good sense of humor. When Beecher wrote him after his interview with the president that Lincoln had told him three stories, two of which he had forgotten and the third which was improper, Bonner was quick to reply "how is it that you remembered the bad one—the one that could not bear telling?"[14] Bonner was pleased by Beecher's oration at Sumter not only because it placed Beecher in the public eye and made him an ideal source for political articles, but also for another reason which he explained in some detail:

> I am, personally, very much pleased that you delivered such a splendid oration because some of your so-called friends (I allude particularly to Tilton) have in a Pecksniffian way been regretting that you were on the decline. Tilton has said to me within two months that you reached the culminating point in your career when you were in England. . . .
>
> In the mean time, I can only say (and I will stake my life on it) that Tilton is not a real friend of you or yours. If he is, he has a queer way of showing it. I would not mention a personal thing like this; did I not consider it my duty as your friend to do so. Tilton has no gratitude in him, or he would not talk as *I know* he does. Every one knows that he owes his position to you. *You may not care anything about such a matter as this*; but *I* hate to see a man constantly following you—hanging on to your coat-tail—identifying himself with you as your righthand man and co-laborer—and behind your back endeavoring to boost himself up at your expense.[15]

Beecher himself was surprised at Bonner's comment. "I hope that his utterances are but the effusions of a heated moment," he replied. "It is painful to doubt any that we have trusted."[16]

Though Beecher spoke occasionally on politics during the summer, not until the late fall did he reassert his position on the main questions of reconstruction: how blacks should be treated, who should be pardoned, and how much control southerners themselves should be given over reconstruction policies.

Like other northerners, Beecher had decided early in the debate that the question of Negro suffrage was to be of central importance in guaranteeing the black man's equality before the law. Yet shortly after the fighting ended, he had commented publicly that to give blacks equality at the ballot box might alienate white southerners. It would be, he stated, "too much for human nature to endure without a great deal of recalcitration."[17] Several months later he changed his position. If blacks were not given the vote, he concluded, the white population of the South would soon place them in a position of complete subordination and subservience. The ballot was to be their major defense. In a speech that was described by the New York *Times* as "Hot Shot from a Very Radical Battery," Beecher advocated the enfranchisement of the black man "not because it is politic, nor on the ground of safety, but because it is his right as a man."[18]

Yet, Beecher was equally opposed to having the federal government defend black rights at the ballot box by taking over southern elections. That action would violate the dominant northern ideology of laissez-faire, to which he also subscribed. Writing to President Johnson in October, 1865, he commented, "Much as I desire to see the *natural* rights of suffrage given to the freedmen, I think it would be attained at too great a price if it involved the right of the Federal Government to meddle with state affairs." Although absolute state sovereignty was a heresy, states rights were "of transcendent value." For the government to help the Negro would violate the "fundamental law of society which says that every-man must help himself."[19] Caught between his commitment to black voting rights and his fear of government control, Beecher hoped that a display of good will on both sides would provide the Negro with access to the ballot box.

Since the government could only play a limited role in helping the Negro in the South, some aid had to come from the white southerner. "The welfare of the freedmen," stated Beecher, "depends far more upon the good will of their white neighbors than it does upon Northern philanthropy or government protection."[20] This attitude toward the Negro reflected Beecher's earlier faith in moral suasion. Just as he had argued in Indianapolis that it was useless to agitate for a reform unless the community would accept it, now he argued that it was pointless to try and legislate equality for the Negro if southern whites would not agree to it. It was of utmost importance, therefore, to use moral suasion to persuade southerners to modify their attitude toward blacks.

Beecher's plan for reconstruction thus had two parts. He argued that first and foremost "the South should be restored at the earliest practical moment to a participation in our common government." To do this there should be an amendment to the Constitution reinstating the rebellious states and a separate oath of allegiance should be drawn up. Second, before the South could be reinstated, it had to create a new body of laws to replace the statutes that were the basis of the slave system. Such laws would "make *Emancipation* real, and not nominal."[21] Beecher's position, as he defined it in the fall of 1865, was remarkably similar to that which President Johnson seemed to be advocating. Like

Beecher, Johnson was a believer in states rights. According to his interpretation of the war, the southerners had never lost the right to regulate their own internal concerns.[22] Johnson, moreover, viewed secession as a gigantic plot by which the aristocrats had duped the people. Through his use of the pardon, Johnson seemed to be following a lenient and conciliatory policy toward the southerners. Beecher strongly supported the president and wrote him in October that "every act of your administration as far as I had been able to judge, seemed wise and patriotic."[23]

During the fall Beecher toured the East delivering a lecture on reconstruction that summarized his previous remarks on the subject.[24] The trip, which lasted several weeks and included more than eight cities, took Beecher away from his church and angered Bonner, who wanted articles on Stanton and Johnson.[25] While in Boston in November, Beecher visited the Union Club, where Governor Parsons of Alabama was soliciting a loan for his state; along with John Andrew, governor of Massachusetts, Beecher defended the southerner from the criticism of Charles Sumner.[26]

In the course of Beecher's tour his remarks were not always reported correctly in the local press, and numerous rumors circulated about his actual views. These rumors were founded in part on the remarks of Mrs. Beecher, who wanted to become a lyceum lecturer and accepted several engagements where she read passages from her husband's speeches. On her first attempt she got carried away and declared that her husband had stated in Charleston that "God was black, that Christ was a Mulatto, that the Devil was white, and that your [Beecher's] greatest regret was that you were not born black yourself." "Now my dear," wrote Beecher to her, "you must allow me to protest against your lecturing if such sentiments are to be propounded."[27] Among those distressed by these rumors was Calvin Stowe, who wrote to Beecher and asked for "an authentic report of his views."[28]

As winter turned to spring, the positions of the Radicals and of the president became more and more evident. On February 19, 1866, Johnson vetoed the first of the congressional reconstruction measures, the Freedmen's Bureau bill. In this action he was supported by Beecher, who contended that the president was objecting to "that particular form of bureau contained in that bill" and not to the concept itself. This was, however, as far as his support went, and Beecher was careful to differentiate his position from that of Johnson, just as he had been careful in the 1850s to remain outside of the antislavery organizations. "I go," he asserted, "neither with the President nor with Congress. He wants them all in at once, and they [the radicals] want them all out at once. I would let in a part, and let the rest wait till they are fit."[29]

Among those who criticized Beecher for his support of the president was Calvin Stowe, Beecher's brother-in-law. Placing Beecher on the level of the New York politician Fernando Wood, the Hartford *Times*, and Beelzebub and company in general, he deplored Beecher's lenient attitude toward the rebels.[30] Stowe's wife, Harriet, came to her brother's defense and accurately described and defended his position. "His policy would be," she wrote to a friend, "to hold over the negro the protection of our Freedmen's Bureau until the great laws of free labor shall begin to draw the master and servant together; to endeavor to soothe and conciliate, and win to act with us, a party composed of the really good men at the South."[31] As Harriet correctly observed, Henry was trying to walk a fine line between providing blacks with some federal support so that they might make an economic and political start and at the same time not overly controlling them, so that the laws of supply, demand, and competition might operate. He assumed that the president shared his point of view.

Calvin Stowe was not the only one to criticize Beecher for his support of the president. Horace Greeley's negrophobe New York *Tribune* attacked him with a fury that increased as time went on. Reacting to this harsh criticism, Beecher felt constrained to write Johnson when the Civil Rights bill came before the president in March. The passage of this legislation, he argued, would frustrate those who had branded Johnson a traitor. Moreover, Beecher had a personal reason for wishing for its passage. "I have strongly and to my own personal inconvenience (for the present) defended your motives," he declared, with the clear implication that Johnson was about to lose a follower. Johnson, nevertheless, vetoed the bill and completely alienated himself from Congress.[32]

When Congress in July took the question of reconstruction into its own hands and passed the second Freedmen's Bureau bill, Beecher discreetly refrained from making any comments on the controversy.

He was, however, far from satisfied with the situation. Congress, divided on the question of the restoration of the southern states, had declared a moratorium on that issue. Beecher had learned of this decision earlier. "Schuyler Colfax told me," he wrote to Leonard Bacon, "last October, in my church, after the sermon . . . that such was the program laid out."[33]

As the fall elections began to draw near, President Johnson made the question of the unqualified restoration of the states the focus of his campaign. Beginning in late August, he set out on the unprecedented speaking tour that gradually alienated the northern public.[34] Meanwhile, a pro-Johnson convention was scheduled to be held in Cleveland, and its leaders wrote Beecher requesting that he be their chaplain. Deeply disturbed about the debate, Beecher used the occasion to answer the request in a public letter that criticized the Radicals.

"Had the loyal Senators and Representatives of Tennessee been admitted at once on the assembling of Congress," he declared, ". . . the public mind of the South would have been far more healthy than it is. . . ." He saw the Radicals, in their fear of losing control of Congress, as purposely delaying reconstruction and making reconciliation more difficult. Moreover, he believed their approach was wrong. "The Federal Government," declared Beecher, "is unfit to exercise minor police and local government, and will inevitably blunder when it attempts it." In their desire to help the Negro, the Radicals erred still further. The freedman, as part and parcel of southern society, could not expect to gain citizenship overnight. "Civilization is a growth," wrote Beecher. "None can escape that forty years in the wilderness who travel from the Egypt of ignorance to the promised land of civilization."[35]

In his letters, Beecher, though favoring the president's position, was attempting to rise above party and take an independent, nonpartisan stand as he had done on the slavery issue during the 1850s, when he favored neither the clerical conservatives nor the Garrisonian radicals. But times had changed and such a position was no longer tenable. The dilemma for Beecher, as for others who wanted to moderate the demands of the more extreme Radicals, was how to accept any part of the president's plan without appearing to be completely pro-Johnson. Although Beecher considered his letter to be above party politics, the general public interpreted his remarks differently. A typical response was that of the New York lawyer George Templeton Strong, who confided to his diary that "Beecher has just published a letter announcing his adhesion to the President and against Congress."[36]

Since Beecher had expressed the same views in his lectures during the winter months, he was shocked and dismayed by the public outcry that greeted his remarks. Criticism came fast and furiously from all directions. Even Beecher's church, which had never before opposed its pastor, was distinctly hostile. Most caustic of all was Horace Greeley, who wrote in the *Tribune* that "Mr. Beecher has achieved a sudden and wide popularity. In the conception of every blackleg, duelist, negro-killer and rowdy, from the St. John to the Rio Grande, he has all at once ceased to be a fanatic, a bigot, a disunionist, and become an enlightened patriot and statesman."[37] More constructive was the criticism of *The Nation* that "nearly every line of it suggests false inferences." As Harriet Beecher Stowe explained in a letter to her brother, "the man who advocated moderate drinking and was backed by a drunkard saying he'd 'spressed his sentiments zackly' is just in your position."[38]

The greatest weakness in Beecher's letter was not its openness to false inferences, but rather its unworkable solution. If southerners were increasingly denying blacks a role in the political process, then the only solution was to have the government play a more active role. As a writer in *The Nation* perceptively commented, "When Mr. Beecher calls upon us to dismiss from our minds the idea that the freedmen can be classified and separated from the white population and nursed and defended by themselves, he is guilty of something very like a sophism. One great cause of the present trouble is that the South insists, in spite of the warning of history, in classifying the freedmen and bases its classification on the absurd distinction of color."[39] The blacks needed the same voting rights as the whites.

But Beecher had his defenders as well as his critics. The New York *Times*, which was the organ of Henry J. Raymond, the president's chief supporter in Congress, declared that "no part of Mr. Beecher's argument for the restoration of the Union is more cogent or suggestive than that in which he dwells upon the identity of interest between the white citizens of the South and the emancipated Negroes."[40] Less partisan were the remarks of Washington Gladden, then an obscure minister in North Adams, Massachusetts, who was later to become the leading exponent of the Social Gospel. As Gladden wrote:

> I find it in my heart to tell you just now, how grateful I am to you for the good you have done me—for the truth you have taught me, for the noble and better views of this life and the life to come you have opened to me. I want to say to you that my faith in your sincerity and devotedness was never stronger than it is today; and though I don't think just as you do in regard to the pending issues, I am grieved and angered beyond measure that any should call in question your motives in taking the course you have chosen. . . . Though hot-headed partisans may malign you, there is a large place for you yet—larger than ever I believe—in the heart of the thousands who have loved and honored you in times past.[41]

To defend his position after these attacks, Beecher wrote a second public letter. Beginning with an affirmation of his place within the Republican party, he denied that he was a "Johnson man" and went on to say that he accepted the "policy which he favors but with modification." He accurately observed that, in Johnson's refusal to defend black voting rights, "unconsciously the President is the chief obstacle to the readmission of the Southern States." Despite the negative public reaction, Beecher continued to reassert his old position and defiantly maintained that the southern states should be readmitted as soon as possible.[42]

The second letter aroused even more criticism than the first. The Beecher family itself was divided over the stand taken by their brother. Harriet defended her brother's motives, but criticized his point of view. "I think (so far as I see)," she wrote, "that you are mistaken (certainly in Johnson's character) but it is the mistake of a noble nature." With his desire to be magnanimous to the South, her brother misunderstood the feelings of the North. "The conquerors are sore with *suffering*," declared Harriet, "too sore to be quite reasonable—you did not know how sore."[43]

Unlike her brother, who talked of vague principles, Harriet was concerned with specific questions—ones that Henry had difficulty answering. Would he admit the southern states without *any* conditions or safeguards for the Negro? Did he think that if the southern states were admitted "on the single condition of the oath of allegiance" they would repeal the Black Codes and elevate the poor whites? What was the experience of men like General Oliver Otis Howard, who were working with the Freedmen? These were important questions that Harriet felt her brother had overlooked.

Since Henry had aroused so much opposition, Harriet urged him to leave the political questions alone and suggested another sphere for activity. Edward Everett Hale of Boston was trying to raise ten thousand dollars for a new common school system in Richmond, Virginia, and Harriet urged Henry to join in the effort. "If we go down with food for their widows and children," she wrote, "with schools for their children, with sympathy for their distresses, will they refuse us? . . . Let legislators do this or that and if we befriend the common people shall we not gain them and have loyal voters?"[44]

Edward Beecher was even more distressed by his brother's letters than Harriet was and wrote a public letter to the Chicago *Tribune* opposing them. "A sense of duty, a universal pressure, not only on you, but on us all as a family, called for this statement from me," wrote Edward to his brother when Henry asked for an explanation.[45] Theodore Tilton, now editor of *The Independent*, seconded Edward's position and declared that "Mr. Beecher, deliberately and officially, under his hand and seal, has entered into league and covenant with the Johnson Party."[46]

Because this criticism from his family and *The Independent* wounded Beecher's pride, he resolved to try a different approach. To Henry J. Raymond, congressman and editor of the New York *Times*, he explained his plans. The first step in preserving the position of the moderates was to get a number of newspapers to support their views. "If the *Times*, *Evening Post*, Springfield *Republican*, Hartford *Courant* and other papers representing anti-radical views, would confer, agree upon a course, and lend every energy to *make it felt*," wrote Beecher, "you will, if you do not gain a political victory, secure a moral one, which, after the election, men will more and more feel and respect." Another tactic to restore the standing of the moderates within the Republican party was to emphasize the temperance movement. "The same men," asserted Beecher, "that work best in the radical movement are mostly found also in the Temperance Movement." Above all, Beecher asserted, the moderates should remain in the Republican

party, "a party better, if we can make it so, but without change and
with all its faults, infinitely preferable to any other, not to be given up,
nor our birthright in it forfeited."[47]

Beecher's attempt to win support for his plan by organizing the leading newspapers in the North and emphasizing the temperance crusade
was a shrewd tactic. It aimed at outflanking rather than confronting the
opposition and rested on the assumption that if he could get both sides
to accept his ideas about social progress, then compromise would be
easy. But the debate had gone too far and had become too heated. Dis-
credited by his association with President Johnson, Beecher was forced
to concede that he could no longer influence the reconstruction policies
of the federal government. It was a bitter blow to a man who once had
clearly exercised national political power. Coming not long after his
Fort Sumter triumph, the public rejection of his compromise position
was a crushing defeat.

Beecher's attempt to play a major role in politics thus ended in disaster. It alienated members of his congregation, created a rift within
his own family, and ultimately lowered his popularity in the eyes of the
public. Yet Beecher weathered the storm. Stubborn and idealistic, he
continued to speak out about a variety of controversial public issues,
but now he resolved to be more careful about becoming identified with
one side or the other. He had made one mistake; he did not want to
make another. From now on he would make sure that his defense of
liberal principles would not alienate any substantial interest group. By
remaining independent, he could act as an impartial judge, and the
public would have more confidence in his statements. Rebuked in his
efforts to influence national politics, he began to search for alternative
ways to influence public policy. Perhaps religion itself might become
the new vehicle for national reform.

NOTES

1. *The Independent*, April 27, 1865.
2. New York *Times*, April 18, 1865.
3. *Ibid.*, April 6, 1865; H. W. Beecher to Abraham Lincoln, Feb. 4, 1865, R. T.
Lincoln Papers, Library of Congress.
4. Paul Buck, *The Road to Reunion, 1865–1900* (New York, 1937), 58; George

Fredrickson, *The Black Image in the White Mind: The Debate on Afro-American Character and Destiny, 1817–1914* (New York, 1971), chap. 5.

5. *The Independent*, Oct. 27, 1864.

6. H. W. Beecher, *Sumter Oration and Sermon on Lincoln's Death* (Manchester, England, 1865), 24–25.

7. *The Independent*, May 11, 1865.

8. H. W. Beecher, *Universal Suffrage and Complete Equality in Citizenship*, pamphlet (Boston, 1865), 6.

9. H. W. Beecher to E. M. Stanton, May 3, 1865, O. O. Howard Papers, Bowdoin College Library. A good account of Beecher's trip to Fort Sumter and his activities there can be found in William S. McFeely, *Yankee Stepfather; General O. O. Howard and the Freedmen* (New Haven, 1968), 58–62.

10. H. W. Beecher, "Conditions of a Restored Union," in *Patriotic Addresses*, ed. John Howard (New York, 1887), 733.

11. *The Independent*, July 6, 1865.

12. Frank L. Mott, *History of American Magazines* (Cambridge, 1939), II, 10, 23.

13. Robert Bonner to H. W. Beecher, Jan. 25, 1865, Yale MSS.

14. Bonner to H. W. Beecher, Feb. 8, 1865, Yale MSS.

15. Bonner to H. W. Beecher, April 22, 1865, Yale MSS.

16. H. W. Beecher to R. Bonner, April 22, 1865, Bonner Collection, New York Public Library.

17. *The Independent*, July 6, 1865.

18. New York *Times*, Sept. 25, 1865.

19. H. W. Beecher to Andrew Johnson, Oct. 23, 1865, Johnson Papers, Library of Congress.

20. New York *Times*, Sept. 25, 1865.

21. H. W. Beecher to ?, Nov. 2, 1865, Beecher Papers, Stowe-Day Foundation.

22. Eric L. McKitrick, *Andrew Johnson and Reconstruction* (Chicago, 1964), 91; Stampp, *The Era of Reconstruction*, 50–52.

23. H. W. Beecher to Andrew Johnson, Oct. 23, 1865, Johnson Papers, Library of Congress.

24. H. W. Beecher, "Reconstruction," lecture delivered Dec. 13, 1865, and other dates, Yale MSS.

25. Robert Bonner to H. W. Beecher, Nov. 11, 18, 1865, Yale MSS.

26. Henry G. Pearson, *Life of John A. Andrew* (Boston, 1904), 272.

27. H. W. Beecher to Eunice Beecher, Oct. 23, 1865, Yale MSS.

28. Calvin Stowe to H. W. Beecher, Oct. 28, 1865, Yale MSS.

29. New York *Times*, Feb. 21, 1866.

30. Calvin Stowe to H. W. Beecher, Oct. 28, 1865, Yale MSS.

31. H. B. Stowe to the Duchess of Argyll, Feb. 19, 1866, quoted in Annie Fields, *Life and Letters of Harriet Beecher Stowe* (Boston, 1897), 275.

32. H. W. Beecher to Andrew Johnson, March 17, 1866, Johnson Papers, Library of Congress. The effect of this letter would have been nullified if Gideon Welles had shown Johnson in the cabinet meetings on the previous day a different letter in which Beecher quoted rumors that Johnson was an alcoholic. See Gideon Welles, *Diary*, ed. H. K. Beale and A. W. Brownson (New York, 1960), II, 453.

33. H. W. Beecher to Leonard Bacon, Sept. 21, 1866 (copy), Yale MSS.

34. William R. Brock, *An American Crisis: Congress and Reconstruction 1865–1867* (New York, 1963), 167.

35. H. W. Beecher to Messrs. Halpine, Slocum, and Granger, Aug. 30, 1866, quoted in *Patriotic Addresses*, 737–41.

36. G. T. Strong, *The Diary of George Templeton Strong*, ed. Allan Nevins and Milton H. Thomas (New York, 1952), III, 101.

37. Horace Greeley, *Tribune Tracts No. 3* (New York, 1966).

38. *The Nation*, Sept. 6, 1866, p. 192.

39. *Ibid.*

40. New York *Times*, Sept. 4, 1866.

41. Washington Gladden to H. W. Beecher, Oct. 2, 1866, Yale MSS.

42. H. W. Beecher to Rev. Tyng, Sept. 8, 1866 (copy), Yale MSS.

43. H. B. Stowe to Eunice Beecher, Sept. 23, 1866, Yale MSS.

44. H. B. Stowe to H. W. Beecher, Oct. 8, 1866 (copy), Yale MSS.

45. Edward Beecher to H. W. Beecher, Oct. 8, 1866 (copy), Yale MSS.

46. *The Independent*, Sept. 6, 1866.

47. H. W. Beecher to Henry J. Raymond, Sept. 19, 1866 (copy), Yale MSS.

9

All the World His Bible

American society at mid-century, as many observers have pointed out, was rent by urbanization, modernization, and vast social change. Thousands moved from the farm to the city. Thousands more entered business and industry as middle-class clerks and managers. Even without the dislocation produced by the Civil War, it would have been a time of enormous anxiety and insecurity; but with the intense and bloody sectional conflict, the emotional crisis became even greater. For Beecher as well as for the rest of the nation it was an anguished period of searching for new ideals and standards. What was needed was a fresh set of guidelines for national policy and private behavior.[1]

Beecher had tried his hand at shaping national policy during Reconstruction and, because of his inability to differentiate his position from President Johnson's, had been bitterly criticized. The abuse heaped upon him both publicly and privately might have incapacitated other men, but it hardly slowed him down. Beecher warded off disillusionment and pessimism largely because he was able to mold his earlier beliefs in romantic Christianity into a full and mature religious system. In coming to terms with his own self-doubts and shortcomings, he created a new religious ethos that spoke directly to the fears and anxieties of a generation. It was a system of faith that was widely accepted because it reassured the public that fixed moral standards existed and could be applied to the ethical questions of everyday life.

The new evangelical liberalism, as Beecher's faith came to be called, developed in response to the social and intellectual changes that threatened Protestant orthodoxy after 1859. The publication of Darwin's *On the Origin of Species* in that year together with the events of the war and the new biblical criticism of David Frederick Strauss and Ferdinand Christian Bauer, which treated the life of Jesus as secular history, all prompted a major rethinking of orthodox theology. In the decade after the war, Beecher became the most conspicuous spokesman for those clergymen who were trying to redefine and remold the traditional Christian message.

Beecher's prominence as a spokesman for evangelical liberalism was closely related to his involvement in several new publishing ventures. Having perceived as early as the 1840s that the press was to have an enormous impact on the American public, he had cultivated his associations with the publishing industry in the 1850s and by the end of the 1860s his name had become a household word. At the end of that decade, Beecher was a regular contributor to the New York *Ledger*, one of the biggest newspapers in the city, with a circulation of four hundred thousand. He was also the editor of a new religious journal, *The Christian Union* (later *The Outlook*). In addition, he published a novel *(Norwood)*, a life of Christ, six volumes of sermons, and a book of lecture-room talks. The new religious periodicals, along with the publication of his own sermons and extensive lecture engagements, provided Beecher with a forum in which he could reformulate and refashion his religious views. The result was his new program of evangelical liberalism.[2]

The process of entry into the publishing business began slowly. As late as 1867, Beecher still spent most of his time preparing sermons and lectures. Eventually, the presure of new commitments forced a curtailment of his speaking engagements. When Elizabeth Cady Stanton wrote Beecher in January asking him to give a speech for women's rights, he was forced to turn her down. "I am to preside and speak on Wednesday night at my own church," Beecher replied. "On Thursday night I preside and introduce a lecturer at the Academy of Music in Brooklyn. On Friday night, at Cooper Institute, I have a speech to make for the starving people of the South; and on Saturday night, at the same place, a speech for the *Cretans*. But these are the *punctuations* of my main business, which just now is, to write a novel for Bonner, at which I am working every forenoon."[3]

Beecher's increased literary activity was prompted in part by the warnings of his publisher. More than a year had passed since he signed the contract with the *Ledger* and he still had not written the first chapter. Delayed by his involvement in the debate over reconstruction and by his dislike of the protracted effort writing a novel required, Beecher procrastinated and stalled from day to day, sending humorous apologies to Bonner's requests for results. By the fall of 1866, Bonner was becoming increasingly annoyed. "I am going to get mad with you," he wrote to the hesitant preacher. "I don't like to be designated Robert Le Diable, Robert Burns, or any Robert, but Robert Bonner."[4]

Spurred on by the promptings of his editor, Beecher at last settled down and began to work on the novel, which he entitled *Norwood: or Village Life in New England*. The first chapter was completed in March, 1867, and appeared in *The Ledger* several months later. The story revolved around the early life and courtship of a young couple in a small town in Western Massachusetts. Separated by the Civil War, they met again during the last days of the conflict and were married.

The novel was not a first-rate work of fiction, as Beecher himself admitted when he wrote to a close friend: "There is something in all this Norwood business which touches my sense of the ludicrous. I can't well explain why—but laughing, you know, has always been one of my strong points. You are not bound to like it. I shall be satisfied if you will only think that I have fairly escaped without loss."[5] Beecher's comment was a classic understatement. Though *Norwood* was not a particularly good novel, it appealed to the public and sold extremely well. Robert Bonner, who commissioned the book and helped to publicize it by writing a highly favorable review of it for the New York *Times*, was satisfied because *Norwood* noticeably increased the subscription list of his paper.[6] Beecher, too, was flattered by the popularity of his novel. Though he realized that it would never rank with his sister Harriet's literary efforts, he was pleased that the publication of the book freed him from all his debts. The mortgages on his house and farm were paid off and his accounts at bookstores were at last settled.[7]

The publicity surrounding the book, which was later adapted for the stage in New York and went through three editions, gave rise to several offers. Bonner agreed to pay Beecher a hundred dollars for each weekly article of general interest, and Harper and Brothers contracted to publish two volumes of Beecher's sermons.[8] Then, in the winter, came the best offer, from a new publishing house that had been created earlier in the year by an Englishman named John B. Ford. A contract was drawn up on January 1, 1868, for Beecher to write a life of Christ. Before Beecher set pen to paper, he was paid a ten-thousand-dollar bonus by the new company. Later the same year, a second contract was negotiated, providing for the monthly publication of Beecher's sermons under the title of the *Plymouth Pulpit*.[9]

Elated by his success as an author, Beecher began to consider the possibility of starting a religious periodical of his own. There was clearly a need for a new Congregational newspaper. The only drawback was that such a venture might alienate Henry C. Bowen and Theodore Tilton, the publisher and editor of *The Independent*, who were members of Beecher's congregation. Since 1867, when Beecher severed his connections with *The Independent*, the paper, under Theodore Tilton's editorship, had become progressively more radical, backing the women's rights movement, attacking President Johnson's policies, and disputing the tenets of evangelical religion. An energetic and clever writer, Tilton devoted his attention to the main reforms of the day and thrived on controversy. "Tilton is his name and tilting his profession," declared *Vanity Fair*.[10] Through his outspoken and caustic editorials, Tilton soon created a number of enemies and alienated many of the paper's subscribers.

Among those most upset by Tilton's editorials were a group of midwestern ministers headed by Beecher's brother Edward. In the fall of 1867, these men met in Chicago with Bowen and Tilton to protest the way *The Independent* was being run. Tilton responded to their criticisms by stating that although he was unable to accept their views of the Gospel, he was willing to stop publishing his own views even though they were supported by Henry Ward Beecher. Upset by these remarks, Edward wrote his brother a long letter setting forth his own views and asking for verification of Tilton's comments. "I fear Tilton more and more," wrote Edward to Henry. "This advice to young men to read Emerson's essays and especially Herbert Spencer's *First Principles* as 'awakeners' is dangerous, and may be ruinous. One is the

teacher of pantheism, the other denies the personality of God, and re-
duces him to an unknown and unknowable force. . . ."[11]

These remarks annoyed Henry, who immediately wrote a hasty reply. "It is well known," he angrily declared, "that I am in positive
antagonism with the general drift of the paper. Mr. Bowen will scarcely recognize me on the street, and feels bitterly my withdrawal from all
part or lot in the paper." As for Tilton, Henry asserted, he was still on
friendly terms with the editor, even though they differed on matters of
public policy and religion. "I do not know what grounds he now rests
upon," Beecher stated. ". . . I do not regard him as of a dogmatic
nature, nor especially precise in his religious philosophy." If Edward
was opposed to *The Independent* and had a quarrel with it, that was his
business, but Henry refused to take part. Since Bowen and Tilton were
members of his church, he did not feel free to enter into the dispute.[12]
Beecher closed his letter by hinting that it was somewhat ironic that
Edward, who believed in the preexistence of souls, should be questioning the orthodoxy of his brother's views.

Although he did not mention it in his letter, Henry himself had worried earlier about Tilton's theological views and during the previous
summer had urged him to refrain from writing editorials on religious
subjects. It would be better, Beecher suggested, for Tilton to wait until
he had reached some firm conclusions before expressing his views. Although Beecher disagreed with Tilton's present religious outlook, he
believed that there was some merit in the writings of Herbert Spencer
and the other social philosophers whom Tilton praised. "It seems to
me," he stated, "that I discern, arising from the studies of natural
science, a surer foothold of these [orthodox religious views] than they
have ever had, in so far as theology is concerned. If I have one purpose
or aim," he continued, "it is to secure for the truths now developing
in the spheres of natural science a religious spirit and a harmonization
with all the great cardinal truths of religion which have thus far characterized the Christian system."[13]

By suggesting to Tilton that he did see an element of truth in the
editor's views and by then denying to his brother that he supported Tilton's views, Beecher placed himself in an awkward position. For when
Edward opened fire on *The Independent*, called for a new periodical to
represent the interests of western Congregationalism, and then insisted
that he was supported in this position by Henry, Tilton felt betrayed.

Relations among Beecher, Tilton and Bowen thus gradually deteriorated. The final blow to the friendship came in 1870 when Beecher decided to become the editor of a new journal owned by J. B. Ford, the company that published his sermons and held the contract for his life of Christ. Beecher set one condition on his acceptance of the editorship. "I should be glad to take hold of a family paper," he wrote to one of the partners, "provided I can do it without being worn out by drudgery. I should expect, for a time, and until it has reached my ideas, to have much personal superintendence. But after that I sh'd want only a Bishop's and not a Curate's place." [14]

In return for editing the paper, Beecher received half the stock of the new journal, which he named the *Christian Union*. Although he was pleased by the financial benefits of his new position, what interested Beecher most was the thought that he would have complete control over the paper's format. The ideas and views that he had developed during his editorship of *The Independent* could now be put to use. Harriet Beecher Stowe, who bought stock in the new enterprise, was also elated by the possibilities the journal offered. "I have all my life but especially lately," she wrote to her brother, "gone with a gospel burning in my bosom which I longed to preach but could not because I was a woman. . . . [I] have had to sit under preaching that didn't hit and didn't warm and didn't comfort when I felt *full* and it seemed so simple and so easy and so blessed to have told the gospel, as it is. But, if we can make the *Union* so distinctively a gospel that seekers and enquirers shall come to it as their natural food. . . , then my ideal of the *C. Union* will be filled up." [15]

Beecher began working on the paper in October, though his name did not appear on it until January, 1870. This was in keeping with his warning to the publishers "not to try to push the paper by using me." [16] The paper itself, he urged, should be its own best recommendation. Beecher spent Mondays at the paper's office, giving instructions to George S. Merriam, the assistant editor, and overseeing the articles that were being considered for each issue.

Publication soon became a family concern. Eunice Beecher wrote articles on domestic economy, while Thomas K. Beecher, Henry's younger half-brother, who was a minister in Elmira, New York, contributed essays on moral subjects. Edward Beecher and Harriet Stowe also sent in articles from time to time. Yet the chief drawing card remained Henry, who wrote most of the editorial comments and contributed weekly lecture-room talks.[17]

From the start, the *Christian Union* set new precedents for the religious press. Smaller in size than the usual magazine, it reflected its editor's liberal views of religion and contained articles on a wide variety of secular subjects. As a surprised reviewer in the Brooklyn *Daily Eagle* wrote, "the editorial page of Mr. Beecher's new journal is almost wholly secular." It was also Beecher's policy not to engage in personalities or in the "perpetual war-whoop" of its competitors. The result was that the growth of the paper far exceeded all expectations. At the end of the first year it had 30,000 subscribers, and by 1872, 132,000.[18]

During the period of his intense literary activity in the late 1860s and early 1870s, Beecher redefined the traditional Christian message and reformulated the social role of the clergy. The resulting theological position known as evangelical liberalism contrasted noticeably with that held by the clerical conservatives who believed in the literal interpretation of the Bible and the scientific modernists who saw science as the final arbitrator of all questions about orthodox religion.[19] It was primarily directed at the new middle class of lawyers, doctors, clerks, managers, teachers, and engineers—a group of people who were both responsible for the increasing industrialization of the period and afraid of it. They sought to humanize the nascent industrial-capitalist order by infusing it with social responsibility, strict personal morality, and high cultural standards. Worried about the corrupting influences of intense competition and the rapid acquisition of wealth, this group, which Daniel Walker Howe has described as "an identifiable segment within the bourgeoisie," sought to sway the public through a massive educational and propaganda campaign.[20] Evangelical liberalism as espoused by Beecher was thus part of a massive Victorian crusade to stabilize American society at mid-century. As such, it reached out to an audience far greater than the small group that originally formulated and supported it.

The first premise of evangelical liberalism as expressed by Beecher was the need to reconcile new developments in science and historical scholarship with traditional religious doctrines. As Beecher wrote in the public announcement for his life of Christ, "at a time when a chill mist of doubt is rising over all the Sacred Records from an excessive addiction to material science, it would seem that good service might be rendered to religion by reasserting, in language and by methods congenial to the wants of modern thought, the Divinity of our Lord and Saviour, Jesus Christ."[21] Beecher's message was clear. By viewing the natural world as emblematic of religious truths, he denied that a conflict existed between science and religion.

Beecher had long found a sense of personal refuge and inspiration in nature. As he wrote to a close friend during one of his lecture trips:

> I have returned from my prairie ride yesterday. I went as far West as the Mississippi, at Quincy. . . . I was surprised and delighted to find that the *American mockingbird* was singing in its full native liberty near the house. . . . I lingered to listen and could not get enough. There is something enchanting to me in the free outdoor singing of birds. That God made such things indicates what thoughts pass through his mind and what his disposition is. How beautiful was the new grass. I longed to lie down on it. I did so. I could not get enough. . . . I think that the Bible is God's spelling-book. After we have learned our letters there, and how to read, *then* the material world and human life reveal more of God than we can learn anywhere else—at any rate, the most dear and touching views of Divine Nature. When John says, *"The world was made by Him,"* he seems to say, that men should know what God was by his *work*.[22]

The lush bounty and incredible richness of the American landscape, long a favorite topic for American writers, became for Beecher a means of fusing American nationalism and religious faith. Religion reinforced patriotism and was in turn supported by the preoccupation with the material conditions of life.

The connection between faith and nature was most fully developed in *Norwood*, where Beecher used the heroine of the novel, Rose Wentworth, and her father, Dr. Wentworth, to express his ideas about the relationship between God and the natural world. As Dr. Wentworth explains to the town minister, "the Bible cannot contain the truth itself, . . . God does not live in a book. Man does not live in a book. Love, Faith, Joy, Hope do not, cannot live in a book. . . . Since I accepted the New Testament, all the world has become my Bible. My Saviour is everywhere—in the book and out of the book. I see Him in Nature, in human life, in my own experiences as well as in the recorded fragments of His own history." Rose Wentworth reiterates this idea when she states that "all of nature is, literally, but a way which God has of making known to us his feelings, tastes, and thoughts."[23]

Beecher's interest in the bounty and inspiration of nature provided a natural foil to his fear and distrust of cities, his view of urban environments as the spawning grounds for hate and greed. "I dread nothing more," Beecher declared, "than to hear young men saying, 'I am going to the city.' . . . There is connected with the business of the city so much competition, so much rivalry, so much necessity for industry, that I think it is a perpetual, chronic, wholesale violation of natural law. There are ten men that can succeed in the country, where there is one that can succeed in the city."[24] In *Norwood*, Beecher repeats this theme and praises the virtues of a rural existence. As he writes in the novel, "commend me to the wisdom of those notable and excellent people who cool the fever of city life under the great elms that spread their patriarchal arms about solitary farm-houses; who exchange the street for mountain streams, make bargains with the brooks, and cast their cheats for trout rather than for men!" Like other nineteenth-century reformers, Beecher saw life in the country not only as a solution for the problems of urban vice and poverty, but also as indicative of a more humane way of life.[25]

Beecher's vision of the natural world as the expression of a living God was a restatement, in popular form, of the second major premise of evangelical liberalism. God was in and of this world, not apart from it. The here-and-now in this conception was the central focus for the divine scheme. Religion and everyday life were not separate. Immutable natural laws were a fact that existed to guide men's actions in the practical everyday world.

Beecher's faith in a system of immutable natural laws underlying and influencing everyday events was an extension of the belief in "higher laws" that had been an important part of the abolitionist crusade and Republican party ideology in the 1850s. The notion that truth did indeed exist and that it rested upon fixed moral principles was thus a major ingredient in the American Victorian effort to improve and civilize the nation. As one of the spokesmen for this vast educational movement, Beecher constantly reassured his audience that the great moral truths were not arcane. They existed everywhere in the natural world and could be discovered through simple common sense.

Beecher not only denied that differences existed between the secular and divine worlds, he continually sought to fuse the two by describing his religious beliefs in terms of the most intensely personal and private relationships. As he told his congregation, "I desire to present to you a clear conception of God as your *personal* God. . . . It is this Christ that I would make more personal to you today." [26] In stressing this personal conception of God, Beecher often used the popular conceptions of the family to reinforce his argument. As he explained to a friend, "the root of my view of truth is that, in forming our ideas of God and moral government we shall take the *family* and not the Civil State as our model, and the Father, and not the magistrate, as our ideal. . . . It is fair to test all questions relative to God on the analogy of a truly Christian family. Of course that will not give a perfect result. *No* method will. But we may be sure we are working in the *right direction*. I regard this not only as fundamental, but as revolutionary." [27] The Victorian ideal of family life, which combined openness with ties of intense love and affection, became the model for Beecher's idealized conception of religion.

Looked at from hindsight, the most unusual feature of Beecher's evangelical liberalism was the tremendous emphasis on nurturing, supporting, and reassuring the anxieties of the Victorian public. The core of the faith rested upon the assumption of God's overwhelming love for man. Over and over Beecher stressed the supportive qualities of faith. Through all troubles and disappointments, men and women could always fall back on their faith in Christ. As he declared on one occasion, "Christ came to save, to rescue, and by his vicarious suffering to redeem them [the people] from their wrong-doing." Or on another, "Not only does God think of us constantly, and love us steadfastly, but there is a healing, curative nature forever outworking from the divine mind upon ours, even though we may not cooperate voluntarily with His will." [28]

Though Beecher's position was sometimes gushy and sentimental, his liberal Protestant faith was not naïve or uncritical. Beecher was aware of the flaws in men, and of the temptations, cheating, and abuse in the world. He did not excuse these actions; rather, he placed the vices and abuses in a context of hope. Things would get better, not by overlooking people's flaws, but by removing them. Beecher, as his sermons attest, was also aware of his own shortcomings—his inability

to visit members of his congregation and to deal with them on a personal level—and he never excused these defects. Like his liberal Protestant faith, which demanded constant self-scrutiny and self-awareness,
he recognized his problems and struggled to deal with them, resting
his efforts on his faith in God's supportive love. This stress on overwhelming, selfless, restorative love as the basis of Christian morality
was enormously appealing to a generation of middle-class Americans
who were as preoccupied with failure as they were with success. Conscious of the financial and social innovations that were taking place
and caught in a boom-and-bust cycle that was to dominate the business
world for the rest of the century, middle-class Victorians found Beecher's message vastly reassuring.

Once Beecher had set forth and defined his own faith in a personal
God whose love was ever present to support mankind, he went on to
draw out the implications of his argument. One implication was that
the meaning and significance of revelation had to be radically altered.
Creeds and dogmas were reduced to guidelines for the individual, and
biblical accounts were considered authoritative only if judged by historical and scientific standards and found to be authentic. A second implication was that, despite occasional reverses, mankind had a glorious
future. "I believe that the human race is being swept in vast aerial
circles toward better climes and nobler societies. . . ," he declared.
"The irresistible power of God is carrying the universe upward and onward to its final perfection and glorification."[29] But the most important implication was that a living faith would bring with it a commitment to social reforms and a reformation of public morality.

Beecher's major contribution to evangelical liberalism was his attempt to redefine the social role of the ministers and the churches. As
he emphasized again and again, the clergy had a duty to speak out on
social issues. "The pulpit is relatively losing ground," he admitted to
his congregation. "You know, as well as I, that the Sabbath day does
not draw forth for religious worship the whole population, nor one
quarter of it. . . . It is not because there is a want of learning, nor because there is a want of sincerity among ministers; it is because they
are handcuffed and manacled with the idea that on Sunday they must
not talk about anything but doctrines and religious truisms. . . ."[30]
Beecher's liberalism was practical and full of common sense. It was
designed to provide a complete ethical system for everyday life.

Beecher was euphoric about the power of religion. If allowed to permeate all aspects of life, it would transform the nature of human relationships. Beecher argued that religion "puts men into connection with God; it brings them into harmonious relations to their fellow-men; it gives them direction for the achievement of duty; . . . it makes them love whatever is good, and abhor whatever is bad; it inspires reverence, obedience, and love toward God and toward our superiors among men; it inculcates justice, mercy, and benevolence toward our fellow-men; it imbues us with courage, with patience, with contentment; it commands industry, frugality, and hospitality; it enjoins honesty, truthfulness, uprightness, simplicity, and integrity."[31] As is evident from these comments, Beecher's religious liberalism was designed to stabilize interpersonal relationships in a society that was becoming increasingly complex and specialized. It encouraged obedience to authority in return for justice and benevolence from those who were in positions of control. It was a calculated attempt to humanize and soften the expansion of industrial capitalism.

Beecher explained his new attitude toward the ministry most systematically in 1872 when he was invited to the divinity school at Yale to give a series of lectures that had been endowed in his father's name. In these lectures he reasserted his distrust of the city, his belief in nature, his emphasis on school and family, his concern for social issues, and his stress on "love as the central element in the Christian ministry." He also urged the students to study the latest developments in science and put them to use. "You cannot go back," he warned, "and become apostles of the dead past, drivelling after ceremonies, and letting the world do the thinking and studying. There must be a new spirit infused into the ministry."[32]

Basic to his new conception of the ministry was his conviction that the clergyman must know and be directly involved in the everyday affairs of his congregation. The minister needed to understand what his parishioners' lives were like and needed to have a fund of illustrations and examples to communicate his ideals. Describing the minister's role as a vehicle for civilization and moral improvement, Beecher continually stressed the wonderful capacity of God's love to heal, restore, uplift, and inspire. The ministry, in his view, was the highest form of service to mankind. It was a noble, idealistic vision of a clergy committed to social action and eager to serve the cause of social justice—

a vision that inspired younger ministers like Washington Gladden and educators like G. Stanley Hall, the psychologist who was to become the president of Clark University.

The lectures were a big success, and the divinity school invited him back for a second year. "My lectures at New Haven have been a famous hit," he exulted to his wife. "The air is ablaze with enthusiasm. They will soon be published in the *Christian Union*."[33] This sentiment was echoed by a writer in the Brooklyn *Daily Eagle* who declared that Beecher's "manly utterance of whatever he believes, no matter who may differ with him, is what constitutes his value to the city and to society at large. . . ."[34]

Beecher's success as an author and newspaper editor was matched by his popularity as a minister. During the decade following the Civil War, his own church grew rapidly. In 1862 the converted members of his congregation numbered 1,460 and contributed $18,443 in pew rents. In the next ten years, the congregation almost doubled in size, adding 1,068 new members and pledging $59,762 in contributions. During these years, the church purchased a new organ, enlarged its Bible and Sunday School classes, established an employment bureau for young men, supported two mission churches, and hired an assistant minister to make pastoral visits and call upon the sick. At a time when the average Congregational church in the country had less than a hundred communicants, Beecher's church with nearly three thousand stood out as an extraordinary exception.[35]

The success of Plymouth Church derived in part from its fortunate location. During a period in which the city of Brooklyn was being flooded by immigrants and many older residents were relocating their homes, the area around Plymouth Church remained upper middle class. Thus, although the congregation increased rapidly in size, the composition of the church changed only slightly. A few rich merchants joined the congregation, like Henry W. Sage, but they were exceptions, and the vast majority of the members remained, as before, moderately well-to-do business and professional people and their families. Because the average church member was not wealthy, the congregation in 1859 had failed to raise $175,000 to construct a larger building, even though a plot of land had been chosen and plans drawn up. Nevertheless, while the rapid increase in membership in the 1860s did not make the church rich, it did substantially improve the church's financial position, and this increase in income enabled it to undertake a wider range of benevolent and missionary activities.[36]

Despite the initial successes of his own church and the popularity of his new books and periodicals, Beecher's evangelical liberalism was not without weaknesses. In his efforts to mediate between inherited Christianity and modern thought, Beecher and the liberals succeeded in making their religious doctrines more relevant to the needs of the times, but in the process they blurred the distinction between religious ideals and the norms of society. The effectiveness of evangelical liberalism was further limited by its essentially middle-class point of view, which restricted its call for social action by seeing reform efforts as largely the responsibility of the individual. Although evangelical liberalism's commitment to social justice was notable, its adherents were rather ineffective in their efforts to help the poor.[37] Beecher himself recognized that "our churches are largely for the mutual insurance of prosperous families, and not for the upbuilding of the great underclass of humanity," yet his own church still failed to help the poor.[38] As the historian of Plymouth Church admitted in 1873, "it is a remarkable coincidence that both the Bethel and Navy missions have, from time to time, removed farther and farther away from the locations in which they were originally established, until they are now situated in very respectable neighborhoods, while the vicinities which they were originally intended to enlighten are still wallowing in darkness."[39]

If Beecher himself had difficulty in living up to the ideals he set before himself, he must nevertheless still be recognized as one of the earliest and most conspicuous spokesmen for the liberal point of view. In his *Yale Lectures on Preaching*, as well as in sermons, newspaper editorials, and other writings, Beecher succeeded in dramatizing some of the most pressing social and intellectual problems that the churches faced in the post–Civil War period. Although his own efforts to modify traditional religious beliefs and to aid the poor were sometimes misguided and inept, the fact that he perceived the crucial issues and took steps to meet them clearly makes him one of the earliest leaders of evangelical liberalism. In his own good-natured and forceful way, therefore, Beecher set a precedent and planted the seeds in the 1860s that were later to flower into the Social Gospel.

NOTES

1. Daniel W. Howe, "American Victorianism as a Culture," *American Quarterly*, XXVII (Dec., 1975), 514–17; Henry Nash Smith, " 'The Scribbling Women' and the Cosmic Success Story," *Critical Inquiry* (Sept., 1974), 45–70.

2. Beecher's nonpolitical articles were gathered into five books: *Star Papers: or Experiences of Art and Nature* (1858), *Plain and Pleasant Talk about Fruits, Flowers, and Farming* (1859), *Life Thoughts* (1860), *Eyes and Ears* (1862), and *Royal Truths* (1866). His political writings were published in 1863 under the title *Freedom and War: Discourses on Topics Suggested by the Times*.

3. H. W. Beecher to E. C. Stanton, Jan. 22, 1867, Huntington Library.

4. Robert Bonner to H. W. Beecher, n.d., Yale MSS.

5. H. W. Beecher to Mrs. Emily Drury, March 12, 1868, Schlesinger Library.

6. Robert Bonner to H. W. Beecher, Nov. 15, Aug. 2, 1867, Yale MSS.

7. Eunice Beecher to H. W. Beecher, Oct. 26, 1867, Yale MSS.

8. H. W. Beecher to Lyman Abbott (typed copy), Dec. 7, 1867, Yale MSS.

9. John Raymond Howard, *Remembrance of Things Past* (New York, 1925), 233.

10. Frank L. Mott, *History of American Magazines* (Cambridge, Mass., 1939), II, 373.

11. Edward Beecher to H. W. Beecher, Dec. 23, 1867, Yale MSS; see also T. Tilton, *Sanctum Sanctorum or Proof-Sheets from an Editor's Table* (New York, 1870), 161–62.

12. H. W. Beecher to Edward Beecher, Dec. 27, 1867, Yale MSS.

13. H. W. Beecher to Theodore Tilton, June 3, 1867, quoted in *Theodore Tilton against Henry Ward Beecher: Verbatim Report of the Trial . . .* (New York, 1875), I, 482.

14. Howard, *Remembrance of Things Past*, 236, 256.

15. H. B. Stowe to H. W. Beecher, n.d., Yale MSS.

16. Howard, *Remembrance of Things Past*, 257.

17. Mott, *History of American Magazines*, II, 423.

18. Howard, *Remembrance of Things Past*, 244; Brooklyn *Daily Eagle*, Jan. 13, 1870.

19. For my account of "evangelical liberalism" I am indebted to Sydney E. Ahlstrom's *A Religious History of the American People* (New Haven, 1972). Winthrop Hudson, *Religion in America* (New York, 1965), 269, correctly sees Beecher as the spokesman rather than the theologian of this movement. Several terms have been used to label those clergy, whom I call evangelical liberals, following the usage adopted by Ahlstrom. Charles H. Hopkins, in his book, *The Rise of the Social Gospel in American Protestantism, 1865–1915* (New Haven, 1940), 19, refers to them as "enlightened conservatives." For a good general discussion of theological developments in this period see Hudson, *Religion in America*, chap. 11.

20. Howe, "American Victorianism as a Culture," 516.

21. H. W. Beecher to ?, Jan. 10, 1868, quoted in New York *Times*, Jan. 13, 1868.

22. H. W. Beecher to Mrs. Emily Drury, April 20, 1859, Schlesinger Library.

23. H. W. Beecher, *Norwood* (New York, 1868), 59–60, 223. For a detailed analysis of the religious themes in *Norwood*, see William G. McLoughlin, *The Meaning of Henry Ward Beecher* (New York, 1970), chap. 3.

24. H. W. Beecher, *Royal Truths* (Boston, 1866), 40.

25. Beecher, *Norwood*, 187; see also Carroll S. Rosenberg, "Protestants and Five Pointers: The Five Points House of Industry," *New York Historical Society Quarterly*, XLVII (Oct., 1964), 326–47.

26. H. W. Beecher, *Sermons by Henry Ward Beecher* (New York, 1869), I, 105–6.

27. H. W. Beecher to Rev. S. S. Martyn, Feb. 18, 1871 (copy), Yale MSS.

28. H. W. Beecher, *Sermons*, II, 168, 46.

29. H. W. Beecher, "Possibilities of the Future," *Plymouth Pulpit*, X, 172.

30. *Plymouth Pulpit*, II, 174–75.

31. H. W. Beecher, *Royal Truths*, 258.

32. H. W. Beecher, *Yale Lectures on Preaching* (New York, 1872, first ser.), 88, 237.

33. H. W. Beecher to Eunice Beecher, Feb. 26, 1872, Yale MSS.

34. Brooklyn *Daily Eagle*, Jan. 5, 1871.

35. Noyes L. Thompson, *The History of Plymouth Church* (New York, 1873), chaps. 10 and 11.

36. *Ibid.*, 36.

37. Robert T. Handy, ed., *The Social Gospel in America, 1870–1920* (New York, 1966), 6–10.

38. H. W. Beecher, "Liberty in the Churches," in *Plymouth Pulpit*, II, 209, as quoted in Sidney Mead, *The Lively Experiment* (New York, 1963), 161.

39. Thompson, *History of Plymouth Church*, 154.

10

The Famous Brooklyn Scandal

By 1872, Henry Ward Beecher was clearly recognized as one of the
most popular and respected clergymen in the nation. For twenty-five
years he had been the pastor of the large and successful Plymouth Congregational Church in Brooklyn and he was generally considered to be,
as *Harper's Weekly* commented, "the most brilliant preacher who has
ever appeared in this country." [1] During his years at Plymouth Church,
Beecher had also attained prominence as a reformer who had cam-
paigned on behalf of the temperance, antislavery, and women's rights
crusades. By 1872 he was nationally recognized as a major spokesman
for Victorian morality. As *Scribner's Monthly* declared in an article
entitled "Mr. Beecher as a Social Force," "his style is himself. . . .
It is unconstrained, free, full, flowing, exuberant, and spontaneous.
. . . [Yet] with all his ideality, he never ceases to teach common
sense." [2]

Prosperous and self-confident, Beecher in 1872 seemed to personify
the Victorian faith in cultural achievements and fixed moral standards.
Yet two years later, Theodore Tilton stunned the nation by bringing
suit against Beecher for having had an affair with Tilton's wife. Tilton's accusation created a sensation, and the trial that followed, which

was covered by the country's leading newspapers and dragged on for half a year, became more than a public scandal; it became a test of public confidence in the Victorian cultural ethos that Beecher represented. If a leading spokesman for Victorian morality was a fraud and a charlatan, then how could anyone still believe in the cultural system he espoused? Thus, the heated controversy over Beecher's innocence or guilt, which attracted vigorous partisans on either side, became a *cause célèbre*, a social debate of unusual importance.

The story of the scandal most properly begins with the personal feuds and struggles for power that took place in the women's rights movement in the preceding two decades. Beecher had long been interested in women's suffrage because he believed that giving women the vote would help redress women's legal inequality. Despite his belief in legal equality, however, Beecher had hesitated to speak out in behalf of women's rights because he feared that doing so might destroy their position within the family. During the 1850s his views on women's rights were dominated by his sister Catharine's belief that the true role of women was to act as "the conservators of the domestic state, the guardians and developers of the human body in infancy, and the educators of the human mind."[3] Like Catharine, he believed that although agitation for women's suffrage was not wrong in principle, it was impractical given the current attitudes in the country on that subject.

In the decade before the Civil War, Beecher had gradually modified his views and in February, 1860, he gave a major speech on women's suffrage at Cooper Institute in New York, Beecher began his address by telling the audience that he had come not to speak about women's rights in general or to debate the question of the equality of the sexes, but rather to discuss whether females should have the right to vote. Women, he argued, should have the privilege of expressing their own gifts. Giving them the vote would not unsex them but would instead make them more domestic. "A woman is better fitted for home who is also fit for something else . . . ," he commented. "No one is a better friend for being ignorant. No one is a more tender companion for being weak and helpless. Our homes demand great hearts and strong heads; but these need the culture of open air and free heavens. They are not of the hotbed or the conservatory."[4] Women deserved the vote to allow them to exercise their potential talents. Giving women the right to vote, furthermore, would help to reform society. "A vote is the simplest, the neatest, the most unobtrusive thing imaginable," he commented. "This white slip of paper drops as quietly and gently as a snow-flake on the top of the Alps; but, like them, when collected, they descend like avalanches. Woe be to the evil which they strike!"[5] The beauty of this argument was that it recommended giving the vote to women on the most conservative grounds possible—on the grounds that the vote would refine public sentiment, cleanse the political process, and, most important of all, educate women to be better mothers and housekeepers. Thus it strengthened the Victorian vision of the home as a place of purity and refinement, and served to make the plea for women's rights respectable.

During the Civil War, Beecher continued to work for the women's rights movement by raising funds for Susan B. Anthony's Women's National Loyal League, and when the conflict ended, he supported Theodore Tilton's suggestion that the antislavery and women's rights reformers unite their efforts and form an American Equal Rights Association.[6] Explaining his views in a major address at the National Woman's Rights Convention in May, 1866, he argued that all people, regardless of race or sex, should share the same civil rights since they all were equal in the sight of God. "The truth that I have to urge. . . ," he declared, is "that *suffrage is the inherent right of mankind.*"[7]

Unfortunately, this view was not shared by many abolitionists who believed that the needs of the Negro were more urgent than those of women. The American Antislavery Society thus refused to join ranks with the women's rights movement and the feminist leaders were forced to set up an Equal Rights Association by themselves. During the next three years while Beecher was fighting with the Radicals, writing his novel, and working on his life of Christ, the women's rights movement underwent a great expansion. Conventions were held throughout the country, and local associations were organized in many states. In the summer of 1867 the Equal Rights Association sent speakers to Kansas to work for an amendment to the state constitution giving women the right to vote.[8]

The rapid growth of the women's rights movement created numerous strains and personal antagonisms. In Kansas, Elizabeth Cady Stanton and Susan B. Anthony aroused hostility when they invited George Francis Train, a wealthy eccentric, to join their cause. Train alienated the New England reformers because he was a racist and had been a

Copperhead during the war. As Mary A. Livermore wrote to her friend Olympia Brown, "Geo. Francis Train cannot be other than a mill-stone around the neck of any cause." [9] The New England reformers were also annoyed by Stanton's newspaper, *The Revolution*, which extolled the superior virtues of women and argued that "men are better fitted than women for all the drudgery of domestic life." [10] In November, 1868—angered by the outspoken and aggressive views of their New York sisters—Julia Ward Howe, Lucy Stone, Thomas W. Higginson, and James Freeman Clarke broke away from the Equal Rights Association and created their own New England Woman Suffrage Association. [11]

Discontent between the two wings of the women's rights movement was further heightened in February of the following year when Congress passed the Fifteenth Amendment. Since the amendment lacked a provision for female suffrage, Stanton and her followers opposed it. The New Englanders, however, agreed with Clara Barton, who wrote that "if the door was not wide enough for all at once—and one must wait, or *all* must wait, then I for one was willing that the old scarred slave limp through before me." [12]

While the controversy in the women's rights movement was brewing, Beecher maintained a neutral position. Though he was friendly with both wings of the movement, however, he had greater sympathy for the conservative aims of the New Englanders. When Lucretia Mott, president of the Equal Rights Association, argued at the association's meeting in Brooklyn in May, 1869, for "dignity and soberness of speech," Beecher could only agree and add that "generations must pass before we should understand the full meaning of 'women's rights,' that is, of the right of woman to be a woman in public as well as in private." [13]

In May, 1869, the animosity between the New England and New York wings of the women's rights movement reached the boiling point and the movement split apart. Stanton, Anthony, and the New York reformers withdrew from the Equal Rights Association shortly after the national convention and formed their own organization, the National Woman Suffrage Association. They were prompted to take this action because of personal rivalries, disillusionment with the Fifteenth Amendment, and their differing conceptions of the scope of the women's rights crusade. More concerned than the New Englanders with organizing working women, liberalizing state divorce laws, and criticizing the conservative attitudes of churches, they believed that the only way they could carry out these aims was to create their own association.[14]

During the early months of 1869, when the antagonisms within the women's rights movement were coming to a head, Beecher managed to remain aloof from the controversy. He carefully stayed away from the debate among the feminists and devoted his spare time and energy to writing his life of Christ. Late in August his attention was distracted, but only momentarily, from this work by the uproar that his sister Harriet created when she wrote an article for the *Atlantic Monthly* accusing Lord Byron, the poet, of incest. A close friend of the late Lady Byron, Harriet published her article to disprove the claim of a recent book that Byron's early death was hastened by the cold, mercenary heart of his wife. Flushed with indignation over the assault on a friend's reputation, Harriet accepted Lady Byron's version of the story without considering whether the older woman might have been using the story to vindicate herself.[15]

Harriet's intemperate article met with widespread criticism in the press. Theodore Tilton commented sarcastically in *The Independent* that "Mrs. Stowe . . . has a weakness for ladies of title," and other periodicals supported his views.[16] Despite the widespread public criticism of Harriet, Henry quickly came to his sister's defense and wrote her a strong letter of support. "I have seen none, of any weight," he asserted encouragingly, "that has seemed even to *see* that it was a question between the saintly purity of a Christian wife and the genius and brilliance of a powerful, but grossly wicked man."[17] Beecher defended his sister without hesitation because he found it impossible to doubt her sincerity. So much did they trust each other that neither Harriet nor Henry was ever able to question the other's motives. Even after the controversy over Lord Byron had died down, Harriet continued to believe that her stand on that issue had been justified. Moreover, she never forgave Tilton for his attack on her character.

Though Harriet spent much of the fall of 1869 defending her views about Byron, she still found time to become a vice-president of the Connecticut Woman Suffrage Association. Her interest in this organization had been aroused by her half-sister, Isabella Beecher Hooker, a devoted feminist and a member of the executive committee of the state women's rights association who went further than demanding the vote and argued that women were intellectually and morally superior to men.[18] In October, perhaps at the request of his sisters, Henry delivered the principal address at the meeting of the Connecticut Woman Suffrage Association in Hartford and insisted that women should have the right to vote and to hold office.[19] Several weeks later he repeated these sentiments at the meeting of the Brooklyn Equal Rights Association.

It was at the Brooklyn meeting that Beecher learned from Lucy Stone that the New England feminists planned to create their own suffrage association at a convention to be held in Cleveland in November.[20] Lucy Stone at that time had also inquired whether Beecher would be interested in holding a position in the new national organization, and Beecher agreed to serve if needed. Beecher was the obvious choice for such a position. He was a well-known public figure and had worked hard to make the movement respectable. As the head of the new organization, he could publicize its views and encourage men of substance to join the crusade. When the convention of New England feminists met a month later, Mary Livermore arose at the beginning of the second day to announce that she had received a letter from Beecher consenting to be president. She then nominated him and he was elected.[21]

The election of Beecher to the presidency of the American Woman Suffrage Association symbolized the search for respectability of the New England feminists. It was a direct affront to the philosophy of Elizabeth Cady Stanton's New York organization (the National Woman Suffrage Association), which excluded men on the grounds that they hindered more than they helped the movement. Beecher's election reassured the public that the new organization wanted the support of men and was not anticlerical. And it marked the organization's determination to stress the virtues of fidelity, decency, and propriety.

It is interesting to speculate about why Beecher consented to be an officer in the new organization. In the past, he had deliberately avoided joining associations, in order to preserve the independence of his views. As *Harper's Weekly* had declared earlier, "Mr. Beecher is identified with various causes, but his independence remains untouched, and he works in his own way."[22] Perhaps he consented now because the new organization was similar to the pre-war benevolent societies. Like these societies, the American Woman Suffrage Association drew most of its members from New England and held its annual meeting in New York during the "May Anniversaries." Or perhaps he joined because he realized that the presidency of the new organization was a token position that would add to his reputation without burdening him with too much responsibility. In either case, Beecher was to have little control over the association's policies during the next few years. He seldom wrote letters to suffragists, and there is little evidence that he had much say in the position that the society took. The influence that he did exert on the women's rights movement came from a different direction. Chosen to give the association the appearance of respectability, Beecher had precisely the opposite effect, for he soon became involved in a public scandal.

The scandal arose from the murder of Albert D. Richardson in the office of the New York *Tribune* in December, 1869, by Daniel McFarland, who was jealous of Richardson's attentions to his divorced wife. The dying Richardson was rushed to the nearby Astor Hotel, where he stated that his last wish was to be married to the former Mrs. McFarland. Someone located Beecher, who was nearby, and he hurried to Richardson's bedside to perform the ceremony. Horace Greeley was the witness, and the service took but a few minutes. Beecher looked upon it simply as performing his ministerial duty and thought little about the incident until the next day.[23]

The wedding aroused a storm of protest from the press. Even the sympathetic Brooklyn *Daily Eagle* conceded that "Mr. Beecher probably erred in consenting to marry these people."[24] Other commentators were more biased and saw the incident as typical of the free-love advocates within the women's rights movement. Perhaps typical was the remark of George T. Strong, a prominent New York lawyer, that "it seems a rule that these popular sensational 'free thinkers' of the pulpit and platform, such as Beecher, Frothingham, Bellows, and others, have a screw loose somewhere."[25]

The public outcry increased even more when it was learned that McFarland's wife had obtained her divorce in Indiana, a state whose laws were not recognized by New York. When this information came to light, Beecher acknowledged that he had legally erred in marrying the couple, but he refused to repent for his actions. At his usual Friday evening prayer meeting, he declared, much to the dismay of some members of his congregation, that he did not wish his church to apologize for him. "If you do not agree with me on this matter," he commented, "then rise up and say so." No one dared to respond.[26]

Fortunately for Beecher, when McFarland's murder trial began a few weeks later, the public soon focused its attention on the trial itself, and most people forgot about Beecher's connection with the case. Those who remembered it probably agreed with the Brooklyn *Daily Eagle*'s conclusion that "none but a sincere, well-meaning man could be so rash, and so often allow himself to be used, for no profit to himself, by more designing people of both sexes. Beecher is all impulse, too warm-hearted to be prudent in his actions or logical in his ideas."[27] This judgment was readily accepted by the New England suffragists, who had feared that the public outcry over the incident would weaken their movement.

Six months after the scandal, Beecher again resumed his activity in behalf of the women's rights movement. In the meantime, Elizabeth Cady Stanton's National Woman Suffrage Association had rescinded its ban against male members and elected Theodore Tilton as its president. This aroused hopes that despite the personal rivalry between the two national organizations they might work together. Beecher himself favored such a plan, but was pessimistic about its chances of success. "The fact is," he wrote to Thomas W. Higginson in April, "the world does not work so smoothly as it would if it had been made on a different pattern. . . . I agree with you," he continued, "that our organization of three or four men as a [part?] of a National Society is ludicrous. But every one works in his own way—and so let Theodore, and Susan, and the rest go on; *only I won't* quarrel with them, and if you do next May, prepare to be talked to like a father."[28] It was an easygoing tolerant attitude, characteristic of Beecher's desire to avoid conflict and his willingness to work with others whose philosophy was different from his own.

The Brooklyn Equal Rights Association provided a meeting place for the discussion of cooperation between the two national women's rights organizations. Both Beecher and Theodore Tilton attended its sessions and Elizabeth Tilton acted as corresponding secretary.[29] When the two national organizations held their annual meetings in New York in May, the National Woman Suffrage Association appointed a seven-member committee to discuss the possibilities of a merger

with the New Englanders and Tilton wrote Beecher a letter express-
ing his organization's views. Later in the month both Elizabeth Cady
Stanton and Lucy Stone spoke before the Brooklyn Equal Rights
Association.[30]

Despite the overtures for a union between the two organizations,
they failed to resolve their differences. Lucy Stone never warmed to
her New York rival, and she refused to accept Elizabeth Cady Stanton's insistence on liberalizing state divorce laws, organizing working
women, and running for public office. The only dialogue that did exist
—that between the two presidents—was eventually silenced by a personal dispute that later broke out between them. The effectiveness of
the women's rights crusade was thus limited for more than two decades
largely by differences in philosophy and by personal rivalries among its
leadership.[31]

The crusade was also hindered in its early years by the social pressure that was exerted on some of its leaders. Beecher himself ran into
strong opposition from his family. Eunice Beecher intensely disliked
Stanton and Tilton, and refused to allow them in her house. She also
opposed her husband's goal of trying "to secure the confidence of the
thoughtful and morally conservative" for the movement.[32] She preferred to see women gain power through their role as mothers and
moral instructors for the home. Catharine Beecher created even more
trouble for her brother. When Henry argued at the National Convention
in May that giving females the vote would not "detract from the beauty
of women's character," Catharine insisted upon sitting on the same
platform and having her opposing remarks read by Henry Blackwell.[33]

Yet of all Beecher's sisters, it was Harriet who created the most
trouble. Harriet had recently read the novels of George Sand and was
shocked by their contents. There was a danger, she feared, that the
illicit views in these novels would be reprinted in *The Revolution* by
"Susan Anthony and other honest old maids who know no more evil
than an old country minister's horse."[34] Harriet wrote to her brother
asking him to expose the danger of these French novelists by printing
in the *Christian Union* an editorial signed by him though written by
her. "For if a *woman* undertakes to utter a protest when licentiousness
is concerned," Harriet confided in an obvious reference to her Lord
Byron troubles, "she is overwhelmed with a deluge of filth."[35]

Although Harriet was a member of the Connecticut Woman Suffrage

Association, she was at heart as conservative in her views on the women question as her sister Catharine was. She opposed her brother's proposal to give women the vote, on the grounds that men were more powerful and should therefore assert their "superior moral force." "The women's rights folks are wrong on one point," she wrote to her brother. "The man *is* and ought to be the head of the woman. He ought to be her head morally as well as physically and intellectually. . . ." "Thank heaven," she added, "*you* can speak on this subject with authority since you are and always have been blameless, since your youth was as pure as a woman's and the seed of your mother remained in you."[36]

Harriet's opposition to giving women the vote was based not only on her belief in male superiority, but also on her conviction that to allow women to visit the polls would undermine their place in the home. The real interest of the woman was in the household, she wrote in the revised edition of *The American Woman's Home* published in 1869. The duty of the woman was to teach her children the Christian virtues of self-sacrifice and self-denial. To take this woman from her children and allow her to participate in politics, Harriet argued, would destroy the purity and refinement of the home.

While Harriet was thus urging her brother to take a more conservative stand on woman's rights, Isabella Beecher Hooker, Beecher's other sister, expressed her hope that he would continue his earlier efforts. Beecher agreed with her on the importance of giving women the vote and wrote to her that "you know my sympathy with you. Probably you and I are nearer together than any of our family."[37] As the year wore on, however, Isabella's opinions became more extreme. In 1870 she went to Washington for a women's rights convention and watched Victoria Woodhull, the spiritualist and advocate of free love, present her suffragist petition to Congress. Shortly thereafter, Isabella became a convert to spiritualism. From then on her brother Henry found her eccentric views increasingly distasteful.[38]

Caught between the divergent views of his three sisters and the growing hostility between the two women's rights organizations, Beecher gradually curtailed his activities in behalf of women's suffrage. As one who had always disliked factional disputes and controversy, he began to look upon the whole movement to give women the vote as a utopian crusade incapable of realization given the existing state of public opinion. Nevertheless, despite all his efforts to the contrary, he soon became enmeshed in another controversy that threatened to ruin his career and discredit the women's rights movement altogether.

Involved as Beecher was in a variety of causes ranging from judicial and educational reform to support for the YMCA and the temperance movement, it was easy for him to reduce his involvement in the women's rights crusade and turn his attention to other issues.[39] The immediate reason for phasing out his participation in the women's rights crusade was the need to prepare for Plymouth Church's festive celebration of its first twenty-five years of service to the community.[40] In recognition of Beecher's prominence as a preacher and his service as a pastor, Plymouth Church decided in 1872 to hold a week-long Silver Anniversary celebration. Although Beecher was embarrassed by the proceedings and tried to focus attention on the church rather than on himself, the celebration, which was widely advertised in the press, became a public testimonial to honor his name. As one of the members of the church stated, "yesterday morning the orders were that we were not to glorify the pastor; I do not know but we had better issue orders the other way."[41] The ceremonies, which lasted for five days, were closed by Beecher with a brief statement of his ideals. "I have endeavored to preach Jesus Christ in all His aspects of mercy to sinful men," he asserted, "and I have never found the time when this message was not the wisdom of God and the power of God unto salvation. To my thought, the whole universe revolves about that blessed Center—that love of God which has in it creation, sustentation, redemption, and everlasting life."[42] The church members ended the week proud of their accomplishments and renewed in their faith.

One month later, Victoria Woodhull shattered the complacency of Plymouth Church by publishing an article in her *Weekly* that accused Beecher of having committed adultery with Elizabeth Tilton, the wife of the editor of *The Independent*. At first, no one could believe the story. Woodhull was a radical women's rights leader who was known for her scandalous reputation. She not only had run for the presidency of the United States, but had also proclaimed herself an advocate of free love, "with an inalienable, constitutional, and natural right to love whom I may, to love as long or as short a period as I can, to change that love everyday if I please!"[43] When she accused Beecher of adultery, therefore, the general public ignored her statements. "There is no better test of purity and true goodness," declared *Scribner's Monthly*, "than reluctance to think evil of one's neighbor, and absolute incapacity to believe an evil report about good men except upon the most trustworthy testimony."[44] The public followed this advice by treating Victoria Woodhull's statements as the malicious libel of a demented woman, and she was later jailed for publishing obscene material. When she was freed and tried to elaborate on her charges against Beecher in a lecture in Boston, the governor himself intervened to prevent her from speaking. Neither Beecher nor Tilton, following the advice of friends, made any reply to Woodhull's accusations, and the scandal died down as quickly as it had begun.[45]

Yet rumors and gossip continued to circulate. Speculation was further increased in April, 1873, when an agreement to refrain from spreading rumors, signed by Beecher, Henry C. Bowen, and Theodore Tilton, was published in the Brooklyn *Daily Eagle*. Nevertheless, the larger daily papers still refused to investigate the stories. Typical was the statement of the New York *Times* that "some very indiscreet friends of Rev. Henry Ward Beecher have obtruded on public notice some inconsequential documents bearing upon a very disgusting controversy."[46] After the publication of these documents, Beecher for the first time broke his silence to assert that the stories were "grossly untrue" and "utterly false." Anyone who had any letters bearing on the controversy, he declared, had his "cordial consent" to publish them.[47]

Because most of the rumors obviously came from Tilton, Plymouth Church dropped him from its rolls in October, 1873. Normally, individuals who were dropped from the rolls of a Congregational church had to appear first before an examining committee and be given the opportunity to defend themselves. But in Tilton's case, the church hoped to take care of the matter as quietly as possible. Since Tilton had not attended the church for four years, they used this fact as a technicality to remove him from the rolls. This aroused the antagonism of two neighboring churches that believed Tilton had not been given the opportunity to state his case. After several months of angry accusations, the other churches called an Advisory Council, which condemned the action of Plymouth Church but did not see the offense as sufficiently reprehensible to remove it from the local congregational association. The matter might have ended here had not Leonard Bacon, a well-known congregational minister from New Haven, Connecticut, delivered a series of lectures in June, 1874, describing Tilton as the villain who caused all the problems. Tilton asserted his innocence and demanded an examination before Plymouth Church. Beecher then established a special committee to hear both sides in the case and offer a decision. The proceedings of the Plymouth Church Examining Committee were closely followed in the press during July and August. Most observers agreed at the end of the investigation with the editors of the *Congregationalist*, who asserted that the investigation renewed their faith in the pastor of Plymouth Church.[48] Convinced justifiably that much evidence had been withheld, Tilton brought suit against Beecher in July, accusing him of adultery and demanding one hundred thousand dollars in damages.

The trial that followed began in January, 1875, and created a public sensation. For the next six months, it was covered in minute detail in the press. Charges and countercharges were traded back and forth by the litigants, and all the details in the sordid affair were made public. Much of the testimony was contradictory and open to different interpretations. Yet the evidence uncovered at the trial provides the best account of a controversy that still remains the source of disagreement among historians.[49]

From the opening day in the crowded room in the Brooklyn City Court, the nation avidly followed the proceedings. Beecher was defended by William Maxwell Evarts, John K. Porter, Benjamin Tracy, and Thomas G. Shearman. The plaintiff had the services of William A. Beach, William Fullerton, Roger Pryor, and former judge Samuel B. Morris. Evarts was clearly the leading counsel for the defense. A tall, lean man with loosely brushed hair and light blue eyes, Evarts was generally adknowledged to be one of the foremost attorneys in the country. He had successfully defended President Andrew Johnson in his impeachment trial in 1868 and later had become the United States Attorney General. Since Evarts did not usually participate in trials of this nature, his presence created the impression that he had accepted the case because of personal sympathy for his client.

Evarts was ably assisted by former judge John K. Porter, a portly man with expansive gestures and a theatrical manner. Porter's impassioned denunciation of Tilton provided an interesting contrast to the cool, reasoned actions of Evarts. The background research for Beecher's defense was handled by Shearman and Tracy, members of Beecher's congregation, who served without fee.

Tilton's chief counsel was William A. Beach, a well-known lawyer who had gained fame in the Erie Railroad's suit againt Cornelius Vanderbilt and in the prosecution of the murderer of Jim Fisk.[50] Beach lacked Evarts's sense of humor, but he was his equal in arguing about the admissibility of evidence. Next to Beach, William Fullerton was the leading attorney for the plaintiff. A former judge, Fullerton was an elderly man whom many regarded as the leading cross-examiner of the day. His easygoing manner and excellent command of detail allowed him to confuse and discredit several of the defense's main witnesses.

The trial began on January 11, 1875. Only ticketholders were admitted to the small court room, and hundreds of would-be spectators were turned away. Plymouth Church was well represented, and Beecher appeared in good spirits as he entered the courtroom with his wife. Judge Joseph Neilson called the court to order and Samuel B. Morris, counsel for Tilton, opened the proceedings by rising to deliver a lengthy speech. Notes in hand, he argued that Beecher had confessed to adultery long ago and that his actions since then, as seen through his correspondence, represented a vain attempt to cover up his guilt. The sternness of his comments threw a hush over the court and there was a moment of stunned silence when he ended. Before anyone could comment on the speech, Evarts rose and declared, "Your Honor, now that the trial is about to begin—would it not be well to have the tables arranged a little better?"[51] It was a clever move that cleared the air and foreshadowed the sophisticated manner in which Evarts was to handle the defense.

The first witness for the plaintiff was Frank Moulton, a friend of Tilton who had acted as an intermediary in the attempts to suppress the scandal. As the "mutual friend" of both parties, Moulton had retained in his possession all the major correspondence. His testimony, which lasted several weeks, covered the complex series of events that had taken place in the controversy between Tilton and Beecher.

Until the debates over Reconstruction, Beecher and Tilton had been the closest of friends. "The debt I owe you I can never pay," wrote Tilton to Beecher during the war. "My religious life, my intellectual development, my open door of opportunity for labor, my public reputation—all these, my dear friend, I owe in so great a degree to your own kindness that my gratitude cannot be written in words, but must be expressed only in love."[52]

Despite their mutual respect, the two men disagreed strongly over President Johnson's program in 1866. Tilton criticized Beecher editorially in *The Independent*, and the preacher responded by withdrawing his sermons from the paper. Yet, even though Tilton's admiration for Beecher was diminished, they remained on friendly terms. At Tilton's request, Beecher continued to call at the editor's home. Tilton was often away on lecture trips, and he repeatedly urged Beecher to look in on his family during his absence.

During the next few years, Beecher began to visit the Tiltons more frequently. Pressed by his literary and clerical duties, he found the Tilton household a place of refuge where he could relax and escape the incessant demands to aid various reform causes.

Tilton, in the meantime, became increasingly disillusioned with his pastor. As he later expressed it, "the fine gold of my idol gradually became dim."[53] Not only did he disagree politically with Beecher, but he also began to question Beecher's religious views. "The old religious teachings, the orthodox view, the dread of punishment, the atonement, have less and less power over my mind," he wrote in 1867.[54]

Because Tilton was editor of one of the largest religious journals in the country, such a change in views created a number of problems. Tilton's rejection of evangelical Christianity, as has been pointed out, provoked a storm of protest from the Congregational clergy, who put strong pressure on him to change his views. This created tension between Tilton and Bowen, the publisher of *The Independent*, who was more concerned with profits than with the religious position the paper took.

Even more important, Tilton's changed religious views distressed his wife and increased the friction that had always existed within his family. The marriage had gotten off to a rough start when they chose to live with Elizabeth Tilton's mother, Mrs. Morse. A domineering woman, Mrs. Morse continued to feel that she should have a say in running the Tilton family even after it had moved into a different house. When Tilton urged his wife to be more careful about spending money, Mrs. Morse protested that he was maltreating her daughter.

Added to the mother-in-law problem was a personality clash between husband and wife. Elizabeth Tilton was stubborn and proud, and she became distressed by her husband's frequent pleas for economy. In 1868, she wrote him a letter that said much about their relationship. "I cannot understand," she commented, "why the demons of weariness, fault-finding, ungenerous selfishness, and many hateful little spirits, perpetually hang about me when you are with me, to modify and lessen our possible enjoyment."[55]

Tilton was himself difficult to live with. Sensitive, egotistical, and intensely ambitious, he constantly worried about his position in the literary world. Behind the facade of the aggressive editor, Tilton was basically insecure. "I am a weak man, supposed to be strong," he wrote to his wife in 1866. "I cannot endure . . . mockery; it breeds agony in me."[56] As the pressure to get ahead increased during the 1860s Tilton became more anxious about his position. He was particularly worried when the western Congregationalists began to agitate for his removal. Bowen, who had never forgiven Beecher for withdrawing from *The Independent*, further troubled Tilton by suggesting that Beecher was behind the western agitation. But Mrs. Tilton doubted that this was so. "I think in reference to Oliver's opinion of Mr. B.," she wrote to her husband, "as his rewards were made to Mr. Bowen, and they are embittered toward one another, that what Mr. B. said of you may appear very different through the coloring Mr. Bowen may give it."[57]

Tilton did not agree. He was angry at Beecher because his wife accepted Beecher's religious views and rejected his own. Soon he became suspicious of his pastor's frequent visits to his house. Elizabeth Tilton, on her part, tried to quiet these fears. "About eleven o'clock today, Mr. B. called," she wrote to her husband who was away lecturing. "Now, beloved, let not even the shadow of a *shadow* fall on your dear heart because of this, now, henceforth or forever. He cannot by *any possibility* be much to me, since I have known you. . . . Do not think it audacious in me to say I am to him a good deal, a rest, and you can understand it if I appear even cheerful and helpful to him."[58]

In addition to his fears of his wife's loyalties, Tilton became worried after 1870 about his deteriorating financial position. Although he had increased his income by extending his lecture tours and taking on the editorship of the Brooklyn *Union*, he remained in debt. Moreover, he began to fear that he might have to sell his house.[59] Then, at the time when his finances seemed most unstable, Tilton learned that two new religious periodicals, *The Advance* in Chicago and the *Christian Union* in New York, had been established to compete with *The Independent*. Beecher, who several years earlier had confided to Tilton that he had given up the thought of starting a religious periodical, now seemed bent on destroying Tilton's literary career.[60]

To make matters worse, Bowen was becoming increasingly dissatisfied with the radical nature of Tilton's editorials. In July, Tilton refused to support in the Brooklyn *Union* the political candidate of Bowen's choice, and Bowen suggested that the only way he might get his way was to assume the editorship himself. In December, Bowen decided to make good his word. The immediate cause for this decision was Tilton's editorial of December 1, which argued for a liberalization of the divorce laws in New York State. The editorial declared: "Marriage without love is a sin against God—a sin which like other sins, is to be repented of, ceased from, and put away. No matter with what solemn ceremony the twain have been made one, yet when love departs, the marriage ceases and divorce begins. This is the essence of Christ's idea."[61] Because of this editorial, Tilton was accused in the public press of being an advocate of free love, and Bowen decided to remove him. Acting judiciously, Bowen informed Tilton that he wanted to edit *The Independent* himself next year. Tilton was given a gold watch for his services and a contract not only to edit the Brooklyn *Eagle*, but also to become a "special contributor" to *The Independent*.[62]

While Tilton was negotiating with Bowen about his new position, his troubles at home came to a head. Elizabeth Tilton left the house and went to live with her mother, sending Bessie Turner, a young woman who had been boarding with the Tilton family, to see Beecher. Bessie Turner explained to Beecher that Bessie had received immoral proposals from Tilton and that Mrs. Tilton wanted advice about separating from her husband. Beecher referred the matter to his wife, and she visited Mrs. Tilton to learn the "indelicate" facts. Eunice returned convinced that Mrs. Tilton should leave her husband. Beecher, who had other business to attend to, then wrote his wife a note to take to Mrs. Tilton saying, "I incline to think your view is right, and that a separation and settlement of support will be wisest and that, in his present desperate state, her presence near him is far more likely to produce hatred than her absence."[63] On December 24, while unsure of what action to take, pregnant and in ill health, Mrs. Tilton suffered a miscarriage.

Several days later Oliver Johnson, managing editor of *The Independent*, asked Tilton to see Bowen about rumors that were circulating about Tilton's marriage.[64] When Tilton met Bowen at *The Independent*'s office, he bitterly denied the accusations and then shocked Bowen with a different story. His wife, Tilton asserted, had admitted to him in July that she had committed adultery with Beecher. If this were true, Bowen exclaimed, Beecher should be driven from his pulpit. Exactly, answered Tilton, who sat down and penned a letter for Bowen to take to Beecher. The letter read: "I demand that for reasons which you explicitly understand, you immediately cease from the ministry of Plymouth Church, and that you quit the City of Brooklyn as a residence."[65]

Beecher was astonished and upset by Tilton's letter, and quickly asserted that its charges were a complete fabrication. He then informed Bowen of the general discontent within Tilton's family and repeated the stories that Bessie Turner had told him. Bowen was convinced. He returned to his office and canceled all his contracts with Tilton, leaving the editor without any job. Thus ended the first events in the long scandal. It is indeed curious that Tilton, who supposedly knew of Beecher's adulterous actions in July, waited six months before he accused him of the deed. But even more puzzling was Beecher's reaction in the succeeding weeks.

After learning about Beecher's negative response to his letter, Tilton obtained from his wife a written confession with which to confront the clergyman. He then sent Frank Moulton, a close friend, to bring Beecher to see him at Moulton's house. It was a Friday night and Beecher was supposed to lead his weekly prayer service, but he found a substitute and went with Moulton. When they met, Tilton was in a rage. He declared that Beecher had dishonored his family and ruined him. (At the trial Tilton asserted that he had then charged Beecher with adultery; Beecher replied that the accusation had been one of "improper proposals," a reference to his advice to Mrs. Tilton to separate from her husband.) As he spoke with Moulton and Beecher, Tilton nervously ripped up his wife's written confession.

Beecher then obtained permission from Tilton to see his wife and walked to Tilton's house with Moulton. During his interview with Elizabeth Tilton, who was still in bed recovering from her miscarriage, she gave him a retraction:

> Wearied by importunity and weakened by sickness, I gave a letter inculpating my friend Henry Ward Beecher, under assurances that would remove all difficulties between me and my husband. That letter I now revoke. I was persuaded—almost forced—when I was in a weakened state of mind. I regret it and recall all its statements.
>
> E. R. Tilton
>
> I desire to say explicitly, Mr. Beecher has never offered any improper solicitations, but has always treated me in a manner becoming a Christian and a gentleman.
>
> Elizabeth R. Tilton[66]

After Beecher left, Elizabeth wrote a letter of explanation to her husband:

> I desire to leave with you, before going to sleep, a statement that Mr. Henry Ward Beecher called upon me this evening, asked me if I would defend him against any accusations in a *council of ministers*. I replied solemnly that I would, in case the accuser was any other than my husband. He (H.W.B.) dictated a letter, which I copied as my own, to be used by him as against any other accuser except my husband. This letter was designed to vindicate Mr. Beecher against all other persons save only yourself. I was ready to give him this letter, because he said with pain, that my letter in your hands, addressed to him, dated December 29, "had struck him dead and ended his usefulness." God grant a speedy end to all further anxieties.[67]

The next day, when Tilton learned from his wife's note that she had given Beecher a letter retracting her confession, he immediately took steps to strengthen his case against the preacher. From his wife he obtained a third note declaring that she feared that her retraction might be used against her husband and asking Beecher to give it to Moulton for safekeeping. Moulton delivered this note to Beecher, who, after some hesitation, complied with its request. Beecher was by now confused and terribly upset. There seemed to be no way to pacify Tilton. As Beecher paced nervously back and forth across the study in his house, Moulton made a suggestion. Perhaps Beecher could send Tilton some sort of apology. Beecher agreed, but was too agitated to write. Moulton therefore drew up a letter and Beecher signed it. At the trial he asserted that he signed it without reading its contents. The letter was as follows:

Brooklyn, January 1, 1871

"In trust with F. D. Moulton"

My Dear Friend Moulton:

I ask through you Theodore Tilton's forgiveness, and I humble myself before him as I do before my God. He would have been a better man in my circumstances than I have been. I can ask nothing except that he will remember all the other hearts that would ache. I will not plead for myself. I even wish that I were dead; but others must live and suffer.

I will die before any one but myself shall be implicated. All my thoughts are running toward my friends, toward the poor child lying there and praying with her folded hands. She is guiltless, sinned against, bearing the transgression of another. Her forgiveness I have. I humbly pray to God that he may put it into the heart of her husband to forgive me.

I have trusted this to *Moulton* in confidence.

H. W. Beecher[68]

This letter later became the key document in the trial. For if Beecher was innocent as he asserted, it seems hardly likely that he would have used such strong language in a letter of apology. On the other hand, as Beecher's defense argued, if he did not dictate or read the letter, then he could not be held responsible for its wording. This explanation nevertheless leaves the question, what was he apologizing for? As General Tracy asked the jury in the opening brief for the defense, "was that letter a confession of adultery as they now say it was, or was it what she [Elizabeth Tilton] says it was in that letter they induced her to sign to Dr. Storrs, a charge of improper proposals? That is the vital question in this case."[69]

Beecher's own explanation of his action was that he had thought at the time that Tilton's accusation, "though entirely untrue," would ruin him and destroy his church. So his first reaction was to try and hush up the matter. "It was in such a sore and distressing condition that Mr. Moulton found me. . . ," he wrote later, "The case, as it then appeared to my eyes, was strongly against me. My old fellow-worker had been dispossessed of his eminent place and influence, and I had counselled it. His family had well-nigh been broken up, and I had advised it; his wife had been long sick and broken in health and body, and I, as I fully believed it, had been the cause of all this wreck by continuing that blind heedlessness and friendship which had beguiled her heart and had roused her husband into a fury of jealousy, although not caused by any intentional act of mine." To make up for these unintentional injuries to Tilton's family, Beecher signed the letter of apology.[70]

A few days afterward, as a further gesture of his repentance, he wrote to Bowen, "I have reason to think that the only cases of which I spoke to you in regard to Mr. Tilton were exaggerated in being reported to me; and I should be unwilling to have anything I said, though it was but little, weigh on your mind in the matter so important to his welfare."[71] Later in the month, Beecher began to pay the tuition for Bessie Turner, the boarder in Tilton's house, who had been sent away to school in Ohio. In general, his efforts to improve Tilton's reputation seemed to have produced results. As he wrote to Moulton, "I am thrown among clergymen, public men, and generally the makers of public opinion, and I have used every rational endeavor to repair the evils which have been visited upon T., and with increasing success."[72]

In the meantime, pressure was placed on Tilton to make him stop spreading rumors. The agent was Samuel Wilkeson, a former correspondent for the New York *Tribune*, who was working as a publicity man for Jay Cooke. "You are in trouble," wrote Wilkeson to Tilton, "I come to you with a letter just mailed to Jay Cooke, advising him to secure your services as a platform speaker, to turn New England, Old England and the great West upside down about our Northern Pacific [Railroad]. Pluck up heart. You shan't be trampled down. Keep quiet. Don't talk."[73]

By February, the discontent on all sides seemed to have disappeared. Tilton wrote to Moulton that he harbored "no malice" toward the preacher and Beecher himself admitted that he felt intensely relieved about the whole matter. As he wrote to Moulton:

> Many, many friends has God raised up to me; but to no one of them has he ever given the opportunity and the wisdom so to serve me as you have. My trust in you is implicit. . . .

Would to God, who orders all hearts, that by your kind mediation, Theodore, Elizabeth, and I could be made friends again. Theodore will have the hardest task in such a case; but has he not proved himself capable of the noblest things?[74]

During the winter, Beecher's activities returned to their normal channels. After his usual lecture trip in February, he spent most of his time working on the second volume of his life of Christ. Later, in March, Harriet Stowe came down to act as his housekeeper for a week, since Eunice Beecher was staying in Florida to improve her poor health. Then, as the snow began to melt, Beecher made several trips to his farm in Peekskill to supervise the preparations for spring planting.[75]

Unfortunately for Beecher, news of the scandal continued to spread. Sometime that spring, Mrs. Tilton told Elizabeth Cady Stanton, who was staying at her house, about the trouble, and Stanton passed the information on to Victoria Woodhull. In May, Woodhull began the first part of her effort to blackmail Beecher by publishing a card in the New York *World* stating that "I know of one man, a public teacher of eminence, who lives in concubinage with the wife of another public teacher of almost equal eminence."[76]

During the summer, Tilton himself formed a close friendship with Victoria Woodhull. An admirer of her ideas on the questions of women's rights and divorce, he frequently visited her at her home or went for rides with her in her carriage. When Woodhull announced her candidacy for the presidency of the United States, Tilton wrote a highly eulogistic campaign biography for her.

On November 11, Woodhull wrote Beecher a letter declaring that "for reasons in which *you* are deeply interested, as well as myself and the cause of truth, I desire to have an interview with you, without fail. . . ." She threatened that if he refused she would expose him in a speech at Steinway Hall in New York.[77] Beecher turned down Woodhull's request on the grounds that he did not want to become involved in the struggle between the two branches of the women's rights movement.[78] But the request, together with the rumors that continued to circulate, began to discourage him. As he wrote to Moulton:

To *say* that I have a church on my hands is simple enough—but to have the hundreds and thousands of men pressing me. . . ; to see tendencies which, if not stopped, would break out into ruinous defense of me; to meet and allay prejudices against T. which had their beginning before this; . . . all this may be talked about, but the real thing cannot be understood from the outside, nor its wearing and grinding on the nervous system.

If my destruction would place him all right, that shall not stand in the way. I am willing to step down and out. No one can offer more than that. This I do offer. Sacrifice me without hesitation if you can clearly see your way to his happiness and safety thereby.[79]

In the meantime, Tilton himself was becoming dissatisfied. Several years earlier, when his contract was broken and he was removed from the editorship of *The Independent*, he had tried to collect his lost wages from Bowen. Now, as his financial position became increasingly insecure, he sought by threatening to write his own account of the events in the scandal and to publish it as the "True Story" in the local newspapers, to force Bowen to pay up.

The threat worked. On April 2, Bowen, Beecher, and Tilton, at Wilkeson's suggestion, drew up a "tri-partitite agreement," vowing to refrain from spreading further rumors. The agreement also provided for the destruction of all the scandal papers in the hands of Tilton and Moulton. Two days later Bowen gave Tilton a check for seven thousand dollars, accompanied by a note that read "spoils from 'new friends' for the enrichment of old."[80] The dispute once more seemed to have been settled.

Thus during the spring and summer, Beecher resumed his regular activities, speaking publicly about political corruption, commenting on the women's rights question, and then retiring to his farm in Peekskill. Later that summer he spent several weeks at the Twin Mountain House in New Hampshire to avoid the hay-fever season. When his sister Harriet visited him there, she found that he "had recovered all the health and spirits of his boyhood and . . . [was] as full of prank as a squirrel." They relaxed and played croquet together, and on Sundays Beecher preached to the hotel guests. When he returned to Plymouth Church in the fall, he had regained his confidence and no longer worried about his reputation.[81]

Then, in December, the scandal was reopened once again. This time the cause was Elizabeth Tilton, who decided to take back her retraction and admit her guilt. Her letter went as follows:

> In July, 1870, prompted by my duty, I informed my husband that H. W. Beecher, my friend and pastor, had solicited me to be a wife to him, together with all that this implied. Six months afterwards my husband felt impelled by the circumstances of a conspiracy against him, in which Mrs. Beecher had taken part, to have an interview with Mr. Beecher.
>
> In order that Mr. B. might know exactly what I had said to my husband, I wrote a brief statement . . . which my husband showed to Mr. Beecher. Late the same evening Mr. B. came to me (lying very sick at the time), *and filled me with distress, saying I had ruined him*—and wanting to know if I meant to appear against him. This I certainly did not mean to do. . . . I then signed a paper *which he wrote*, to clear him in case of trial. In this instance, as in most others, when absorbed by one great interest or feeling, the harmony of my mind is entirely disturbed, and I found on reflection that this paper was so drawn as to place me most unjustly against my husband, and on the side of Mr. Beecher. So, in order to repair *so cruel a blow to my long-suffering husband*, I wrote an explanation of the first paper and my signature. Mr. Moulton procured from Mr. B. the statement which I gave to him in my agitation and excitement, and he now holds it.[82]

This letter would have been disastrous to Beecher's defense had not Elizabeth Tilton changed her mind at the trial and written yet another statement denying Beecher's guilt.

At the time, however, the letter was enough to make Beecher extremely upset, especially since it was followed by a note from Tilton to the Brooklyn *Daily Eagle* in which he stated that he refused to defend himself only because to do so would mean telling the whole story.[83] Beecher was worried, too, by the attitude of his half-sister, Isabella Beecher Hooker, who had become a spiritualist and wanted a confession from her brother. Troubled by his sister's wild ideas and outspoken nature, he tried to get her to drop the subject. "Of some things *I neither talk nor will I be talked with*," he wrote to her. "For love and sympathy I am deeply thankful. The only help that can be grateful to me, or useful is *silence*, and a silencing influence on others."[84] Isabella's questions not only troubled her brother, but they also angered Harriet, who refused to believe her brother capable of commiting any evil. The resulting dispute soon threatened to split apart the Beecher family.[85]

The continuous pressure from Tilton and his family gradually wore down Henry's spirits. Despite a successful lecture trip through the Ohio River Valley in February and March, 1872, and the completion of his divinity school lectures in New Haven, Beecher's spirits remained low, and the feelings of insecurity that had plagued his early career now reappeared. With his wife in Florida and his children married or in college, he fell into melancholy moods. As he wrote to his wife, with "the family broken up—one's wife gone, the children scattered, one feels quite alone in the world, and at times, would be glad to be out of it. It may be that my life long wish of sudden death will be gratified. Many are dropping about me suddenly. But God knows best."[86]

In these periods of despair, Beecher began to question the usefulness of Moulton and the merits of the policy of silence. Nevertheless, when in March Moulton suggested to him that Tilton's new publication, *The Golden Age*, was in financial difficulty, Beecher agreed to give Tilton a gift of five thousand dollars, even though he was forced to mortgage his house to raise the money.[87] When Tilton still threatened to publish the documents in his possession, Beecher suddenly changed his tack. "I have determined to make no more resistance," he wrote to Moulton. He was tired of trying to appease Tilton's anger. "Theodore's temperament is such that the future, even if temporarily earned, would be absolutely worthless, filled with abrupt changes, and rendering me liable at any hour or day to be obliged to stultify the devices by which we have saved ourselves. It is only fair that he should know that the publication of the card which he proposed would leave him far worse off than before."[88] Thus, when Tilton went ahead and sent the tri-partite agreement and several letters to the press, Beecher at last broke his silence and sent a letter to the Brooklyn *Daily Eagle*, declaring that Victoria Woodhull had two business letters from him and no others. "I will only add, in this connection," he continued, "that the stories and rumors which have, for a time, been circulated about me are grossly untrue, and I stamp them, in general and in particular, as utterly false."[89]

The letter helped to quiet the critics and restore peace within the

Beecher family. One brother wrote to express his "love and admiration and sympathy," while Harriet resolved to crush forever any family critics. "It is difficult to offend me," she wrote to her daughter, "but there are things which strike my *very life* and these accusations against my brother are among them. I cannot hear that subject discussed as a *possibility* open for inquiry without such an intense uprising of indignation and scorn and anger as very *few* have ever seen in me these late years. But if ever I should hear those who ought to know better wandering out insinuations and doubts about him I think there will be the eruption of a volcano that has for years been supposed to be extinct. They *will see what* I am when thoroughly aroused." [90]

By 1874, the conflict between Beecher and Tilton had become public. The controversy had become further complicated by Tilton's dismissal from the rolls of Plymouth Church and by the Church Council that investigated the action taken by Beecher's congregation. But the basic question remained: was Beecher guilty of having committed adultery? Mrs. Beecher, for one, never doubted her husband's innocence, and she was instrumental in exposing the ambiguous role that Frank Moulton played during the investigation of the charges against Beecher by the special examining committee of his church in August, 1874. As she wrote to her daughter:

> Why, there is *now* no fear that father will not fight. His eyes are at last opened and he sees both Tilton and Moulton in their naked depravity and bareness. It has been hard work to convince the dear guiltless simple-hearted man that such baseness and treachery could exist . . . and the process of opening his eyes was like dividing soul and body. . . . For a week he suffered terribly and sunk into a state of despondency that alarmed me. . . . But at last Moulton's insincerity and treachery stood [exposed?] and after one or two days of sharpest agony, . . . the noble old *Lion* roused himself. . . . Father is now roused to the fullest extent of indignation and holds back nothing. Many things that it is very hard for him to expose—as they show to what extent and how weakly he has trusted—how fearfully he has been muted or blackmailed—not through *fear* but through *kindness and sympathy*. Now is explained his stern appeals to me *to be more careful*—to *economize*. He was on the verge of financial ruin and he was just finding out that his sympathies had carried him too far. . . . He yet began to see on the verge of what precipice he stood and then—finding their supplies cut off, Tilton began to threaten—

bringing up all the old Bowen and Woodhull slanders. But mind you, *to father* only claiming that father had ruined his (Tilton's) family happiness by advising Mrs. Tilton to get *letters of separation*—when in truth they were before that advice, he claimed, very happy together save every few weeks she was a little unsettled in mien! . . .[91]

This letter is even more remarkable because Mrs. Beecher's relationship with her husband had itself been difficult and somewhat unsettled. Eunice Beecher's health had been poor since her illness and frequent pregnancies in Indianapolis, and in 1859 she was severely injured when thrown from her carriage in Brooklyn. Because of her poor health, she had often been cross and moody. As Beecher wrote to a close friend in 1867, "My poor wife is a barometer, and registers the changes in atmosphere on a scale of aches and pains."[92] The trial proved to be a great burden to her, and even after her husband was acquitted she remained upset. "I live in the past over and over and every little while when talking most cheerfully, such a flood of fiery indignation sweeps over me that I am constantly on the watch lest I lose my self-control and show it," she wrote to a friend.[93] It was a terrible weight to bear, but she withstood it strongly and without protest.

By 1874, then, all the basic evidence that was used in the trial had been collected. The question thus remains: do the documents and testimony in court substantiate the charges of adultery? The answer is no. The problem is that contradictory interpretations are possible of every major document and the testimony of those involved is itself ambiguous. Elizabeth Tilton, to take the most important example, changed her mind about Beecher's guilt four times before the trial and then in 1878 reversed her position once again to declare that he was guilty. It was not surprising, therefore, that the jury, after listening to six months of contradictory and conflicting testimony, was unable to reach a decision. It divided nine to three in favor of Beecher's innocence. No one at the time should have been surprised by the verdict. As E. L. Godkin commented in *The Nation*, "the truth is that only a very small portion of the stuff contained in the various 'statements' can, under the rules of evidence, be laid before the jury. . . . What *will* be laid before the jury is, in the main, 'questions of veracity' between three or four persons whose credit is already greatly shaken, or in other words, the very kind of questions on which juries are most likely to disagree. . . ."[94]

Given the contradictory nature of the evidence, it was at the time and is now impossible to judge whether Beecher had actually committed adultery. Although he admitted making improper proposals, it will never be known whether these included an invitation to have sexual intercourse. It is clear, nevertheless, that in his efforts to hush up the controversy, Beecher's actions, as the New York *Times* put it, were "entirely unworthy of his name, position, and sacred calling."[95] His payments to Tilton, his refusal to answer accusations, and the use of a personally chosen committee of his church to investigate the claims against him were clearly cowardly acts. It is difficult, moreover, to believe that he could have been deceived so easily by the "mutual friend," Frank Moulton. The payment of more than twelve thousand dollars to Tilton appears to be an attempt to buy silence rather than the expression of generous feelings.

While Beecher's actions were inconsistent and contradictory, so, too, were those of Tilton and Moulton. Tilton was in financial difficulty throughout the period, and he clearly used the documents in his possession to extort additional funds from the preacher. As *Harper's Weekly* commented, "the key to the comprehension of this whole case is Mr. Tilton's frank declaration, 'I resolved to smite Mr. Beecher to the heart.' The arrow was well fashioned, the bow well bent, but the destroyer has failed of his purpose; and when posterity, wiser than we, reads the history of this case, it will honor, not less than the noble achievements of Henry Ward Beecher's noble life, the no less noble failure of the patience and magnanimity of his only too chivalric and unhappily unsuccessful endeavor to shield 'all the other hearts that would ache' from the publication of the famous Brooklyn scandal."[96]

The general attitude of hostility toward Tilton and admiration toward Beecher that was expressed by *Harper's Weekly* was shared by the general public. As the poet John G. Whittier wrote to Beecher, "any man, but more especially any man in thy position is liable to be slandered, to find his very virtues of love and kindness and generous feelings made to take the appearance of Evil. No man is absolutely perfect, and he who wishes an occasion for plausibly impugning his neighbor will not have long to wait for it."[97] *Scribner's Monthly* agreed and added that "the majority of the jury in the late trial, like the majority of the public, held Mr. Beecher guiltless of the crime charged against him, and the result of the trial is virtual acquital."[98]

But the real significance of the trial goes far beyond the dispute over whether Beecher committed a crime. The crucial question is not whether he acted improperly, but rather why so many people refused even to entertain the notion that he might have been guilty. In this respect, the comment of *The Congregationalist* "that the spiritually psychological aspects of it imperatively forbade the theory of Mr. Beecher's guilt," was typical.[99] Or, as *Scribner's Monthly* commented, "the idea that Mr. Beecher, who had carried a pure name through life, should, after having lived to be nearly sixty years old, [and] reared a family, . . . [have] gone out of his way to seduce an innocent member of his own flock,—the wife of a personal friend, to whom he had married her,—was simply preposterous."[100] As these statements indicated, most Americans simply refused even to consider whether Beecher might have been guilty.

The refusal to doubt Beecher's integrity is not difficult to explain when one looks at his position as a spokesman for the Victorian cultural ethos. For more than thirty years, Beecher had warned against political and economic corruption and had stressed the value of Christian ethics. At a time when industrialization and the growth of cities were changing the face of the nation, he had reaffirmed the morality of an earlier, more rural, America. For those who were frightened by the rapid and chaotic social change, his views became a reference point by which they could evaluate the events taking place around them. Beecher had thus come to symbolize the strength of middle-class Victorian values.

When Beecher was accused of adultery in the 1870s, therefore, Victorian Americans could not bring themselves to question his innocence because to do so would undermine many of their most cherished values. If Beecher was a mountebank and a charlatan, then they, too, had been duped for years. To admit Beecher's guilt would bring into question many of the values that he had exalted. Could it be that honesty, thrift, and hard work were not the best ways to attain success? For many Americans, to admit that Beecher might have been guilty, in other words, was to admit that their own moral perspective on life might be wrong and they were simply unwilling to entertain this thought.

The refusal to believe in Beecher's guilt, moreover, was closely tied to the middle class's conception of the family. Since Victorian Americans believed that sexual relationships should only exist within a marriage, the subject of illicit sex was a social taboo. Normal relations within the family were important not only for the stability of society (hence the smearing of Irish and other immigrant groups with assertions of sexual promiscuity), but also for the furtherance of a wide range of status goals and aspirations. Since for Horatio Alger's heroes as well as for clerks and business personnel, marriage to the boss's daughter represented the quickest and easiest road to advancement, illicit sexual relations could interfere with social mobility. Even wealthy Boston Brahmins, secure in their Back Bay mansions, used the marriage of their sons and daughters to advance their business connections and their position in high society. Since sexual promiscuity threatened the sacred ideal of family life, even to entertain the thought that Beecher had had an extramarital affair, therefore, was inconceivable to many Americans for to do so would violate the sacred ideal of family life.

The trial itself, together with the investigations that preceded it and the Church Council that followed it, were thus elaborate rituals by which these Americans reaffirmed their faith in Victorian values. They believed, as *Harper's Weekly* argued, that

> under a careful analysis the evidence against Mr. Beecher utterly fails. It would not suffice against a man much less strongly entrenched in public esteem than he: against his pure life and noble character it breaks in vain, as the foam of the angry ocean against the cliff which it can obscure but cannot destroy. The case is one of conspiracy against a good and great, though careless, man, but a conspiracy which grew rather than was formed, which was the natural product of the jealousy of self-conceit rather than the deliberate contrivance of greed. On the one side is a man the greatness of whose heart and the credulity of whose sympathies are at once his genius and his weakness; on the other hand is a man whose insane jealousy is the natural though deadly fruit of insane self-conceit, embittered by a spirit of personal and fell revenge. . . .[101]

That most Americans believed Beecher to be innocent is borne out in his subsequent career. His church raised $100,000 to pay the expenses of the six-month trial, and Beecher turned down an offer to deliver a series of lectures for $75,000. When he did consent to speak, he was mobbed by enthusiastic admirers. As Beecher described his lecture trip in 1876, "next to *Brattleboro* fine audience and cordial. . . . Next, (April 20) Boston, Temple full, received me with prolonged clapping and afterward shook hands with forty or fifty. . . . Night, in Boston for Wright, 10,000 people couldn't get in, shook hands with the whole audience. . . . went to Congregational minister's meeting on Monday morning—cheered and clapped when I entered. After the paper for the day finished, it was moved that I address the meeting. I did so, and closed it with prayer. All wept—and it broke up like a revival meeting."[102] This was indeed an unusual greeting for a clergyman who had been accused of committing adultery.

Not everyone, however, believed in Beecher's innocence. Edwin L. Godkin, the editor of *The Nation*, was appalled by the scandal. Placing flowers from well-wishers in the courtroom during the trial, he commented, was like placing "wreaths round the man-hole of a sewer." What particularly disturbed him about the affair was the shoddiness and sentimentality of popular culture that it revealed. Godkin was one of a new breed of intellectuals who, like Thomas W. Higginson, Charles Eliot Norton, and Henry Whitney Bellows, came out of the Civil War with a disgust for the romantic and sentimental outlook of the earlier years and a faith in the efficacy of reason and science. Godkin saw the trial as characteristic of the worst aspects of popular culture, or, as he phrased it, the "chromo civilization":

A large body of persons has arisen, under the influence of the common-schools, magazines, newspapers, and the rapid acquisition of wealth, "who are not only engaged in enjoying themselves after their fashion, but who firmly believe that they have reached, in the matter of social, mental, and moral culture, all that is attainable or desirable by anybody, and who therefore tackle all the problems of the day—men's, women's, and children's rights and duties, marriage, education, suffrage, life, death, and immortality—with supreme indifference to what anybody else thinks or has ever thought, and have their own trumpery prophets, prophetesses, heroes and heroines, poets, orators, scholars, and philosophers, whom they worship with a kind of barbaric fervor. The result is a kind of mental and moral chaos, in which many of the fundamental rules of living, which have been worked out painfully by thousands of years of bitter human experience, seem in imminent risk of disappearing totally.[103]

What Godkin wanted was a new toughness in human relations based upon scientific expertise and the use of clean-cut logic. He believed that Beecher was a fraud and should be called one. If men like Beecher, the false prophets of popular culture, could be exposed, then men of Godkin's quality, the intellectual and scientific elite, could achieve their rightful influence in public affairs. Godkin's comments are particularly significant because they reveal the antagonism that existed in the post–Civil War period between popular culture and high culture. The one was sentimental, romantic, and moralistic, the other was tough-minded, logical, and scientific. The conflict between these two outlooks was to lie at the heart of the intellectuals' discontent in the Gilded Age.[104]

Although Godkin's view was shared by only a few intellectuals, the trial and scandal did significantly change Beecher's life. The pressure and strain of trying to hush up rumors and of having the whole affair displayed before the public in a six-month trial changed Beecher's personality. Where he had been frivolous, witty, and playful, he now became quiet, restrained, and thoughtful. As Mrs. Beecher wrote to her daughter, ''Father bears up bravely but I see that the last two years [in] which he has been gentle and forebearing to his foes has [*sic*] given him at home a colder, more abrupt way of speaking—less tender and loving—that I miss more than tongue can tell. It is not strange, but I long for the old tones—the old cheery smiles. It would not be strange—if when all is over, this struggle should have him much changed.''[105] In addition to subjecting him to an intense emotional strain, the trial crippled Beecher financially. Despite the hundred thousand dollars raised by his church and the expenditure of all of his savings, Beecher still remained more than fifteen thousand dollars in debt. To help meet these expenses, he invited his son Henry and daughter-in-law to live with him and Eunice and pay rent. His son, who was working in Brooklyn, accepted his father's offer and moved in with his parents, much to the dismay of Mrs. Beecher. Mrs. Beecher thereafter felt as if she had been deprived of her position as head of the household, and she became increasingly bitter about living with her son and his wife and children.[106]

Despite the emotional and financial strain of the trial, Beecher was still able to maintain his central position in the community. That he could continue to preach and lecture was testimony to the resiliency of his character. Although he appeared several times to come close to having a breakdown, he managed to keep going. The ability he had developed in the West to cover up and hide his feelings now became an invaluable asset.

Encouraged by the praise and enthusiasm that greeted his first efforts on the lecture platform after the trial, Beecher decided to expand his public engagements in order to repair the damage that had been done to his reputation. Although the task was not an easy one, he now believed that it would be possible to rebuild his national position as a leading spokesman for liberal Protestantism and he resolved to devote his energies to that cause for the remainder of the decade.

NOTES

1. *Harper's Weekly*, Aug. 11, 1866.

2. "Mr. Beecher as a Social Force," *Scribner's Monthly*, IV (Oct., 1872), 754.

3. H. W. Beecher to T. W. Higginson, May 28, 1853, Higginson Papers, Harvard University; Catharine E. Beecher, *The True Remedy for the Wrongs of Women* (Boston, 1851), 28.

4. H. W. Beecher, *Women's Influence in Politics*, pamphlet (Boston, 1870), 6.

5. *Ibid.*, 12.

6. Alma Lutz, *Susan B. Anthony* (Boston, 1959), 103; Robert E. Riegel, "The Split in the Feminist Movement in 1869," *Mississippi Valley Historical Review*, XLIX (Dec., 1962), 487.

7. H. W. Beecher, *Women's Duty to Vote*, pamphlet (New York, 1867), 27.

8. James M. McPherson, "Abolitionists, Women's Suffrage, and the Negro, 1865–69," *Mid-American*, XLVII (Jan. 1965), 42.

9. Mary A. Livermore to Olympia Brown, April 28, 1868, Olympia Brown Papers, Radcliffe Archives.

10. New York *Times*, June 13, 1869.

11. *Ibid.*, Nov. 19, 1868.

12. Andrew Sinclair, *The Better Half* (New York, 1965), 189.

13. New York *Times*, May 15, 1869; Brooklyn *Daily Eagle*, May 15, 1869.

14. Eleanor Flexner, *Century of Struggle* (Cambridge, 1959), 153; Robert E. Riegel, *American Feminists* (Lawrence, Kans., 1968), 89–92.

15. Forrest Wilson, *Crusader in Crinoline: The Life of Harriet Beecher Stowe* (Philadelphia, 1941), 535.

16. *Ibid.*, 539.

17. H. W. Beecher to H. B. Stowe, Sept. 1, 1869 (copy), Yale MSS.

18. New York *Times*, Oct. 20, 1869.

19. Brooklyn *Daily Eagle*, Oct. 29, 1869.

20. New York *Times*, Nov. 16, 1869; Brooklyn *Daily Eagle*. Nov. 16, 1869.

21. New York *Times*, Nov. 26, 1869.

22. *Harper's Weekly*, July 17, 1858.

23. Lutz, *Susan B. Anthony*, 174.

24. Brooklyn *Daily Eagle*, Dec. 1, 11, 1869.

25. G. T. Strong, *The Diary of George Templeton Strong*, ed. Allen Nevins and Milton H. Thomas (New York, 1952), III, 262.

26. Brooklyn *Daily Eagle*, Dec. 11, 1869.

27. *Ibid.*, Dec. 13, 1869.

28. H. W. Beecher to T. W. Higginson, April 11, 1870, Higginson Papers, Harvard University.

29. Brooklyn *Daily Eagle*, April 5, 1870.

30. New York *Times*, May 12, 1870; Brooklyn *Daily Eagle*, May 14, 26, 1870.

31. For a discussion of the split, see Riegel, "The Split in the Feminist Movement in 1869," 485–96.

32. H. W. Beecher to T. W. Higginson, April 11, 1870, Higginson Papers, Harvard University.

33. New York *Times*, May 13, 1870.

34. H. B. Stowe to H. W. Beecher, n.d., Yale MSS.

35. H. B. Stowe to H. W. Beecher, n.d., Yale MSS.

36. H. B. Stowe to H. W. Beecher, n.d., Yale MSS.

37. H. W. Beecher to Isabella B. Hooker, April 25, 1872 (copy), Yale MSS.

38. Kenneth R. Andrews, *Nook Farm* (Cambridge, Mass., 1950), 55.

39. New York *Times*, July 11, Sept. 1, 9, 1868.

40. Brooklyn *Daily Eagle*, Oct. 9, 1868, Jan. 24, 1869.

41. *An Account of the Services of the Silver-Wedding Week in Plymouth Church*, ed. Horatio C. King (New York, 1873), 21.

42. *Ibid.*, 90.

43. Frank L. Mott, *A History of American Magazines* (Cambridge, Mass., 1939), III, 446.

44. *Scribner's Monthly* (Vol. V, 1873), 384.

45. Mott, *History of American Magazines*, III, 449.

46. New York *Times*, April 30, 1873.

47. *Ibid.*, July 1, 1873.

48. *The Congregationalist*, Sept. 3, 1874.

49. For a brief, though biased, narrative of the events in the scandal, see William C. Beecher and Samuel Scoville, *A Biography of Henry Ward Beecher* (New York, 1888), chaps. 24 and 25. For differing recent points of view, see Robert Shaplen's *Free Love and Heavenly Sinners* (New York, 1954), which argues that Beecher was guilty, and Edward Wagenknecht's *Ambassadors for Christ* (New York, 1972), which asserts he was innocent.

50. Chester L. Barrows, *William Maxwell Evarts* (Chapel Hill, 1941), 268.

51. *Ibid.*, 270.

52. Theodore Tilton to H. W. Beecher, Nov. 30, 1865, quoted in Beecher and Scoville, *Biography*, 489.

53. *Theodore Tilton versus Henry Ward Beecher: Verbatim Report of the Trial . . .* (New York, 1875), I, 478.

54. Theodore Tilton to Elizabeth Tilton, Feb. 12, 1867, *ibid.*, I, 494.

55. E. Tilton to T. Tilton, Jan. 26, 1869, *ibid.*, I, 450.

56. T. Tilton to E. Tilton, Dec. 6, 1866, *ibid.*, I, 494.

57. E. Tilton to T. Tilton, Jan. 25, 1867, *ibid.*, I, 496. "Oliver" was Oliver Johnson, one of the editors of *The Independent*.

58. E. Tilton to T. Tilton, Feb. 1, 1868, *ibid.*, I, 489.

59. T. Tilton to E. Tilton, Jan. 15, 1869, *ibid.*, I, 502.

60. H. W. Beecher to T. Tilton, June 3, 1867, *ibid.*, I, 485.

61. *The Independent*, Dec. 1, 1870; *Verbatim Report*, I, 163.

62. *Verbatim Report*, I, 509.

63. *Ibid.*, III, 132.

64. *Ibid.*, I, 16; II, 231.

65. T. Tilton to H. W. Beecher, Dec. 26, 1870, *ibid.*, I, 515.

66. E. Tilton to ?, Dec. 30, 1870, *ibid.*, II, 42.

67. E. Tilton to T. Tilton, Dec. 30, 1870, *ibid.*, III, 37.

68. *Verbatim Report*, I, 65.

69. *Ibid.*, II, 42.

70. Beecher and Scoville, *Biography*, 504–5.

71. H. W. Beecher to H. C. Bowen, Jan. 2, 1871, *Verbatim Report*, I, 66.

72. H. W. Beecher to F. Moulton, Feb. 5, 1871, *ibid.*, I, 86.

73. S. Wilkeson to T. Tilton, Jan. 11, 1871, *ibid.*, II, 308.

74. *Verbatim Report*, III, 66.

75. H. W. Beecher to Eunice Beecher, March 14, 1871, Yale MSS.

76. *Verbatim Report*, I, 86.

77. *Ibid.*, III, 121.

78. H. W. Beecher to F. Moulton, Jan. 2, 1872, *ibid.*, III, 122.

79. H. W. Beecher to F. Moulton, Feb. 2, 1872, *ibid.*, III, 92.

80. *Verbatim Report*, II, 290; III, 140.

81. H. B. Stowe to her twin daughters, Sept. 16, 1871, Schlesinger Library.

82. New York *Times*, *The Beecher Trial: A Review of the Evidence*, pamphlet (New York, 1875), 7.

83. *Verbatim Report*, I, 92.

84. H. W. Beecher to Isabella B. Hooker, April 25, Nov. 9, 1872, Yale MSS.

85. Harriet B. Stowe to her sister (?), Dec. 26, 1872, Yale MSS.

86. H. W. Beecher to Eunice Beecher, March 23, 1873, Yale MSS.

87. *Verbatim Report*, I, 269.

88. H. W. Beecher to F. Moulton, June 1, 1873, *ibid.*, III, 53.

89. *Verbatim Report*, I, 101.

90. (?) Beecher to H. W. Beecher, July 23, 1873, Yale MSS; H. B. Stowe to Elisa Stowe, May 11, 1873, Schlesinger Library.

91. Eunice W. Beecher to Anne B. Scoville, Aug. 9, 1874, Yale MSS.

92. H. W. Beecher to Mrs. H. B. Claflin, March 12, 1867, Rutherford B. Hayes Library.

93. Eunice B. Beecher to ?, Aug. 8, 1875, Yale MSS.

94. E. L. Godkin, "Chromo Civilization," *The Nation*, Sept. 24, 1874.

95. New York *Times*, *The Beecher Trial*, 1.

96. *Harper's Weekly*, June 5, 1875.

97. John G. Whittier to H. W. Beecher, Dec. 26, 1874 (typed copy), Yale MSS.

98. *Scribner's Monthly* (Vol. X, 1875), 636.

99. *The Congregationalist*, Sept. 3, 1874.

100. *Scribner's Monthly* (Vol. VIII, 1874), 744.

101. *Harper's Weekly*, June 5, 1875.

102. New York *Times*, Jan. 6, 1875; Eunice Beecher to her daughter Harriet Scoville, Sept. 26, 1875, Yale MSS; H. W. Beecher to Eunice Beecher, April 25, 1876, Yale MSS.

103. *The Nation*, Sept. 24, 1874.

104. This change in outlook among the intellectuals is best described in George Fredrickson, *The Inner Civil War* (New York, 1965), chap. 13.

105. Eunice Beecher to Harriet Scoville, Jan. 16, 1876, Yale MSS.

106. Eunice Beecher to Harriet Scoville, Sept. 26, Oct. 3, 1875, Yale MSS.

11

The Wastes and Burdens of Society

Henry Ward Beecher's trial for adultery in 1874 was but one of the shocks that troubled Victorian Americans in the 1870s. Corruption and fraud seemed rampant at all levels of government. The revelation that the Crédit Mobilier construction company, which had gotten a good deal of help from Congressman Oakes Ames, was transferring much of the money it received from railroad contracts to a few major shareholders was matched by the news that President Grant's private secretary had participated in the notorious "Whiskey Ring," a conspiracy of major distillers who had bribed treasury officials to evade federal taxes. These and other scandals made it appear that fixed moral standards, so widely extolled in the pulpit and the press, were systematically being violated and undermined. To add to the trouble, the country entered a major depression in 1876. Almost a million workers lost their jobs, and many people were on the verge of starvation. As conditions became worse during the following summer, railroad strikes broke out in New Jersey, Pennsylvania, and Maryland, and the president called out the troops. Americans who had long prided themselves on the material abundance of the continent now began to have major doubts about the economy. Cheats and crooks seemed to be destroying the natural advantages conferred by the environment. To many Americans, the nation seemed to be on the verge of a class war.[1]

The confusion and despair that were generated by the political corruption and spiraling depression provided a new opportunity for Beecher to restore his reputation as a public speaker. Hoping to improve his finances and refurbish his position as a popular spokesman for Victorian morality, Beecher took to the lecture trail in the summer of 1876, traveling across the continent and speaking in town after town. With lectures on "The Wastes and Burdens of Society" and "The Reign of the Common People," Beecher explained why society seemed to be falling apart and what could be done about it. Always sensitive to the public mood, he recognized the urgency of the crisis and used the occasion to rebuild and refashion his earlier ideas about private morality and social progress.

The new message proved to be an instant success. What started as a limited engagement soon became an extended popular campaign. The audiences were ecstatic. As he wrote to a friend, "the general effect of continuous work and a wonderful reception, full of enthusiasm, affection, and even pathos, stands out with ineffaceable distinctness. In the balmiest days of my life, I never had such audiences."[2] In Chicago the house was sold out a few hours after the box office opened. In Madison, Wisconsin, and in Springfield, Illinois, his lectures were so popular that he was invited to repeat them before the state legislatures. In St. Louis he filled the largest auditorium in the city.[3] He also received an enthusiastic welcome in the smaller towns, where admission was fifty cents instead of a dollar. Encouraged by the success of his first lecture tours, Beecher kept enlarging his schedule until he was away from his church for almost four months each year. In this fashion, he covered more than twenty-seven thousand miles and visited eighteen states as well as Canada in the nine months between September, 1876, and June, 1877.[4]

The unusual success of his lecture tours proved to be a windfall in several respects. Financially, they were a gold mine.[5] Because of the extraordinary demand, Beecher could earn a thousand dollars for a single lecture and as much as four thousand dollars for a ten-day trip.

As Samuel Clemens grudgingly admitted, he was one of the few men who knew his value as an orator and exacted it.[6] Although it is impossible to determine how much he actually earned, it is probable that Beecher made in the neighborhood of sixty thousand dollars from his lectures, a sum which, when added to his twenty-thousand-dollar church salary, would have made him the best paid clergyman in America.

A more indirect benefit of the lecture tours was the opportunity they provided for redefining his earlier ideas about success and social progress in a way that made them appeal more directly to the middle class. Although Beecher's espousal of Victorian values in the 1850s and '60s crossed class lines and appealed to some degree to all segments of American society, his message was now more closely directed at the salaried, middle-class professionals—teachers, clerks, lawyers, and small businessmen who were upset by the growing power of labor unions and the aggressive tactics of large business corporations. Using an appeal to the middle-class ideals of efficiency, good management, and self-control, Beecher devised a general program that promised an end to the financial depression, the destruction of class antagonisms, and a restoration of faith in fixed moral standards.

Buoyed by his enormous success as a lyceum lecturer, Beecher then reentered the political arena, fighting corruption and supporting the Republican party. Some reformers might have hesitated before exposing themselves to the invective and personal abuse of the political process, but not Beecher. Convinced of the righteousness of his own position, he refused to shy away from moral questions and quickly became a political force in his own right. In the hotly disputed presidential election of 1884, Beecher was to play a prominent role.

By 1884 then, Beecher appeared to have completely recovered from the tension and abuse that had been heaped upon him during his trial for adultery. Not only were his debts paid off, but he was even able to fulfill his lifelong dream of designing and building a new summer house. But success was not achieved without a price. The extensive lecture tours and heavy involvement in politics, when added to the duties at his church, took him away from home for long periods of time. Gradually the relationship with his wife became more strained. Although a compromise of sorts was eventually arranged, the affection that had earlier existed was only slowly restored.

Beecher's analysis of the 1876 depression and the subsequent labor unrest was simple and direct. He assumed, along with other middle-class Americans, that the natural abundance of the landscape was inexhaustible. Thus, any major economic decline could not be attributable to the system itself. There had to be a problem with the people. To Beecher, the depression of 1876 was the product of two forces: misguided and deceived labor organizations and aggressive, corrupt corporations.

Beecher was particularly concerned about what he perceived to be new developments within the labor movement. Although he conceded that laborers had the right to organize to protect themselves against accidents, disasters, and "the natural selfishness of employers and of capital," he nevertheless asserted that a poisonous "foreign element" was gaining control of the unions and creating discontent. "It is said that a dollar a day is not enough for a wife and five or six children," he commented. "No, not if the man smokes and drinks beer. . . . It is not enough to enable them to live as perhaps they would have a right to live in prosperous times. But is not a dollar a day enough to buy bread with? Water costs nothing and a man who cannot live on bread and water is not fit to live."[7]

This statement, delivered in a heated moment after one of the most violent strikes, provoked a public outcry and Beecher was forced to qualify it the next day. He did not mean, he said, "to undervalue the trials of the laboring classes," but simply to argue that their resort to strikes and violence was unacceptable. "You never can readjust the thoughts of God in that matter," he continued. "He has meant that the great shall be great and that the little shall be little. Men are distributed on a long scale, and no equalizing process will take place till you can make men equal in productive forces." This was a callous statement that clearly revealed Beecher's fear that conspiratorial forces were plotting to overthrow society.[8]

Although Beecher worried about the influence of foreign elements within the labor movement, he nevertheless opposed the restriction of immigration. Writing to President Hayes in 1879, he urged him to veto the Chinese exclusion bill:

> Besides the wrong to the Chinese, the dishonour to our Nation, [and] the great damage to our commerce, there is a consideration yet more threatening, in my judgment. You are aware of the progress of socialism

among our laboring population, especially our foreign people. . . . This California craze is another carbuncle. If by combination and by political leverage, the ignorant population can drive competition from their midst, it will give courage all over the land, to men who hold theories of rights of labor wh[ich] are destructive of the rights of property—of the freedom of industry, and of the predominance of virtue and intelligence in managing the affairs of state.

If the president refused to allow aliens to enter the country, the source of free labor would be cut off and the strength of the radicals within the labor movement would be increased.[9]

At the heart of Beecher's dislike of labor organizing then, was the middle-class belief in the self-sufficiency of the free individual. Accepting the laissez-faire argument of the day that economic progress could only occur when marketplace transactions were free and unrestricted, Beecher resisted the notion that labor should organize to pressure business corporations into making concessions over wages. Yet he retained his faith in the basic integrity of the working class. Exclude the radicals and socialists and the system would return to its earlier balance and equilibrium.

Beecher's faith in the integrity of the working classes was occasionally overridden, however, by his dislike of violence. Beecher was so afraid of labor unrest that he advocated calling out the army to quell disturbances. "The world is not yet Christian enough to trust the Sermon on the Mount as our only policy," he told an audience in Springfield, Massachusetts. "If men will not respect each other's property, liberty, and rights by moral suasion, they must be compelled to do so by physical suasion."[10] Government officials should not hesitate to use force, if necessary, to crush the strikes and stop violence and disorder. This statement marked a significant shift in Beecher's attitude toward coercion. He no longer considered it sufficient to try to control the public's behavior by persuasion and rational argument. This view was shared by many other clergymen. The editors of the *Congregationalist* agreed that drastic measures were needed to stop violence. "Bring on then the troops—the armed police—in overwhelming numbers," they cried. "Bring out the Gatling guns. Let there be no fooling with blank cartridges. But let the mob know, everywhere, that for it to stand one moment after it has been ordered by proper authorities to disperse, will be to be shot down in its tracks. . . ."[11]

Although Beecher feared the violence of the labor movement, he also shared the middle-class hostility toward business leaders who used their wealth to bribe legislatures. Special contempt was reserved for railroad executives and stockbrokers, individuals who seemed to be manipulating the system for their own gain. "Capitalists and corporations find it more economical to trade by wholesale than by retail," he asserted.

> The days are near at hand when money is to bear a relation to politics scarcely yet suspected, notwithstanding our recent experiences of corruption. If it were in the interest of these four vast [railroad] corporations that a certain policy should be pursued, and that certain men should be put in power to execute them, their concentrated councils and their enormous wealth and influence would go far to counterbalance all resistance. I do not assail the system of the general management of railroads. They are young, they are lion cubs; and it is wise to consider, while we play with them as kittens, what they will do when their nails and teeth are grown and their haunches are strong.[12]

Beecher's hostility toward organized labor and corporate wealth undoubtedly added to his popularity in the 1870s, but it would be a mistake to picture this hostility as the main source of his appeal. The real basis for Beecher's popularity was not his attack on business corporations and labor radicals, it was his prescription for overcoming hostility and class differences. This prescription was presented in two of his most popular lectures: "The Wastes and Burdens of Society" and "The Reign of the Common People."[13]

These lectures, like Beecher's newspaper articles, begin by repeating many of the themes found throughout his earlier writings: the duty of the clergy to speak out on social issues, the importance of industry and thrift, the need for public education, the necessity for temperance, and the faith that America was still a land of opportunity where anyone could be successful if he worked at it. They continue, moreover, to stress the importance of the family. As Beecher commented to a friend, "I have found that those whose love is deepest and warmest [for me] represent families who look at everything in the world from the standpoint of the household—who judge of preaching, of ethics, and of methods by the relation which they bear to the bringing up of the young, and to the founding and maintaining of Christian homes."[14] Beecher's idealization of family life, so often mentioned in his letters

_____

and lectures, is somewhat ironic, since he was at that time having increasing difficulty maintaining harmony within his own household. Perhaps his glorified vision of the family was a way of compensating for his own failures at home.

What was new about Beecher's lectures was not his stress on education, temperance, self-help, and the family, but rather the way in which these themes were presented. Influenced by the emphasis on expertise that had developed during the crisis of the Civil War, Beecher placed his views in a more "scientific" context, stressing rationality and efficient management, and adding an appeal for honesty and involvement in community affairs.

Beecher wrote the first draft of his lecture on the wastes and burdens of society in the summer of 1877. His interest in this subject had been aroused in July by an article in the *North American Review* by the laissez-faire economist David A. Wells on the causes of the depression. Wells had argued that the depression resulted from the overproduction and underconsumption of goods. The difficulties created by this imbalance had grown until they reached crisis proportions. To avert a disaster in the near future, Wells urged the statesman, the merchant, and, more especially, the clergyman to try to siphon off discontent. "If half the time spent [by the clergy] in preaching sermons and singing hymns, and in metaphysical discussions . . . ," he declared, "were spent in inquiring *why it is* that in this country, with all the elements of abundance, we have enforced idleness, increasing poverty, and, consequently, increasing crime; why it is that people who pass out of churches and tabernacles where sermons are preached and hymns sung, pass out into an atmosphere so crammed with unnatural necessities that overcome virtue, and with artificial temptations to do wrong so powerful that human nature, as ordinarily constituted, cannot resist, there would be more souls made happy in this world, and more probably saved for the next, than there now is."[15] Beecher agreed with this criticism and wrote to Wells to ask for more information on economic and social problems.[16] Using the materials provided by Wells and gathered from the writings of Herbert Spencer, Beecher then sketched an outline for his lecture. There were clear reasons why the nation's growth and prosperity had been reduced in recent years. One major problem was the increase of sickness and ill-health. The failure to maintain standards of neatness and cleanliness, Beecher asserted, had resulted in an alarming increase in illness. "There are two things that God made the most of in this world that men are more afraid of than anything else—fresh air and cold water," he wrote. When men failed to use these agents of health, sickness and disease increased and valuable man-hours of work were lost.

By stressing the need for neatness and cleanliness, Beecher reiterated what came to be one of the classic features of the middle-class ethos in the late nineteenth century. The intense preoccupation with good health and neatness, which could be seen in the newspaper advertisements for soaps and patent medicines, was directly related to two social changes of the period—the fantastic growth of cities and the strains of the industrial revolution. The enormous urban expansion after the Civil War created basic sanitation problems that could not be avoided. As Beecher warned his audiences, ". . . the upper classes have a great deal more risk than they are apt to suppose; though they keep themselves in a sanitative condition, yet there is [a danger] in this reeking influence that is coming up directly or indirectly from society everywhere."[17] Unless men took quick action, their families might be wiped out by diphtheria, smallpox, and other epidemics that periodically swept through the cities. Although there were important medical reasons for stressing cleanliness and neatness, they were more than matched, in the eyes of the middle class, by reasons of social respectability. In a period when the United States was undergoing vast industrial changes, neatness and cleanliness of dress and appearance were a mark of social distinction, a sign that the individual was not associated with manual labor. Thus, Horatio Alger insisted in his dime novels that before the newspaper and shoeshine boys could begin to climb the ladder of success, they had to wash their faces and buy new sets of clothes. Care in grooming and personal appearance became the sine qua non of respectability.

Having described the loss to society created by sickness and ill-health, Beecher went on to list the other factors that had limited the growth-rate of society in recent years. In addition to illness, Americans had been plagued by ignorance, corruption, religious bigotry, lying, drunkenness, and war. Burdened by these evils, they had been unable to work efficiently and the nation had gone into a depression. The worst aspect of these problems was that they affected the lower classes more than the upper stratum of society. "The care," Beecher asserted, "should be at the bottom of society, first and mainly, and not at the top. If you go into a community and see beautiful mansions, you have a right to rejoice in them. I like to see fine streets, well shaded; I like to see comfortable dwellings, surrounded by flowers, and all the elements of taste; but, after all, I can form no idea of the Christian civilization of any community till I go down and see where the working men live, where the mechanics live. The test of civilization is not at the top, it is the average, but more especially the bottom of society."

The lower classes had become discontent because of ignorance, poor health, and intemperance. If these evils could be remedied, he asserted, the most pressing social problems of the times would be solved. To restore prosperity, however, it was necessary to do more than simply aid the poor. Middle-class Americans had to take a more active part in community affairs and develop a sense of trust. To neglect general social problems like sanitation was to place the entire community in danger. No man could safely isolate himself in his home. "For their own sake and for the sake of humanity," declared Beecher, "every thinking man and citizen well off should see to it that the great body of society should be taken care of and that a preventable disease should not be allowed to ravage the community." It was necessary, furthermore, to stamp out dishonesty and develop a sense of trust in the community, "for lying disintegrates society."[18] Without faith in the truthfulness of other men, the social fabric would be ripped apart.

Beecher's analysis of the perils society faced rested upon two fundamental assumptions. The first, which he adapted from the writings of Herbert Spencer, was that the evolution of society depended upon the efficiency of its members. This evolutionary view of social organization coincided with the outlook of intellectuals such as E. L. Godkin, Brooks Adams, and Henry Adams, but unlike these men Beecher placed his hopes for the future on the character of the common people and not on the expertise of their leaders. He made fun of the intellectuals who continued to lament that they had been neglected. As one of Beecher's friends wrote to him, "Brooks Adams . . . was pretty honest. No Adams being nominated for any office, he warns the dear people that they are by no means sure of escaping the bow-wows during the next century. What would become of us if we had neither

Brooks Adams nor Godkin to guide our benighted souls? I draw the veil."[19] Beecher agreed with this view. Shared values, not leadership by the elite, were the only solution to America's problems.

Beecher's second assumption was that the character of the common people determined the rate at which the nation progressed on the scale of civilization. Having grown up during the Age of Jackson, Beecher shared that period's faith in the intelligence and ability of the common man. Since that time, this central assumption had become a basic part of his social outlook. Thus, when war broke out in 1861, Beecher blamed it on the aristocratic plantation leaders of the South who had duped the common people. Similarly, when the conflict ended, he attributed the success of the northern war effort to the industry and determination of the common man.

In 1877, Beecher used this assumption as the basis for a popular lecture entitled "The Reign of the Common People." It was wrong, he now asserted, to be overly fearful of the unrest among the lower classes. Although certain elements, particularly the labor leaders, were dangerous and he worried about them, the trouble was that "the great undermass of society, and the underparts of society, less fortunate in every respect than those that are advanced, are seeking room to develop themselves; they are seeking to go up, and no road has been found along which they can travel as far yet."[20] The common people were lower-class Americans and immigrants who were trying to work their way up the social ladder. Their only faults were that they desired "excessive property" and worked too hard. "The great majority are born poor and in order to succeed devote too much time to business," commented Beecher. "Those who live in Brooklyn, the dormitory of New York, spend so much time [at work] that they don't know their children. They use Sunday as a railroad uses its repair shop."[21]

Despite these shortcomings, Beecher was optimistic about the future growth of the nation. Although there were problems with self-government and difficulties with giving immigrants the vote, "it is better," he believed, "that we should have sixty millions of men learning through their own mistakes how to govern themselves, than it is to have an arbitrary Government. . . ." He was convinced, moreover, that the present troubles would find a solution because the nation was in the hands of God. As he declared at the end of his lecture, "I believe that the Hand that has steered this vagrant world through all the dark seas and storms of the past has hold of the helm yet, and through all seeming confusions He will guide the nations and the people safe to the golden harbour of the millennium. Trust Him: love Him; and rejoice!''

As his closing comments revealed, Beecher was able to overcome his fear of social unrest because he believed that the destiny of the nation was ultimately in the hands of God. In the individualistic, competitive, exploitative society of the late nineteenth century, God's love for man absolved guilt, melted class conflict, bound society together, and led to the triumph of justice and truth. Beecher's continual emphasis on God's love and beneficence helped to reassure millions of Americans that progress was still possible and that the nation still had a glorious future.[22]

The lectures further increased Beecher's popularity, which was already widespread, and his name became a household word throughout the nation. But the popularity was not achieved without some sacrifices. In order to undertake his extensive lecture tours, Beecher was forced to leave his church for long periods of time. During his absence, the church was run by his brother Edward, who was now a resident of Brooklyn, and by Samuel B. Halliday, the assistant minister. As Beecher's tours became longer and more extensive, these men and the trustees gradually came to control the everyday affairs of the church. Without a strong leader, Plymouth Church failed to adapt itself to the needs of the time and became increasingly out of touch with the problems of the lower classes in Brooklyn. This loss of direction was in contrast to the church of Beecher's half-brother Thomas in Elmira, New York, which created a new precedent for helping the poorer members of the parish by providing kitchens, lounges, reading rooms, and places for recreation.[23]

Beecher's extensive lecture tours also forced him to give up his newspaper activities. Since 1870 he had been editing the *Christian Union*, but the scandal, together with the onset of the depression and a fire in the company's plant, drove the paper into bankruptcy in 1875. Ownership was then transferred to the Christian Union Publishing Company, a new corporation supported by some of Beecher's wealthy friends. Beecher remained the editor in name, but Lyman Abbott, the former editor of the *Christian Illustrated Weekly*, came to control the publication of the paper. Beecher agreed to this arrangement because

Abbott had edited two volumes of his sermons a decade earlier and was a close friend. When Beecher was accused of adultery, Abbott had defended him by writing a highly favorable review of the trial for *Harper's Weekly*.[24]

From 1876 on, Lyman Abbott ran the *Christian Union* and wrote most of the paper's editorials. Beecher contributed his weekly sermons and lecture-room talks, but otherwise had little to do with the daily affairs of the paper. He trusted Abbott completely and frequently shared his thoughts with him. As he wrote to a friend, "the very central element of my theologic life has been, to bring men into personal, conscious, and direct intercourse with God. That has been the impelling motive, in attacking all doctrinal statements which blurred and misinterpreted the divine nature, and kept men from going to God directly—soul to soul. The immanence of the Divine spirit—the essential and perpetual play on the human soul has been a foundation of faith with me. All this Abbott knows better, or as well as anybody living."[25] In 1881, Beecher retired from the paper and Abbott became the editor-in-chief. Although his association with the *Christian Union* had never been financially rewarding, Beecher had gained the satisfaction of having a paper that expressed his own views and distributed them to a national audience.

In addition to the decline in his literary activities, Beecher's extensive lecture engagements created problems at home. Shortly after the trial had ended in 1876, Beecher's son and family had moved in with them as an economy measure. When he was away on his lecture trips, Mrs. Beecher frequently wrote to complain about the inequities of such an arrangement. When Beecher's financial situation started to improve, she began to feel that his refusal to reorganize the household was proof that he now believed that she was incapable of running the house. Her discontent was further accentuated by her husband's insistence that she go to Florida for the winter months to improve her health. "It is very bitter to go away from you," she wrote to him on one occasion, "worse now than years ago, because while under this mysterious cloud, whatever it may be, and feeling its cruelty, I am in danger of that which will be far worse than death, that my love and trust in you may grow cold or waver. . . . If your heart had not changed woefully, you would not—you could not subject me to the torture of the last four years."[26] As this letter implied, the pressure of the scandal had changed the relationship between Henry and Eunice and she wanted to restore the earlier mutual trust and confidence.

Mrs. Beecher was particularly bitter because her son's wife, by taking over the supervision of the house, deprived her of a role that gave her a sense of self-respect and usefulness. For many years she had identified with the ideal of domesticity that Catharine Beecher and Harriet Beecher Stowe had described in their book, *The American Woman's Home*. Like her sisters-in-law, Mrs. Beecher believed that the home should be an enclave protected from the vicissitudes of the outside world by a kind and devoted mother. Henry had further strengthened his wife's identification with this ideal by giving her complete control of the household. Absentminded and careless about details, he preferred to let his wife pay the bills and look after the family finances. Thus, when he agreed to let his son's family move in and asked his son's wife to take over the direction of the household, he deprived his own wife of a role that had been a chief source of her identity.

To improve his wife's spirits and restore her confidence, Beecher at last consented to take her with him on his lecture tours. He hoped that the change of scenery would do her some good. Unfortunately, instead of becoming more cheerful, Mrs. Beecher remained in a grim mood and spent most of her time telling others of her troubles. As she wrote to a close friend, "if I could only see one rag of hope that . . . someday I shall find my husband's eyes opened—and ready to do me justice —and reinstate me in my proper place [in the house], I could be more patient."[27] Beecher viewed his wife's discontent as the sign of a martyr complex and tried to keep her in the background, but in Iowa they were invited to visit a local family and Mrs. Beecher told them all her woes. "I do not think she spoke of the *housekeeping*—tho' I do not know but she did," wrote Beecher to a friend, "but my money matters —my new house, the mortgages, her unwillingness to have me build, the extravagances of everybody—her holding a tight rein and preventing ruin, etc., etc., etc. . . . This morbid craving for sympathy over fictitious woes seems like the appetite of the inebriate."[28] After this embarrassment Beecher was uninclined to invite his wife to join him again on his lecture tours.

Eventually, Beecher found a more tactful way of restoring his wife's role as the manager of the household; in 1878 he decided to build a new summer home that Eunice could help design and run. Though at first his wife was hesitant and feared the extra expense, she eventually agreed and came to appreciate the home that *she* could run.

For almost twenty years Beecher had owned a small farm in Peekskill, New York, where he raised a wide variety of fruits and flowers. The farm served both as a summer retreat from the muggy heat of Brooklyn and as his favorite form of amusement. As soon as the snow left the ground each spring, Beecher would travel to Peekskill to give his gardener instructions about the planting and cultivation of the fields. He delighted in competing with his neighbors to see who could produce the earliest crops, and he made frequent gifts of flowers and fruit to his friends in Brooklyn.

As Beecher's children were married and started to raise families of their own, they outgrew the house on the farm. Beecher, therefore, began to think of replacing it. He was encouraged to do so by his sisters Harriet and Catharine, who had given much thought to the different forms of domestic architecture in their books about domesticity. Harriet herself had recently purchased new houses in Mandarin, Florida, and Hartford, Connecticut, and she urged Henry to try his hand at designing a new summer home of his own. After much thought, Beecher decided to take her advice, assured that the income from his lectures would more than pay for the new building.

It took several years to design and construct the house in Peekskill and the supervision of the project became for Beecher a welcome diversion. Working closely with the architect, he became well-versed in the details of building and made frequent trips to Peekskill to check upon the work of the contractor. The final product, sitting on a hill overlooking the Hudson River, clearly reflected his ideas. As he had written a decade earlier in one of his Star Articles, "a house is the shape which a man's thought takes when he imagines how he should like to live. Its interior is the measure of his social and domestic nature; its exterior, of his esthetic and artistic nature. It interprets, in material form, his ideas of home, of friendship, and of comfort." [29]

The house was built of wood and stone in a neo-Gothic style. Three stories high, it was topped with steep-pitched roofs that overlapped each other and were pierced with dormer windows. A long porch, supported by wooden arches, extended across the front of the house and around one side. The front door opened into a large hall, richly furnished with carved oak paneling and heavy Victorian furniture. The hall led into rooms of different sizes, many of which had fireplaces. The house, with its thick stone walls, ornate oak beams, irregular roof, and profusion of windows created a sense of strength and respectability as well as of individuality and distinctiveness. Like Beecher himself, it seemed at once unique and yet typical of the architecture in vogue at the time. Imagination seemed to be balanced and held in check by the need for respectability.

The completion of the house in 1878 gave Beecher particular satisfaction. As he wrote to a friend, "The house at Peekskill goes on prosperously. . . . I am laying up money diligently so as to meet every bill as it comes due. I have a pride in building the house, in one year, and earning every penny that pays for it, without a cent of debt, and that after the world, the flesh, and the devil conspired to put me down."[30]

The great advantage of the new house, once Eunice was put in charge, was that it could easily accommodate the families of his children, who were invited to spend the summer and the fall months there. Most of Beecher's children lived within traveling distance. Harriet, the eldest, had married Samuel Scoville, a clergyman in Norwich, Connecticut, and had several children of her own. So, too, did his son William, who worked for Henry W. Sage's lumber company and lived in Brooklyn. The only member of the family who could not be expected to visit was Herbert, the youngest son who had recently graduated from Amherst College and was now married and working on the West Coast.

In addition to financing the construction of his house, Beecher's lecture tours paid for his three-week vacations in New Hampshire, where he and Eunice went to avoid his attacks of hay fever in late August and September. As he humorously commented to a friend, "My tour is completed. I am on my way home. . . . The Hay Fever is at the door. The symptoms are advancing, I must run for my life. I see whole regiments of sneezes in ambush waiting for me to pass. I am repacking my trunk, with all my handkerchiefs on top. My voice is rusty and grates like an unoiled hinge but, by the time you get this, I shall be in the White Mts. . . ."[31] In New Hampshire, he and Eunice usually stayed with his sister Harriet at a resort hotel called the Twin Mountain House. There brother and sister could relax and share their ideas about religion. In the afternoons, they would dominate the croquet court and take on all comers. With mallet in hand, each displayed the characteristic Beecher aggressiveness. On Sundays, Henry would preach to hotel guests and other visitors, who gathered in a large tent on the lawn. The trip to the White Mountains became such a regular occasion that Beecher eventually agreed to preach every Sunday. After two or three weeks in New Hampshire, he would then return to Brooklyn, rested and ready to begin the new year at his church.

Once his house was completed and his debts were paid off, Beecher no longer needed the extra money supplied by his lecture tours and he began to limit his speaking engagements to the summer months. This gave him more time during the year to resume his former activity as an advocate of reform. He was particularly interested in local political developments. With the election of President Hayes in 1877, Beecher gained access to the national administration through William Maxwell Evarts, the chief counsel during his trial for adultery, who was now the secretary of state. Unsure about the national party leadership, Beecher frequently wrote to Evarts to express his opinion about the distribution of patronage in Brooklyn. "I am not in political life and do not feel at liberty to have much to do with appointments," he declared apologetically in his first letter. "As far as I know the only single thing I have asked is that my friend Freeland shall hold the office of Collector in Brooklyn where more than 30 millions of dollars have passed through his hands without loss to the government of a penny. . . ." It was important to Beecher that Freeland be retained, because the opposition was pushing for a man named French, who was Frank Moulton's partner and a threat to Beecher's influence in the city. "For the administration to promise me bread, and then break my head with stone," he added, "will not I am sure agree with the President's wish nor with his intentions."

In March of the following year, with the decision about the Brooklyn patronage still up in the air, Beecher visited Washington to talk with the president about the matter. No sooner had his request been granted, however, than the opposition began to renew its efforts to win the post once more. "Those who sympathize with me," wrote Beecher to Evarts in 1879, "desire to keep that important office *out of the hands of politicians* and to make it a model of fiscal management, to the honor of this Administration and of Civil Service Reform, and whoever will help us we mean to act solidly for him."[32] The implication was clear. Beecher and his friends would support the national administration in the coming election only if the administration reciprocated and gave them support in the struggle for patronage in Brooklyn.

Despite his worries about patronage and party leadership, Beecher's comments to Evarts clearly revealed his commitment to the Republican party. When Rutherford B. Hayes refused to run for a second term of office in 1880 and the Republicans nominated James A. Garfield of Ohio and Chester A. Arthur of New York, Beecher reaffirmed his belief in Republicanism in a major speech at Cooper Institute. "The great end of the Canvass is not the election of a *President*," he shouted to the large audience, "but for the ascendency of the *Party*." He then went on to argue that the Republican party, which had "sprung from the *spirit of liberty*," "inspired and sustained the government for 4 war years," and "guided the nation back to sound currency," deserved to be reelected. There were dangers, he admitted. Some Republicans exaggerated the strife between capital and labor. They wanted to meddle with wages, and asked the government to provide work for men. This was clearly an "attempt to change republican government into paternal government." These men had to be silenced by electing Garfield and Arthur. "Let all feuds cease!" he shouted. "Let all factions end for party, for the country, for humanity."[33]

The speech brought down the house and aroused considerable enthusiasm among Republicans. Mrs. Garfield was so impressed that she wrote Beecher a personal letter of thanks. "General Garfield has just finished reading aloud to me your address at Cooper Institute on Wednesday evening last," she commented, "and I must presume enough upon your kindness to say to you how indebted we are to you for it. The high ground to which you lift up political discussion and your broad philanthropic views show there are yet strong hands to hold up the majesty of our Government, and watchful hearts to stand guard against all destroying powers. All you have said is so in harmony with General Garfield's own views and feelings that it has given him new strength to read your inspiring words. . . ."[34]

The praise from Mrs. Garfield and the subsequent election of her husband to the presidency in November bolstered Beecher's faith in Republicanism, but he never entirely regained his former commitment to the party leadership. The exposure of corruption in the 1870s, together with a lingering evangelical distrust of politicians, made him wary of the party professionals, and he continued to question their motives. When Garfield was assassinated during the following summer and Arthur became president, Beecher again became uneasy. This uneasiness deepened in October, 1882, when the party regulars defeated the bid of Governor Alonzo B. Cornell of New York for another term in office. Angered by what appeared to be a flagrant disregard for public opinion, Beecher decided to criticize publicly the party leadership. Speaking at a mass meeting in Brooklyn, he scathingly rebuked President Arthur for using the power of the federal government to force his views on the state. Beecher's attack was so intense that the Republican "candidates on the platform turned all the colors of the rainbow," much to the glee of the opposition.[35] Beecher later explained his position by arguing that "a great middle class" had developed, "composed of men who are determined to act in the future with regard to municipal affairs in Brooklyn upon local considerations as distinguished from National politics."[36]

Beecher's independent stand during the 1882 gubernatorial election made the Republican party leaders in Brooklyn distrust his loyalty. As the time for the next presidential race drew near, they therefore tried to obtain an explicit pledge of support. As early as February, 1884, General Benjamin Tracy, a member of Beecher's defense counsel during his trial for adultery, wrote to Beecher to offer him a position within the local leadership if Beecher would promise to support the party. Though the offer was tempting, Beecher nevertheless refused to commit himself. "I love my personal independence," he replied, "and on the whole had better keep it. Yet I feel that it was kind of you to propose—and that it would be an honor to me to accept. But after 70 honors are at a discount."[37]

In March the invitation to support the Republican party was renewed, but this time it came through higher channels. During one of Beecher's periodic lecture trips to Washington, President Arthur invited him to the White House. "I was very graciously received by the President, who hopes to be the candidate for the next election, and reckons on my services," wrote Beecher to his daughter.[38] Convinced by the passage of the Pendleton Civil Service Act and by the president's apparently nonpartisan conduct in office that Arthur had broken with the professional politicians in the party, Beecher agreed to speak in his behalf during the coming campaign.[39] But this commitment proved to be premature, for in July Arthur was passed over by the national convention in favor of James G. Blaine, the former Speaker of the House. Thus the question of Beecher's loyalty to the party was again reopened and the competition for his services was again renewed.

The nomination of Blaine by the Republicans and of Cleveland by the Democrats placed Beecher in an awkward position, since unpleasant rumors were circulating about both candidates. Blaine was accused of using his position as Speaker of the House for personal gain by giving a land grant to a railroad in 1876, and Cleveland was rumored to have fathered an illegitimate child. Because both candidates had unsavory reputations, Beecher at first refused to back either one.

Beecher's reluctance to commit himself made both candidates increase their efforts behind the scenes to obtain a pledge of support. Writing to Harriet Beecher Stowe, Blaine made ties of friendship the basis of his appeal. Having complimented Harriet on "her warm support of those whom we feel entitled to claim as personal friends," he went on to assert that "I never was more surprised in my life than when I found your gifted and eloquent brother opposing me. We had been friends for so many years that it came upon me as a sore disappointment. . . . Please tell the Rev. H.W.B. that he should not turn his back on his own connections."[40] Blaine's approach was clever, but he made a major mistake in thinking that Beecher could be won over by threats. Such tactics simply reinforced Beecher's misgivings about Blaine's ethics.

In contrast to Blaine's heavy-handed attempt to win Beecher's support, the efforts of Cleveland's backers were more subtle. Cleveland worked through Carl Schurz, the articulate leader of the Independent Republicans, who was known for his honesty and integrity. "The more I study the case," wrote Schurz to Beecher, "the more I become convinced that Gov. Cleveland is a much calumniated man; that the stories as told bear all the signs of artful invention, and that those who started them, persuaded themselves that the fourteen year old affair which forms the substratum, would deter Gov. Cleveland and his friends from ever attempting to challenge the fabric of falsehood built upon it." Despite the forcefulness of Schurz's arguments, Beecher at first refused to act, because a number of clergymen in Buffalo assured him that Cleveland had not changed his ways. "The Independents of all men," wrote Beecher in reply to Schurz, "being the advocates of moral reformation in politics cannot uphold a grossly dissipated man and they ought not to wait to be *driven* from their position, but [should] retreat in good order, before being charged, from an untenable ground."[41]

Notwithstanding Beecher's initial misgivings, several days after writing to Schurz he agreed to support Cleveland. The decision to back Cleveland was influenced by a variety of considerations. The first was a letter from George W. Curtis, a prominent Mugwump reformer and the editor of *Harper's Weekly*, who argued convincingly that Cleveland's affair had ended years ago and that Cleveland had paid for the child's support from that time on.[42]

Although Beecher was impressed by Curtis's comments, what really induced him to change his mind about Cleveland was his annoyance at letters from friends who urged him to think of his own reputation and stay away from politics.[43] He was particularly angered by a letter from the assistant minister of his church urging him to remain neutral so that his position would not divide the congregation. "The alarm of friends, the party excitement of others, has no effect upon me whatsoever," declared Beecher in a strongly worded reply. "Any *new* and *real information*," he added, "I shall be grateful for; but to tell me nothing, and only to express amazement, wonder, concern, etc., etc., and to let me know how damaging to my reputation, and my interest it will be, if I follow my judgment and not theirs, . . . indicates how far gone in political excitement they are and how little they understand the man whom they love. . . . I am ready to resign my pastorate," he continued, "at an hour's notice, when I no longer have freedom to follow my convictions or when doing so, divides the church and scatters the congregation."[44]

Angered by the thinly disguised way in which his friends appealed to his self-interest, Beecher decided to take a stand, and he launched a major attack on Blaine. "Unsound in statesmanlike judgment, unscrupulous in political methods, dim-eyed in perceiving the distinction between truth and untruth; absorbingly ambitious, but short-sighted as to the methods of gratifying it, . . . Mr. Blaine makes a charming candidate, but would make a dangerous President," he declared in a public letter to R. A. Alger, a candidate for governor of Michigan. The local newspapers greedily snatched up the story. Beecher's accusation, declared the New York *Times*, ''cannot be lightly dismissed; and certainly it cannot be readily disproved.''[45]

Having at last taken a stand, Beecher now entered into the campaign in earnest. A week after he sent his letter, he spoke in favor of Cleveland at a rally at the Brooklyn Academy of Music. He defended the stand of the Independent Republicans by asserting the country would be in grave danger if Blaine were elected. "It is the whole style of his statesmanship that I am opposed to," Beecher declared. "And at this time with more than a hundred millions surplus on hand, with a large and active body of manufacturing men that want to keep that hundred million on hand and find ways to use it without disturbing monopolies—with this vast treasury that would make an honest man almost tremble for his integrity I do not wish to see a man as President whose opinions of the power of money are in the slightest degree doubtful."[46] The danger of political corruption was paramount, and Beecher wanted to make sure that a corrupt politician like Blaine would be kept out of office.

Beecher further developed his views about political corruption in a second speech, delivered on October 22, 1884, to a huge gathering at the Brooklyn Rink. He began by recounting his services to the Republican party during the Civil War. "I am now opposing the party whose cradle I rocked," he declared, "because I do not mean to be a pall-bearer to carry the coffin of that party to the grave." The problem was that the party refused to consider the main issues of the day—Civil Service reform, the defense of the rights of the common people, freedom of commerce, and liberty of thought. "The rights of labor as against combined capital, and the defense of the individual against the despotism of corporate bodies" were concerns that the Republican party had totally neglected. Thus, he thought, it was imperative to elect Cleveland rather than Blaine.

Having described what he believed to be the basic issues in the election, Beecher ended his speech on a personal note. During the previous week his wife had written to Cleveland asking him to explain the rumors about his personal life that continued to circulate in the press. Cleveland answered by sending a frank letter in which he insisted that the rumors were "utterly and in every shape untrue." Beecher read the letter to the audience and then went on to make a direct comparison between his own scandal and the rumors about Cleveland:

> When in the gloomy night of my own suffering, I sounded every depth of sorrow, I vowed that if God would bring the day star of hope, I would never suffer brother, friend, or neighbour to go unfriended, should a like serpent seek to crush him. That oath I will regard now. . . . Men counsel me to prudence lest I stir again my own griefs. No! I will not be prudent. If I refuse to interpose a shield of well-placed confidence between Governor Cleveland and the swarm of liars that nuzzle in the mud, or sling arrows from ambush, may my tongue cleave to the roof of my mouth, and my right hand forget its cunning. I will imitate the noble example set me by Plymouth Church in the day of my own calamity. They were not ashamed of my bonds. They stood by me with God-sent loyalty. It was a heroic deed. They have set my duty before me, and I will imitate their example.[47]

By deliberately connecting the accusations against Cleveland with his own trial for adultery, Beecher consciously tried to cast himself in the role of the martyr. He deliberately risked his reputation in the defense of a friend so that he would appear so honest and forthright no one would ever doubt his integrity again. He hoped thereby to convince his audience that he was a man who was willing to sacrifice his reputation and career for a just and noble cause. And the ploy worked. By playing the role of the martyr, he won over the audience and aided Cleveland's campaign. He also proved to himself and to the public that the scandal that had plagued his own name was dead and that his reputation had survived intact.

Moreover, even near the end of his long career, Beecher continued to search for new ways to add to his popularity. Not satisfied by the acclaim that greeted his efforts in the pulpit and on the lecture platform, he constantly looked for new methods to appeal to the public. In almost haphazard fashion, therefore, he continued to play an important role in politics. Although he exerted little influence within the parties themselves, his enormous personal following made him a man worth fighting over. Conscious of the power that derived from his popularity, Beecher continued to interject his views about the struggle between capital and labor into the political arena, even when doing so threatened to alienate members of his congregation.

NOTES

1. Robert V. Bruce, *1877: Year of Violence* (Indianapolis, 1959), chap. 7.

2. H. W. Beecher to Mrs. H. B. Claflin, March 11, 1877, Rutherford B. Hayes Library.

3. H. W. Beecher to Eunice Beecher, Feb. 8, 9, 21, 26, March 15, 1877, Yale MSS.

4. H. W. Beecher to Mrs. H. B. Claflin, June 5, 1877, Rutherford B. Hayes Library.

5. J. B. Pond to H. W. Beecher, n.d., Yale MSS.

6. Samuel Clemens, *Mark Twain's Autobiography* (New York, 1924), I, 157.

7. H. W. Beecher, *The Strike and Its Lessons: Two Addresses*, pamphlet (New York, 1877), 18–19.

8. *Ibid.*, 28, 34.

9. H. W. Beecher to Rutherford B. Hayes, March 4, 1879, Rutherford B. Hayes Library. Hayes agreed and vetoed the exclusion bill.

10. H. W. Beecher, "Address before the Society of the Army of the Potomac," in *Patriotic Addresses*, ed. John Howard (New York, 1887), 815.

11. *Congregationalist*, July 25, 1877, p. 236, quoted in Henry F. May, *Protestant Churches and Industrial America* (New York, 1963), 93.

12. H. W. Beecher, *Patriotic Addresses*, 819.

13. These lectures are contained in H. W. Beecher, *Lectures and Orations*, ed. Newell D. Hillis (New York, 1913), chaps. II and III.

14. William C. Beecher and Samuel Scoville, *A Biography of Rev. Henry Ward Beecher* (New York, 1888), 104–5.

15. David A. Wells, "How Shall the Nation Regain Prosperity?" *North American Review*, CXXV (July, 1877), 131–32.

16. H. W. Beecher to D. A. Wells, July 24, 1877, David A. Wells Papers, Library of Congress.

17. H. W. Beecher, *Lectures and Orations*, 48, 54–55. On the attitudes toward cleanliness, see Leonore Davidoff, "The Rationalization of Housework," in *Dependence and Exploitation in Work and Marriage*, ed. D. Barker and S. Allen (London, 1976), 121–51.

18. *Ibid.*, 52–54, 78.

19. Thomas G. Shearman to H. W. Beecher, July 5, 1876, Yale MSS.

20. H. W. Beecher, *Lectures and Orations*, 102.

21. *Emporia* [Kansas] *Daily Republican*, Sept. 22, 1883. Although the title of the lecture remained the same, the content of it frequently changed.

22. Beecher, *Lectures and Orations*, 119, 126–27. I am indebted to William G. McLoughlin for the central arguments in this paragraph. See his book, *The Meaning of Henry Ward Beecher* (New York, 1970), 246–47.

23. Thomas K. Beecher to Leonard Bacon, Feb. 2, 1878, Leonard Bacon Papers, Yale University Library.

24. Ira V. Brown, *Lyman Abbott: Christian Evolutionist* (Cambridge, Mass., 1953), 66–77.

25. H. W. Beecher to S. B. Halliday, Sept. 12, 1882 (typed copy), Yale MSS.

26. Eunice Beecher to H. W. Beecher, n.d., Yale MSS.

27. Eunice Beecher to Mrs. C. Beach, July 24, 1878, Yale MSS.

28. H. W. Beecher to Mr. White, Aug. 6, 1878, Yale MSS.

29. H. W. Beecher, *Star Papers, or Experiences of Art and Nature* (New York, 1855), 285.

30. H. W. Beecher to Eunice Beecher, April 20, 1877, Yale MSS.

31. H. W. Beecher to ?, April 15 (no year; typed copy), Yale MSS.

32. H. W. Beecher to William M. Evarts, Oct. 18, 1877 (copy); H. W. Beecher to Mrs. H. B. Claflin, March 3, 1878, Rutherford B. Hayes Library; H. W. Beecher to William M. Evarts, Oct. 10, 1879, Evarts Papers, Yale Library.

33. H. W. Beecher, Speech Notes, n.d., Library of Congress.

34. Lucretia Garfield to H. W. Beecher, Oct. 17, 1880; Chester A. Arthur to H. W. Beecher, Nov. 8, 1880, Yale MSS.

35. New York *Times*, Oct. 2, 1882: Brooklyn *Eagle*, Nov. 4, 1882.

36. New York *Tribune*, Nov. 12, 1883.

37. H. W. Beecher to General Benjamin F. Tracy, Feb. 27, 1884 (typed copy), Yale MSS.

38. H. W. Beecher to Harriet B. Scoville, March 5, 1884, Yale MSS.

39. New York *Times*, May 21, 1884.

40. James G. Blaine to H. B. Stowe, July 25, 1884, Schlesinger Library.

41. Carl Schurz to H. W. Beecher, July 30, 1884; H. W. Beecher to Carl Schurz, July 29, 1884, Yale MSS.

42. George W. Curtis to H. W. Beecher, July 30, 1884; see also the letter from L. S. Metcalf, editor of the *North American Review*, to H. W. Beecher, Aug. 2, 1884, Yale MSS.

43. Rossiter W. Raymond to H. W. Beecher, July 31, 1884, Yale MSS.

44. H. W. Beecher to S. B. Halliday, Aug. 9, 1884, Yale MSS.

45. H. W. Beecher to General R. A. Alger, Oct. 6, 1884 (typed copy), Yale MSS; New York *Times*, Oct. 7, 1884.

46. New York *Times*, Oct. 16, 1884.

47. H. W. Beecher, "Patriotism above Party," in *Lectures and Orations*, 311.

12

Evolution and Morality

Henry Ward Beecher had long been interested in the controversy over evolution that arose after the publication of Charles Darwin's *Origin of Species* in 1859, but, in characteristic fashion, he refrained from speaking publicly on that subject until the theory had gained a degree of general acceptance. As he explained to his congregation in 1884, "until recently he had not preached what lay on the horizon of his mind forty years ago. He was very cautious in regard to enunciating new truth. He did not want to break off a man from the old truths before he was ready for the new."[1]

The controversy over evolution centered on the social and intellectual implications of Darwin's theory. Darwin had argued that the different species of plants and animals in the world had their origin not from an act of special creation, as had been previously argued, but from a process of "variation and natural selection" during which "the less improved forms of life" had died out. In a single theory, he thus organized a mass of hitherto uncorrelated and unknown data and put forth a hypothesis that seemed to explain the pattern of change throughout the natural world. The difficulty in Darwin's hypothesis lay not in the hypothesis itself, though that was open to question because it did not explain the cause of variation, but rather in the differing and contradictory implications of the theory when applied to the world of man.[2]

The clergy were among the first to recognize the potentially harmful implications of Darwin's theory. Although Darwin himself believed in God and had at one time considered entering the ministry, he struck at the heart of orthodox theology when he argued that the variety of species in the natural world had come about through "natural selection" rather than by special creation. Swiftly and devastatingly, his theory contradicted the biblical account of creation, and, by extension, undermined the orthodox conception of sin as the heritage of Adam's fall. Adam's violation of God's authority clearly could not have taken place if there had not been a Garden of Eden. Darwin's theory, moreover, cast doubt on the authority of the scriptures and brought into question the argument for the existence of God based on the evidence of design in the world. Because Darwin's theory threatened cherished Christian beliefs and seemed to encourage a relativistic attitude toward standards, the more orthodox clergy were quick to label it as a fraud and a heresy.

This was the position taken by Charles Hodge, a professor at the Princeton Divinity School and the chief spokesman for the conservative wing of the Presbyterian church. Hodge had long asserted that no new idea had ever been introduced into his classes at Princeton, and he now substantiated his claim by attacking the theory of evolution. In a book entitled *What Is Darwinism?* published in 1874, Hodge argued that Darwin's theory was "virtually atheistical" because it denied the existence of design in the natural world. Evolution was simply another heresy, developed by scheming men to undermine traditional religious values.[3]

Hodge's unflinching attack on Darwinism had considerable appeal for more conservative members of the Presbyterian church, but it was stoutly opposed by many liberals who sought to reconcile the latest developments in science with the basic tenets of evangelical theology. Speaking for these liberals, James McCosh, the president of the College of New Jersey (later called Princeton University), argued that evolution was not an atheistic theory, because the Creator had "stacked the deck with purposeful variations and thus [had] guarded the selective process." He was supported in this view by John Fiske, a professor of philosophy at Harvard, who declared that "the doctrine of evolution asserts, as the widest and deepest truth which the study of Nature can disclose to us, that there exists a Power to which no limit in time or space is conceivable. . . ." That power was God himself, the "first cause" of the universe. Thus, both McCosh and Fiske insisted that the theory of evolution, instead of discrediting traditional religious beliefs, actually provided a new and more scientific basis for faith.[4]

The debate between Hodge and Fiske over the implications of Darwin's theory for religion was matched in the 1870s by the controversy that arose over evolution in the field of social ethics. The debate began when Herbert Spencer, an English social philosopher, seized upon Darwin's theory as a new technique for getting rid of what he considered to be the romantic sentimentalism of his day. Tired of seeing indiscriminate aid doled out to the poor and convinced that science could bring a new objectivity into the field of social ethics, Spencer argued that "natural selection" was but another name for the "survival of the fittest." Progress resulted when the "unhealthy, imbecile, slow, vacillating, faithless members" of society were weeded out and allowed to die. It made no sense to help the sick and infirm, he added. Charity, either from the government or from private sources, simply reduced the efficiency of natural selection.[5]

Spencer's views were enthusiastically endorsed in America by William Graham Sumner, a Yale professor who found in the theory of evolution the key to a new science of society. Using the Malthusian doctrine that the population of the world was increasing faster than its means of support, Sumner argued that "if a man comes forward with any grievance against the order of society so far as this is shaped by human agency, he must have patient hearing and full redress; but if he addresses a demand to society for relief from the hardships of life, he asks simply that somebody else should get his living for him. In that case he ought to be left to find his error from hard experience."[6] Life was tough and brutal, and those who lacked the strength to overcome its burdens did not deserve to survive.

The harshness of Sumner's views was rejected by most Americans, who agreed with Lester Frank Ward, a sociologist working for the Treasury Department, who asserted that men had progressed out of the stage where the struggle for survival determined their social outlook. Unlike animals, men were intelligent enough to cooperate and help one another. Charitable impulses, it followed from this view, were the mark of a higher stage of civilization. They were not, as Sumner had argued, simply the sign of maudlin sentimentality.

It was the conjunction of the controversy over the religious and ethical consequences of Darwinism with a social crisis caused by the influx of immigrants, the growth of cities, and the expansion of business and industry that made the debate over Darwinism so serious, so consequential, and so crucially important for Victorian Americans. The debate between Lester Frank Ward and William Graham Sumner was far more than a squabble between two intellectuals; it was implicitly a debate over the meaning of individualism and success in America. For the acceptance of Darwin's theory forced both to reject a basic assumption that lay at the heart of pre–Civil War Emersonian individualism. This was the assumption that a natural order existed apart from and independent of society. For Emerson, this natural order was the harmonious and benign world of nature, a place where the individual, freed from the restraints of social institutions, might most fully realize his creative potential. For Sumner and Ward, in contrast, the natural world was an arena filled with conflict, strife, violence, and terror. In such a world, the battle to survive became the greatest necessity.[7]

The acceptance of Darwinism not only destroyed the Emersonian vision of the natural world as harmonious and beneficent, it also forced Americans to reassess the value of institutions. For once the natural world was portrayed as cruel and violent, institutions had to be seen in a different light. Depending upon one's perspective, they could now be considered either as necessary devices to control the aggressive instincts within human nature or as artificial restraints that retarded the progress of the superior species.

The acceptance of evolution, in a similar fashion, brought into question the traditional conception of the relationship between wealth and success. In the years before the Civil War, success had been defined primarily as the development of character. Wealth was a mark of achievement only if one could prove that it had been earned through diligent industry, careful planning, and hard work. After the Civil War, the acceptance of Darwinism together with the creation of new fortunes of unimagined size forced a rethinking of the earlier attitude toward wealth. Once again, two differing views were possible. Darwinism could be used either to defend the fortunes as the product of superior ability or to attack them as clear evidence of cunning and ruthlessness. In either case, the acceptance of the theory of evolution in the decades after the Civil War forced a redefinition of the relationship between wealth and success.[8]

As early as the 1860s, in his attempt to develop a new, more romantic conception of Christianity, Henry Ward Beecher had indirectly tried to meet the challenge to the faith caused by Charles Darwin's discoveries. As he admitted to a close friend:

> I do not think Science, as it will be, is without its Calvary. But, *as it now is*, in the hands of Mill, Spencer, Huxley, Tyndall and I may add, Charles Darwin, it has gone only so far as to have lost the cross, and not far enough to have found it again. I am entirely confident that the truths of the *New Testament* are perfectly at one with the truth of nature. Both are divine. They will never collide in any such sense as to be interchangeably destructive. We are in a transition. Such periods are apt to be barrens and deserts for religious feeling. I am anxious to maintain the religious sentiment and fervor of men during these changes, and that recasting of philosophy which impedes.[9]

Beecher's answer to the conflict between religion and science, as we have seen, was to develop a new conception of Nature. God was immanent in the natural world and had ordered the world in terms of natural laws. As William G. McLoughlin has pointed out,

> Mutual dependence—man upon Nature, Nature upon Man, society upon order, the world upon control, the garden upon cultivation—this was the lesson Beecher drew from the new discoveries of science. But he had faith both in God's benevolent superintendence and upon man's will to mastery of his fate. Because God is greater than man and thus even better able to "drive" the laws of Nature; because he is in Nature and guiding it every moment and not a clockmaker God who exists outside the world He has made; because He has given man the power to discern the laws by which the universe works and the intuition to perceive His hand at work in them, there is no need to be fearful either that Nature will overwhelm us or that God has forsaken us or that science will lead us away from God.[10]

Beecher accepted the theory of evolution not only because it was in harmony with his conception of nature, but also because it appeared to be compatible with the ideas of reason, progress, and divine immanence. Darwin's theory, as far as the Brooklyn preacher was con-

cerned, made change understandable, demonstrated the utility of suffering and hardship, and supported the doctrine of "Christian Nurture,"
the view that an individual's devotion to God should develop gradually
rather than spring forth suddenly at the time of conversion. The only
difficulty for Beecher with Darwin's theory was the reluctance of the
public to accept it. Thus, although he early incorporated an evolutionary perspective into his lectures and sermons, he deliberately waited
until the 1880s before he spoke directly to the controversy raised by
Darwin and his followers.

Then he entered the ranks of the controversy with an article entitled
"Progress of Thought in the Church" in the August, 1882, *North
American Review*. As he stated in his introduction, Beecher wrote the
article not only to study the nature and direction of the "great change
. . . passing over the public mind, in matters of religious beliefs," but
also to attack the religious beliefs of conservative congregational clergymen. Beecher began his essay by distinguishing between churches
and theology. Churches were increasing in numbers, he argued, because they were "organized centers" for morality, education, and
public spirit. But theology was undergoing a major transition, a change
from "creeds of the past to the formation of creeds adapted to the present wants and present knowledge of truth." These were changes forced
by the new developments in science. "It matters little that upon some
points the great doctrine of evolution is yet in discussion," Beecher
stated reassuringly. "The debate is not about the reality of evolution,
but, of the influences that produce and direct it." Since the reality of
evolution could be accepted as a fact, all that was needed was to correct the errors of orthodox theology. "Our time is one of transition,"
Beecher emphasized. "We are refusing the theology of Absolute Mon-
archy—of Divine Despotism and [are] framing a theology consistent
with the life and teachings of Jesus Christ."

As these comments reveal, Beecher was most interested in Darwin-
ian theory because evolution could be used as a new weapon to combat
the "hideous doctrines" and the "crustacean shell" of the orthodox
Calvinist theology that he had long opposed. For years he had espoused an evangelical liberalism—a faith based on the teachings of
Jesus—only to have his ideas challenged and opposed by conservative
church leaders like Hodge. Now, convinced that "science is truth,"
Beecher felt that he could refute for once and for all the older notions

of original sin and divine judgment. In their place, he offered his new theology based on Christ's love. "Changes must come and old things pass away," he asserted in a veiled reference to the older Calvinism, "but no tree sheds its leaf until it has rolled up a bud at its axil for next summer."[11]

Beecher's ready acceptance of evolutionary theory in the pages of the *North American Review* created little stir even though it was his first direct statement on that subject. The reason was obvious. Other clergymen had already argued the case for Darwin's theory in a more detailed and extensive manner. Even the debate over creeds had somewhat died down after William J. Tucker, a professor at Andover Seminary in Massachusetts, had asserted that no creed could ever "be the final expression of truth."[12] The only criticism that did arise came from clergymen in the New York area who had long disagreed with Beecher's theological views and resented his attack on orthodoxy. That criticism, too, would have been inconsequential if it had not prompted Beecher to resign from the local Congregational ministerial association. Tired of controversy and fearing that his acceptance of evolution would lead to a battle among the local churches, Beecher handed in his resignation in October, 1882. With this step, he severed the last of his ties to the national church and formally rejected the vision of cooperation that had sparked the Second Great Awakening. Cooperation among the churches had too often been shattered on the rocks of theological controversy. It no longer seemed to be a viable ideal.[13]

Once freed from his ties to the local ministerial association, the organization that had censured Plymouth Church for its dismissal of Theodore Tilton before the scandal, Beecher was able to develop his ideas about evolution without fear of censure from other Congregational churches. Thus, when invited later that fall to speak at a dinner in honor of Herbert Spencer, he accepted without hesitation. The dinner, held at Delmonico's in New York, was a gala affair, attended by more than one hundred and fifty educators, civic leaders, and clergymen. Wine flowed freely and the audience remained enthusiastic as they listened to seven after-dinner speeches. Spencer himself, who was unable to attend the dinner because of ill health, had just completed a three-month tour of the states. During his tour, he had somewhat revised his earlier views about government and now argued that it should play a more active role in protecting the rights of the individual.

"Everywhere," he commented, "along with the reprobation of government intrusion into various spheres where private activities should be left to themselves, I have contended that in its special sphere, the maintenance of equitable relations among citizens, governmental action should be extended and elaborated."

What Americans needed most, Spencer continued, was a "revised ideal of life." "Hereafter," he asserted, "when this age of active material progress has yielded mankind its benefits, there will, I think, come a better adjustment of labor and enjoyment. Among the reasons for thinking this, there is the reason that the process of evolution throughout the organic world at large, brings an increasing surplus of energies that are not absorbed in fulfilling material needs, and points to a still larger surplus for humanity of the future." The struggle for survival had become less urgent, and it was now time to consolidate the benefits an industrial society could provide for the common man.

Spencer's remarks, which combined a mild criticism of the American social system with a belief in progress, were enormously appealing to Beecher, who had long been troubled about the quality of American life. But, as the seventh speaker of the evening, he wisely decided to limit his comments to less serious questions. After humorously discussing the difficulty of tracing one's ancestry back to the monkeys, he concluded by thanking Spencer for his contribution to science and expressing his hope that they both might meet again in the world to come.[14]

The extensive press coverage of the Herbert Spencer dinner prompted Beecher to make evolution the topic for his lecture tour the following summer. After considerable thought, he entitled his talk "Evolution or Revolution." The title foreshadowed his approach, which was first to scare the audience with the idea that evolution was a radically new doctrine and then to reassure them that "the revolutionary tendencies of the doctrine of Evolution are more in seeming than in fact, and, though extremely radical, are radical in the right direction."

The lecture itself was divided into two parts. In the first, Beecher explained the compatibility of evolution and religion, as he had done in his article in the *North American Review*. In the second, he went on to explore the social implications of Darwin's theory. The real advantage of the theory of evolution, Beecher explained to his audience, was that it threw new light on some of the most pressing social issues of the day. For the radicals who sought to equalize the position of each member of society, evolution provided a new answer. Success depended upon brain power. You cannot make the intellectually feeble man equal to the man of real ability, he argued. That would be going against the laws of nature. "The way out from poverty and insignificance and all the miserable experiences of undercast men is . . . development, education, more brain, better brain. . . . Send your children higher. The elevation of mankind in moral and intellectual culture is the only way to cure the evils of society."

This advice on how to succeed was essentially a recast version of Beecher's earlier statements about self-help, brought up to date and given a more scientific basis by the doctrine of evolution. Having reaffirmed his earlier view of social change, Beecher ended on an optimistic note by asserting that the human race was daily improving in reason and moral sense. By casting off superstition and embracing the doctrine of evolution, society was progressing and true religion was being strengthened.[15]

Once again, Beecher's lecture proved to be an immense success, since while posing as a radical and an innovator, he reaffirmed the earlier American faith in education and self-help. It mattered little that he dodged the more troublesome aspects of Darwin's thought. What mattered was that Beecher's explanation enabled his audience to be at once daring and respectable, open-minded and yet socially conservative. For nothing could be more reassuring than to learn that the latest developments in science simply reaffirmed the age-old truths of Christianity.

The irony of Beecher's lecture was that while reassuring the general public of the benefits of Darwinism, he himself continued to have doubts about its application to social problems. In particular, he worried about the growing rift in American society between the rich and the poor. As the decade wore on, the increasing evidence of poverty among the lower classes made him more and more critical of the rich. "If the rich were wise," he warned in one lecture, "they would lay aside the idea that they could swell before society and look down upon and treat with contempt the struggling poor." The indignities of affluence were even more offensive because of the existence of large-scale corporate organizations. "Capital has no right to be unjust and inhuman," he complained. "The human element must be considered."[16]

Beecher's concern for the poor became so intense that by 1882 he was willing to accept the organization of labor and the use of strikes. He believed that unions like the Knights of Labor were a form of popular education and should be supported. Labor had the right to organize for self-defense. "One thing is certain," he declared in a sermon reprinted in the New York *Times*, "our sympathies should be with the multitude, with the poor and weak against the rich and strong. The duty of the rich was to be on the side of the less fortunate—the mass of men—and to hold their wealth as a trust from God for the benefit of the poor." [17]

Beecher's anger at the rich and his concern with the plight of the poor, when added to his earlier misgivings about the social implications of evolution, eventually led him to revise his conceptions of individualism and success. His earlier beliefs had rested on the assumption that American abundance was so readily available and American society so open that anyone could get ahead if he worked. Failure, according to this belief, had to be the result of personal faults. But now Beecher became convinced that the power of the rich had limited the openness of the American enterprise system. Class war threatened because of the greedy, hostile actions of men like Cornelius Vanderbilt who ran the industrial giants. Since he no longer believed that the ideals of pre–Civil War America were applicable to a society dominated by teeming cities, aggressive corporations, and ruthless politicians, he began to search for a more effective set of social values. His findings were published in 1884 in a volume entitled *Evolution and Religion*. [18]

Calling himself a "cordial Christian Evolutionist," Beecher began his book by restating the arguments that he had earlier used in the *North American Review* to reconcile evangelical liberalism with evolution. He then quickly moved to what he considered to be the more important subject, "the application of the evolutionary principles and theories to the practical aspects of religious life." Following the path traced by Lester Frank Ward, Beecher argued that man had reached a stage where survival was no longer open to question. Moral force had replaced physical force and men were now being asked to help the less fortunate. The rich, therefore, because of their position in society, were faced with new responsibilities. "Today," Beecher wrote, "the rich are about to learn, if they have not yet learned it, that they cannot separate themselves from the welfare of the whole great laboring multitude. . . . Men who are to have large properties are coming rapidly under the responsibility of using them for the public welfare, and not alone for their own selfishness. The man that stands to-day upon a pedestal simply because he is rich, will in another fifty years stand in the pillory if he does not make his riches serve mankind."

What Beecher wanted was the development of a new kind of social conscience, one which included not only the stewardship of wealth but also the involvement of the rich with the problems of the poor. "If the top of society bends perpetually over the bottom, with tenderness, if the rich and strong are the best friends of the poor and needy, that is a civilized and a Christian community . . . ," he argued.

Stated in another way, what Beecher wanted was a new conception of individualism. As Beecher himself phrased it:

> In the individual, then, is needed not an individuality that quarrels with itself, not a conscience eternally quarreling with benevolence . . . , but a character that throws out in strength every part of the man and harmonizes these around about the element of love; and who, moreover, can lead men together by combinations, exterior unions; for if every human career were individual to its extremity, there would be no such things as uniting in common labor for the purpose of forming communities and nations. Therefore, the harmonization must be such that the man is reconciled in all parts with himself, and by that same love is able to suppress so much of himself that he can march with others.

The individualism Beecher described was not that of Emerson's independent, self-reliant man; it was an individualism that pictured man as a part of a larger community whose needs took precedence over his own. The ideal was modeled after Jesus Christ, the great exemplar of man's love for man, whose philosophy was eloquently summed up in the simple statement: "Thou shalt love the Lord thy God with all thy heart, and thy neighbor as thyself." [19] To follow this ideal, man had to sacrifice his own needs and work for the good of others. The significance of the individual was measured in terms of his contribution to the good of society. [20]

Beecher's redefinition of individualism, with its denial of autonomy and self-sufficiency, appears to be a perversion of the original meaning of the word. How can the individual have any independence if he continually has to support the public good? Beecher's answer was not

to deny independence but rather to encase it in a larger ethical frame-
work. His argument, which was to become the classic middle-class
managerial ideal, was to allow the middle-class professional the freedom to make decisions at one level of the organization to which he
belonged, realizing always that the validity of his decisions must be
based on their contribution to the public good. The freedom to choose,
so crucial to the middle-class notion of individualism, is maintained,
but this freedom is to be exercised only within a narrowly defined context.

By redefining the traditional conception of individualism, Beecher
also modified the earlier conception of success. Achievement had to be
measured in social as well as in individual terms. While life was a
struggle, a continual battle between good and evil, reason and passion,
benevolence and selfishness, it was necessary to remember that the
good of the community was more important than that of the solitary
man. As Beecher declared, "Every man should learn to look upon his
business as a calling that, while it brings to him support, . . . affluence,
and even distinction, in the main is a factor of benevolence, and is
developing him by methods that very largely multiply the happiness,
the convenience, and the welfare of his fellow-men."

Although progress could not be achieved without strife, Beecher
was nevertheless optimistic about the general improvement of mankind. "When I see the changes taking place," he stated, "I see that
this is a part of that gradual struggle which has been running on through
thousands of years, and very likely will run on through thousands of
years yet to come. It is a struggle which has an inevitable termination
—namely, in such an exaltation of the race that all these animal elements will be finally purged out of it, and a larger intelligence, and a
better, more transparent moral element shall reign, to the glory of God
and the joy of the universe."[21]

To say that Beecher had modified his conceptions of individualism
and success, however, should not imply that he had totally changed
his earlier social philosophy. He still believed that poverty was as
much the product of a lack of motivation as it was the result of a harsh
environment, and he still displayed his dislike for institutions. Yet
Beecher's new social ideals were not simply abstract expressions of
good will, full of altruism but lacking in substance. For in 1885 and

1886 he began to apply them to the most pressing social issues of the day.

When a wave of strikes swept the country in the spring of 1886, for example, Beecher refused to condemn them. "I am glad of this row," he commented to his church. "Out of the war of conflicting things great good will come. . . . I am not disturbed in this evolution by fears of anarchy or violence, except for the moment. God never steers by men's fears. . . . Times of excitement, disturbances, anxiety and turmoil are always times of progress. Patriotism, hope, courage will adjust all things. We can afford to wait."[22] Beecher's optimism contrasted strongly with the hysteria of the upper classes, who saw the strikes as clear evidence that the country was going to pieces. Similarly, when the upper classes labeled the labor unrest as the work of a foreign conspiracy, Beecher replied, "Let the Anarchist come. Let the Socialist come. Let the Communist come. . . . They are men yet, though misdirected men, born under despotism, under a throne. Our institutions and sentiment can cure them."[23]

Although Beecher found in the concept of evolution a theory which made conflict between capital and labor less threatening, the general public did not share his optimism. The strikes, which culminated in the Haymarket bombings in Chicago on May 4, simply confirmed public distrust of the labor movement. People agreed with the view expressed by *The Congregationalist* that "when anarchy gathers its deluded disciples into a mob, as in Chicago, a Gatling gun or two, swiftly brought into position and well served, offers, on the whole, the most merciful as well as effectual remedy."[24]

Beecher's attempt to redefine middle-class social values, in some respects, was similar to that undertaken by Andrew Carnegie in his article on the gospel of wealth, published in 1889 in the *North American Review*. Carnegie shared many of Beecher's views: the belief in evolution, the interest in character development, the distaste for display and extravagance, the faith in education, and the concern for the stewardship of wealth. The difference was that Carnegie was less impressed than Beecher by humanitarian concerns and was more deterministic in outlook. He worried most about the "progress of the race," the "law of competition," and the problem of "indiscriminate charity."[25] Beecher's concern, in contrast, was over the reconciliation of evolution with Christian ethics in a way that would preserve a humanitarian perspective. As he commented about the charity movement in New York City: "A sympathetic heart doubles the value of a liberal hand. To relieve external trouble is less than half. Personal sympathy is sometimes better than material relief. A man is often more disordered than his affairs. When both hand and heart go forth the relief is perfect. So great is the sum of misery, especially in great cities, that organization becomes indispensable. The danger of organized charity, to be watched and avoided, is the substitution of mechanical help for personal cordial kindness."[26] Although Beecher accepted the theory of evolution, he realized, far more than Carnegie did, that it had to be softened by the addition of personal sympathy for the sufferings of the less fortunate. With the growth of industry and the rise of cities, human relationships were becoming increasingly formal and impersonal. It was therefore of crucial importance to retain a sympathetic and humanitarian perspective.

Because Beecher was acutely aware of the erosion of personal relations by mass society, he was able to capture the loyalties of the middle class to a far greater degree than Carnegie did. Although Carnegie is frequently singled out as a typical representative of the social ideals of the Gilded Age, he was in fact an exception even among the rich, who preferred to use more traditional arguments to defend their wealth.[27] Beecher, not Carnegie, best represented the middle-class social views of the period. Worried about the growth of corporate wealth and the rise of a militant labor movement, he used the theory of evolution to justify his optimism that the current social problems would eventually be solved. Society was improving, he believed, and might someday reach the stage where violence and strife would cease.

In addition to retaining an optimistic view of the future, Beecher tried to modify the traditional American ideals of individualism and success to bring them more in line with the social realities of the age. Since the members of society were becoming increasingly interdependent on one another, individual fulfillment now had to be seen in a more social context. The good of the individual had become less important than the good of society. Success, in a similar fashion, now had to be defined in a way that would emphasize social responsibility. Riches could be considered as a sign of virtue only if they were used to help others.

Ultimately, Beecher was only partly successful in his attempt to modify the social ideals of the period. Although he influenced Lyman Abbott and Washington Gladden and helped pave the way for the Social Gospel, he did not greatly affect the social behavior of most Amercans. What he did do was to redefine middle-class ideals in a way that made them more understandable and realistic, and that in itself was a major contribution.

The theory of evolution, as interpreted by Beecher, thus served two purposes for the middle class. It reassured them that the world was governed by immutable natural laws, that progress, though not inevitable, was yet a reality that could be achieved, and that society itself was everyday becoming more refined and perfect. Second, Darwin's theory increased the faith of Victorian Americans in the churches themselves, which, once freed from the bonds of orthodox theology, were becoming the new forces of cohesion for society. As Beecher stated in his lecture on evolution, "the churches that mollify the manners, cure the prejudices, extract the poison of hatred and bring men together, and not separate them, produce concord, sympathy, mutual love and helpfulness, are divine institutions."[28] Churches helped to bind people together and restore a sense of community at a time when labor unrest, the growth of business, and the expansion of industry seemed to be dividing society and setting man against man. Therefore, although Beecher's vision of the future contrasted starkly with the social realities of his day, it enabled the middle class to adjust to the social unrest of the period and to retain its faith in the mission of America. At a time when the nation was confronted by a crisis of values, Beecher's message helped to dissipate hostility and restore confidence in democracy and progress.

NOTES

1. New York *Tribune*, Jan. 28, 1884.

2. Charles Darwin, *The Origin of Species by Means of Natural Selection or The Preservation of Favored Races in the Struggle for Life* (Modern Library ed., New York, 1948), introduction, 371; see also Theodore Baird, "Darwin and the Tangled Bank," *American Scholar* (Autumn, 1946).

3. Charles Hodge, *What Is Darwinism?* (New York, 1874), 46, quoted in Ira V. Brown, *Lyman Abbott: Christian Evolutionist* (Cambridge, Mass., 1953), 140.

4. Stowe Persons, "Evolution and Theology in America," in *Evolutionary Thought in America*, ed. Stowe Persons (New Haven, 1950), 427; John Fiske, "Speech," in E. L. Youmans, *Herbert Spencer on the Americans* (New York, 1883), 55.

5. Donald Fleming, "Social Darwinism," in *Paths of American Thought*, ed. Morton White and Arthur M. Schlesinger, Jr. (Boston, 1963), 124–25.

6. W. G. Sumner, "Sociology," in *Darwinism and the American Intellectual*, ed. R. J. Wilson (Homewood, Ill., 1967), 146.

7. My understanding of the antebellum conception of individualism is heavily indebted to John William Ward's essay, "The Ideal of Individualism and the Reality of Organization," in his book, *Red, White, and Blue: Men, Books, and Ideas in American Culture* (New York, 1969).

8. Contrary to the popular view, Darwinism was used more often to attack new wealth than to defend it. See Irvin G. Wyllie, "Social Darwinism and the Businessman," *Proceedings of the American Philosophical Society*, CIII (Oct., 1959), 629–35.

9. H. W. Beecher to ?, May 8, 1867, as quoted in *Henry Ward Beecher as His Friends Saw Him*, ed. J. H. Tewkesbury (New York, 1904), 87.

10. William G. McLoughlin, *The Meaning of Henry Ward Beecher* (New York, 1970), 45.

11. H. W. Beecher, "Progress of Thought in the Church," *North American Review*, CXXXV (Aug., 1882), 100–109, 114, 117.

12. D. D. Williams, *The Andover Liberals* (New York, 1941), 28.

13. H. W. Beecher, *Statement before the Congregational Association of New York*, pamphlet (New York, 1883), 14.

14. E. L. Youmans, ed., *Herbert Spencer on the Americans* (New York, 1883), 18, 34, 61–62.

15. New York *Times*, Jan. 14, 1883; New York *Daily Tribune*, Jan. 7, 1883; Boston *Weekly Transcript*, Jan. 30, 1883.

16. New York *Times*, June 12, 1882; New York *Tribune*, June 12, 1882.

17. New York *Times*, June 27, 1881, June 26, 1882.

18. Brown, *Lyman Abbott*, 141; Frank H. Foster in *The Modern Movement in American Theology* (Chicago, 1907) devotes a chapter to the "School of Henry Ward Beecher," but this is an overstatement as Winthrop Hudson points out. Beecher's views were never systematic enough to be the basis for a "school."

19. H. W. Beecher, *Evolution and Religion* (New York, 1885), 147, 209, 309, 393.

20. For an excellent discussion of the changing conceptions of individualism in the nineteenth century, see Ward, *Red, White, and Blue*.

21. H. W. Beecher, *Evolution and Religion*, 335, 217.

22. New York *Times*, March 29, 1886.

23. New York *Times*, May 17, 1886; New York *Tribune*, May 17, 1886.

24. *Congregationalist*, May 13, 1886, quoted in Henry F. May, *Protestant Churches and Industrial America* (New York, 1963), 101.

25. Andrew Carnegie, "Wealth," *North American Review* (1889), 653–64.

26. H. W. Beecher, *Evolution and Religion*, 393.

27. Wyllie, "Social Darwinism and the Businessman."

28. H. W. Beecher, "Evolution or Revolution," New York *Tribune*, Jan. 7, 1883.

13

Symbol for a Middle - Class America

By 1885, Henry Ward Beecher at seventy-two years of age was at the height of his career, and his daily schedule, if anything, was even more hectic than it had been in the past. In addition to his usual busy routine at Plymouth Church, he wrote an article on former president Grant, sent numerous letters to the administration in an effort to secure a customs position for his son Herbert, and in the spring toured the South on an extensive lecture trip.[1] As he explained to a close friend,

> . . . I am more like a pine tree that must keep green both summer and winter. Take for instance a few weeks back. I lectured four nights, one of them in Boston, and rode home at night, to conduct my Friday meeting. Preached twice on Sunday—and then on Tuesday night presided and spoke at Brooklyn Academy of Music—Wednesday dined and spoke at the dinner in New York of the Friendly Sons of St. Patrick—of which I am an honorary member; on Thursday I was present and spoke at the annual dinner of the Baptist Union of Brooklyn—Friday prayer meeting—Sunday preached twice, on Monday opened a fair in Plymouth Church, and spent afternoon and evening there talking to all

comers, and wasting myself on nonsense, universal and unmitigable—last Sunday [preached] twice and now for three weeks you see my chart laid out! Do you wonder that I have no time to grow old?—No—I am *yet* young.[2]

As these comments attest, Beecher took great pride in his ability to sustain a hectic schedule of church work and lecturing. Quite clearly, too, by the end of his career he had come to think of himself primarily as a public figure. With so many speaking engagements, he had little time for either family or friends. Increasingly, as his wife had noticed, he had lost interest in his private life. He had become more concerned about his public image and role as a social commentator.

Despite his claims to boundless energy, however, he was beginning to show signs of age. For one thing, he no longer prepared new lectures for his lyceum tours. While speaking in England during the following summer, for example, he took as his subjects the "Reign of the Common People" and the "Wastes and Burdens of Society," topics that he had first prepared nearly a decade earlier. In politics, too, his interest diminished and he lost touch with the affairs of the Independent Republicans in Brooklyn. He now devoted his energies only to those causes he considered to be matters of principle. Thus, when Oscar Strauss's nomination as minister to Turkey came under attack in February, 1887, Beecher quickly wrote a letter of support to President Cleveland. "The bitter prejudice against Jews which obtains in many parts of Europe," he commented, "ought not to receive any countenance in America. It is because he is a Jew that I would urge his appointment as a fit recognition of this remarkable people, who are becoming large contributors to American prosperity, and whose intelligence, morality and large liberality in all public measures for the welfare of society, deserve and should receive from the hands of our government some such recognition."[3]

Later that same spring, Beecher contracted to write his autobiography. Though he still enjoyed the full use of all his faculties, he realized that sooner or later he would have to slow down. He therefore decided, following the example set earlier by his father, to put his reminiscences on paper before his memory became dim. Accordingly, he organized his personal papers and began to write. But he never completed more than a page or two, because on March 7, 1887, he suffered a stroke. Two days later he died quietly in his sleep.

Beecher's death stunned the nation and brought forth an immediate public response. The city of Brooklyn declared a day of mourning, the state legislature recessed, and the president and other national leaders sent telegrams of condolence. During the public funeral that followed, services were held at four churches and the entire city turned out for the solemn procession to Greenwood Cemetery. It was a somber occasion, during which hundreds of thousands of mourners paid their respects to the clergyman who had served Plymouth Church for forty years.

In the weeks after Beecher's death, many of the country's leading writers and newspaper men tried to assess his influence as a man and a preacher. All the writers without exception agreed that Beecher had been the most popular orator of his day, but they differed widely in their analysis of the sources of his appeal. Some attributed it to his oratorical ability, others to his personality, and still others to his talent as an actor. But few recognized the major source of his popularity, which was the way he spoke to the hopes and fears of millions of Americans.

Beecher's pastorate at Plymouth Church in the years between 1847 and 1887 coincided with a period in which Victorian Americans experienced a profound and traumatic crisis of faith.[4] At the heart of the crisis was not only a disillusionment with the church, but also an intense questioning of the mission and destiny of the nation. Indeed, many Americans in the mid-Victorian era felt as if they had lost a sense of community and purpose. In a society where impersonality and anonymity were becoming increasingly prevalent, these Americans began to lose their faith in progress, social ethics, and democracy itself.

Henry Ward Beecher devoted his career to meeting the crisis of faith by setting forth in his sermons and lectures a new middle-class ethos built around a more personal and intuitive belief in Christianity. In a society where the specter of socialistic and communistic conspiracies lurked on the horizon, in a society that appeared to have lost its meaning and purpose, Beecher preached a new romantic Christianity that healed wounds, promised forgiveness of sins, and urged love for one's fellow man. It reassured Americans that the universe was governed by moral laws, that Truth and Justice did exist, and that the American nation had a glorious future as the vehicle for God's chosen people. Romantic Christianity was thus a broad, catholic, liberal faith that saw all religions as working to strengthen the individual and bind society together. Religion, according to Beecher, was the cohesive force that prevented the fragmentation and disintegration of the social order. "It is," he once remarked, "refining social life, not simply by the progress of elegance, but by a larger good will and a truer fellowship than ever before existed. It is developing individuals in purity, self-denial, benevolence, and true moral heroism. It is at work in society, restraining the outrage of passions, inspiring indolence with activity and enterprise, building up schools, cleansing the ways of business, and producing an intelligent morality."[5]

Romantic Christianity helped not only to restore men's faith in church and state, but it also helped them to internalize habits of self-repression and self-control. Where the earlier generation of Evangelical Protestants had used the social pressure of mass revivals to force the individual to act in a socially correct manner, the leaders of romantic Christianity turned to the family, the school, and the church as the proper instruments for controlling men's aggressive behavior. Thus, Beecher's liberal Protestantism was both pragmatic and idealistic. It helped to restore the faith of middle-class Americans in the future growth of the nation while at the same time it reassured them that order would be maintained within society.

During Beecher's forty years at Plymouth Church, he came to be identified with the Victorian values that he so constantly extolled. To many Americans he became the symbol for their new faith, a man of practical experience, not theory, who seemed to exhibit in his own life and career the middle-class virtues of honesty, industry, health, sobriety, education, culture, refinement, patriotism, and benevolence. He was the man who exemplified the value of self-direction and dedication, a living example of the opportunities open to those individuals who wanted to reform and remake society. In the words of George William Curtis, editor of *Harper's Weekly*, Beecher was "a man of strong virility, of exuberant vitality, of quick sympathy, of an abounding humor, of a rapid play of poetic imagination, of great fluency of speech; an emotional nature overflowing in ardent expression, of strong convictions, of complete self-confidence; but also not sensitive, nor critical, nor judicial; a hearty, joyful nature, touching ordinary human life at every point, and responsive to every generous moral impulse."[6] Beecher was the symbol of crusading idealism and moral convictions and grass roots democracy in a society troubled by massive immigration and chaotic social change.

Curtis's identification of Beecher's energy and enthusiasm as a major source of his success was astute. The preacher's strength, however, was also at times his major weakness. Impatient about details, careless about personal matters, and passionately concerned about injustice and social reform, Beecher occasionally got carried away and lost his sense of balance. If Beecher had difficulty in maintaining his sense of proportion, so, too, did the generation of Americans who shared his beliefs. What began as an imaginative search for truth and progress often could become bogged down and misinterpreted. Self-confidence could become smugness, emotional sympathy and sensitivity to the needs of others could easily degenerate into sentimentality and gush, manners and conventions could become rigid and stiff, and a concern for education and high culture could end up as a preoccupation with social status. That Beecher did avoid, to a great extent, the tendency to become set in one's ways was a testimony to the openness and broadmindedness of his outlook. With a few exceptions, Beecher achieved the balance that was so crucial to the Victorian outlook. Optimistic but not naïve, sympathetic but not sentimental, he became a reference point and popular prophet that others could look up to and respect.

The ultimate test of Beecher's practical, open-minded approach was his own assessment of his career. He was a man who had few misgivings about his own limitations and purpose in life. "I am not one of the largest natures," he admitted to a friend shortly before the Civil War. "I know my place and rank, I think. I belong to the second place [among] men. I shall do good while I am alive, not so much in *discovering* or organizing truth as in *applying* it, and rousing men to activity." [7]

And Beecher was in this respect as good as his word. As the spokesman for Victorian morality, he preached for forty years a message of love and hope that helped to relieve the fears and anxieties of mid-Victorian Americans as they entered the first stages of the industrial revolution. Though he was often inconsistent, he nevertheless helped to renew the faith of middle-class Americans in traditional values at a time when lying, cheating, and corruption seemed to have become a way of life.

NOTES

1. H. W. Beecher to Eunice Beecher, March 21, 1885, Yale MSS; H. W. Beecher to President Grover Cleveland, June 9, Sept. 18, Dec. 11, 1885, Jan. 11, March 27, 1886, Cleveland Papers, Library of Congress; H. W. Beecher to E. L. Godkin, Sept. 21, 1885, Yale MSS.

2. H. W. Beecher to Mrs. Emily Drury, March 29, 1886, Schlesinger Library.

3. H. W. Beecher to Grover Cleveland, Feb. 12, 1887, Yale MSS.

4. This idea comes from William G. McLoughlin, *The Meaning of Henry Ward Beecher* (New York, 1970).

5. H. W. Beecher, "National Unity," in *Patriotic Addresses*, ed. John Howard (New York, 1887), 766.

6. *Henry Ward Beecher as His Friends Saw Him*, ed. J. H. Tewkesbury (New York, 1904), 135.

7. H. W. Beecher to Mrs. Emily Drury, n.d., Schlesinger Library.

A Note on Sources

MANUSCRIPT COLLECTIONS

This book is based on the extensive writings and personal papers of
Henry Ward Beecher, which are scattered in many libraries. The
largest collection of material, given to the Yale University Library in
the early 1940s, has not been used by any of Beecher's biographers in
the twentieth century. The Beecher Family Papers at Yale are substantial and include most of the family correspondence during the
nineteenth century. In addition, they contain sermons and sermon
books, yearly date books, financial papers, and Beecher's journal, or
private diary.

Smaller in size, but equally important, is the Beecher-Stowe Collection in the Arthur and Elizabeth Schlesinger Library on the History of
Women in America at Radcliffe College. Although this collection is
devoted primarily to the letters of Harriet Beecher Stowe, it contains
the most complete family correspondence for the 1820s and 1830s,
including several of Henry's early letters. This collection should be
supplemented with the Henry Ward Beecher Papers at the Library of
Congress. These papers contain seventeen boxes of sermons, business
correspondence, and a large scrapbook containing clippings of articles

which Beecher wrote for *The Independent* and the New York *Ledger*. The clippings are, for the most part, without date. The few Beecher letters in the Robert Todd Lincoln Papers and the Andrew Johnson Papers at the Library of Congress are also important.

Smaller collections of Beecher manuscripts are available at many different institutions. The Robert Bonner Papers in the New York Public Library are helpful for the Civil War years. Bonner was the editor of the New York *Ledger* and Beecher corresponded with him almost weekly in the 1860s. The Stowe-Day Foundation in Hartford, Connecticut, also has many family letters, as well as Beecher's own copy of his *Seven Lectures to Young Men*. The Julia Merrill Papers at the Indiana Historical Society Library and the "Reminiscences of Jane Merrill Ketcham" at the Indiana State Library contain materials about Beecher's pastorate in Indiana. Since Beecher's journal makes few references to this period of his life, these sources are invaluable for learning what his congregation thought about him. Two other manuscript collections that are helpful because they reveal the private views of New York clergymen toward Beecher are the Henry Whitney Bellows Papers at the Massachusetts Historical Society and the George B. Cheever Papers at the American Antiquarian Society.

Finally, there are scattered letters in the following libraries: Amherst College Library, Cornell University Library, Columbia University Library, Rutherford B. Hayes Library, Boston Public Library, Henry E. Huntington Library, University of Georgia Library, Fiske University Library, Cincinnati Historical Society Library, Historical and Philosophical Society of Ohio Library, and Houghton Library of Harvard University.

References to the secondary materials which have shaped my understanding are to be found in the notes to each chapter.

Index

death of George Lyman, 64; birth of daughter, Catharine, 64; unhappiness in Midwest, 69; birth and death of twins, 114–15; birth of ninth child (1854), 115; as lyceum lecturer, 172; causes confusion on husband's postwar views, 172; articles on domestic economy for *Christian Union*, 186; dislike of Stanton and Tilton, 205; letter to daughter on adultery scandal, 222–23; pressures after adultery trial, 244; attitude toward women's role, 245

Beecher, George (brother), 10, 11, 12; minister in Batavia, Ohio, 29; death of, 56; influences HWB on slavery issue, 65–66

Beecher, Harriet (sister). *See* Stowe, Harriet Beecher

Beecher, Henry Barton (eldest living son): birth of, 53; desire to fight in Civil War, 152

Beecher, Henry Ward: source of appeal, 2, 3; critics of, 2–3; early childhood, 6–7, 10; death of mother, 10; early importance of Harriet to, 10, 24; early interest in nature, 11; youthful struggle over religious beliefs, 11–12; education, 11–12, 15–18, 30; conversion, 14–15; meets Eunice Bullard, 19; engaged to Eunice Bullard, 21; at Amherst, 24; letter to Harriet about future, 24; differs with father on view of God, 24–25; moves to Cincinnati, 29; literary interests, 30–32; development of preaching style, 31–32; humor, 32; popularity with women, 32–34; sensitivity to criticism, 33, 119–20; leaves Lane Seminary, 40; marries Eunice Bullard, 41; moves to Lawrenceburg, 41; birth of first child (1838), 42; ordination, 43–44; moves to Indianapolis, 45–46; early experiences in Indianapolis, 51–53; death of son, George, 64; on slavery and the Bible, 67–68; decision to return East, 69–73; four themes of early career, 71; death of daughter, Catharine, 79; joins *The Independent*, 87; refuge in illness during periods of stress, 93–94; outward success, family discontent, 114–16; literary activity in 1850s, 182–84; charged with adultery by Tilton, 197–98, 207–29; significance of adultery trial, 225; themes in lectures, 238; and family tension, 244–45; constructs summer home, 245–47; and middle-class ideals, 271; last years, 273–74; as symbolic of Victorian values, 276; self-assessment, 277

Beecher, Lyman (father): revivalist activity for Congregational Church in Litchfield, 7–9; religious philosophy, 8–9; conversion of

own children, 10–11; move to Cincinnati, 19–22; and abolitionist movement, 22–23; religion, politics, and destiny of nation, 23; heresy trial, 34–36; on moral government, 38–39; and son Charles's loss of faith, 54–56

Beecher, Mary (sister), 11

Beecher, Roxana (mother): death of, 10

Beecher, Thomas K. (half-brother): letter about Bushnell, 82; disagreement with criticism of government, 154; essays on moral subjects, 186; successes in Elmira, N.Y., 243

Beecher, William (brother), 10; minister in Putnam, Ohio, 29

"Beecher's Bibles," 123

Bellows, Henry Whitney (Unitarian minister): on HWB's antislavery lecture (1855), 122; concern for education of blacks, 125; changes attitude on Beecher, 133; reaction to early Union reverses, 155

Beman, Nathaniel S., 34

Birney, James G., 36–38

Blacks: education of, 96, 125; inconsistency in HWB's definition of rights of, 139; rights of free Negroes in the North, 140; change in HWB's attitude toward, 167; legal equality and social inequality, 168; suffrage for, 170–71, 175–76; citizenship issue, 174–75

Blaine, James G., 251–53

Blair, Francis P., 125

Bonner, Robert: offers HWB contract for novel, 169; demands *Norwood* manuscript, 183

Bowen, Henry C.: and HWB's move to Brooklyn, 71–72; opposition to business community over slavery issue, 92; financial problems with *The Independent*, 152; involvement in adultery scandal, 214; pays off Tilton, 219

Brooklyn, N.Y.: rapid expansion at mid-century, 76–77

Brooklyn Equal Rights Association, 202, 204

Brooklyn Phalanx, 151

Buchanan, James, 125

Bullard, Ebenezer, 19

Bullard, Eunice. *See* Beecher, Eunice Bullard

Bushnell, Horace: author of *Views of Christian Nurture* (1846), 81–82; compared to HWB, 82–86; on Beecher, 133–34; initial reaction to Civil War, 148–49

Butler, Benjamin, 116–17, 118

Byron, George Gordon: Harriet B. Stowe's controversial article on, 201